EARLY CHRISTIANITY

Editor

John M. G. Bai

Editorial Board
Loveday Alexander, Troels-Engberg-Pedersen, Bart Ehrman, Joel Marcus,
John Riches, Matthias Konradt

LIBRARY OF NEW TESTAMENT STUDIES

450

Formerly Journal for the Study of the New Testament Supplement Series

Editor

Chris Keith

Editorial Board
Dale C. Allison, John M.G. Barclay, Lynn H. Cohick, R. Alan Culpepper,
Craig A. Evans, Robert Fowler, Simon J. Gathercole, John S. Kloppenborg,
Michael Labahn, Love L. Sechrest, Robert Wall, Steve Walton, Catrin H. Williams

THE EARLIEST CHRISTIAN MEETING PLACES

Almost Exclusively Houses?

Revised Edition

Edward Adams

Bloomsbury T&T Clark
An imprint of Bloomsbury Publishing Plc

B L O O M S B U R Y

LONDON · OXFORD · NEW YORK · NEW DELHI · SYDNEY

Bloomsbury T&T Clark
An imprint of Bloomsbury Publishing Plc

Imprint previously known as T&T Clark

50 Bedford Square	1385 Broadway
London	New York
WC1B 3DP	NY 10018
UK	USA

www.bloomsbury.com

BLOOMSBURY, T&T CLARK and the Diana logo are trademarks of Bloomsbury Publishing Plc

First published 2013. This Revised Edition published 2016

© Edward Adams, 2016

British Library Cataloguing-in-Publication Data
A catalogue record for this book is available from the British Library.

ISBN: PB: 978-0-56766-314-6
HB: 978-0-56728-257-6
ePDF: 978-0-56715-732-4

Library of Congress Cataloging-in-Publication Data
A catalog record for this book is available from the Library of Congress.

Series: Library of New Testament Studies, volume 450

Typeset by Newgen Knowledge Works (P) Ltd., Chennai, India

CONTENTS

Part II
EVIDENCE AND POSSIBILITIES
FOR NON-HOUSE MEETING PLACES

PREFACE TO THE REVISED EDITION

I am delighted that this monograph, published in 2013, has been deemed worthy of a paperback edition, which will make the book available to a wider readership (at a more affordable price!). I have taken the opportunity to correct some typographical errors that slipped through the net the first time round (and for which I am entirely to blame!) and to make a small number of stylistic changes. I have also added an update which takes account of reviews of my book in academic journals and notes some relevant research that has appeared since my book was finished.

I want to thank Dominic Mattos for commissioning this paperback version, Miriam Cantwell for her work as general editor and Srikanth Srinivasan for copy-editing. I also want to re-thank my wife, Ruth, to whom this book is dedicated, and my children, who have increased in number since the publication of the hardback edition. So I now record my immense appreciation for my daughter Naomi as well as my boys.

31 August 2015

ACKNOWLEDGMENTS

This project has dominated my research activity over the period covered by the Research Excellence Framework (2008–13). The main research was carried out during a period of study leave in 2009–10 made possible by a Leverhulme Trust fellowship. I am extremely grateful to the Leverhulme Trust for this award, which included an allowance to spend a week at the archaeological excavations of Pompeii. In the autumn of 2012, I was granted sabbatical leave by my university, King's College London, to enable me to complete the writing of the book. I want to thank my (then) Head of Department, Paul Janz, for facilitating this sabbatical and for his support of my project all the way through.

The Maughan Library, King's College London, together with the Warburg Institute Library and the Institute of Classical Studies Library, provided the main resources for my research. I made use of Tyndale House library and Glasgow University Library as well. I also took advantage of my university's electronic resources. The excellent websites, Pompeii in Pictures, http://pompeiiinpictures.com/pompeiiinpictures/index.htm, and Ostia – Harbour City of Ancient Rome, http://www.ostia-antica.org, allowed me to revisit Pompeii and Ostia at the convenience of my home or office.

I am glad to have had a number of opportunities to present my research, as it developed, at conferences (the British New Testament Conference, Durham, 2008; the Annual Meeting of Society of Biblical Literature, Book of Acts unit, New Orleans, 2009; the Irish Biblical Association Annual Meeting, Dublin, 2010) and university research seminars (the New Testament Senior Seminar, Cambridge, 2011; the New Testament Research Seminar, Durham, 2011; the Centre for Biblical Studies research seminar, Exeter, 2009, 2011, 2013; the Biblical Studies Research Seminar, King's College London, 2010; the Department of Biblical Studies research seminar, Sheffield, 2011). I am most grateful for the feedback I received on those occasions.

I wish to record my thanks to Richard Burridge, who, in his capacity as my line manager at King's, monitored my progress throughout the period of my Leverhulme Trust award. He read and reacted to (very rough!) draft chapters written during this time, offering positive criticism seasoned with encouragement. My King's colleagues, Joan Taylor and Markus Vinzent, also read through (more polished) drafts of this book, and I am grateful to them for their valuable comments and suggestions.

I am tremendously indebted to David Horrell for his support of this research project from its beginnings. Conversations with David, going back to our research visit to Corinth in 2002, helped stimulate my interest in this topic, and I benefited greatly from discussing my findings with him on a regular basis over the period of my research. David read and commented on every chapter of the manuscript at various stages of composition, and gave vital advice for improving the structure and argument of the book. I am grateful to Siri Sande for discussing her own ideas about early Christian meeting places with me in email correspondence and in a personal meeting at the Norwegian Institute in Rome in 2008. I also thank John Barclay for reading the manuscript and accepting it for the ECC subseries of LNTS. I am grateful to Rosie Ratcliffe for proofreading the work. Other academics I must thank for helping in some way include: Loveday Alexander, David Balch, Stephen Barton, Siam Bhayro, Oliver Davies, Lutz Doering, Troels Engberg-Pedersen, Cherryl Hunt, Larry Hurtado, Judith Lieu, Peter Oakes, the late Graham Stanton, and George van Kooten.

A portion of my article, 'The Ancient Church at Megiddo: The Discovery and an Assessment of its Significance' (*ExpTim* 120 [2008], pp.62–9, doi: 10.1177/0014524608097822), is reprinted with some changes in Chapter 5. The reuse of this material meets SAGE's Global Journal Author Reuse Policy. Parts of my essay, 'Placing the Corinthian Communal Meal' (in C. Osiek and A.C. Niang, eds., *Text, Image, and Christians in the Graeco-Roman World: A Festschrift in Honor of David Lee Balch* [Eugene, OR: Wipf & Stock, 2012], pp.22–37), reappear in Chapter 1 and Appendix 1. This material is used by permission of Wipf & Stock Publishers (www.wipfandstock.com).

I am very grateful to Dominic Mattos and Caitlin Flynn at Bloomsbury T&T Clark, and especially to Duncan Burns, the commissioned copy-editor, for their excellent work in taking the manuscript quickly through the publication process so that the book could appear in time for REF 2014. I want to thank Duncan additionally for compiling the indices.

It is, though, to my wife Ruth, and my boys, Jacob, Caleb and Daniel (the latter being born during my sabbatical leave in autumn 2012), that I owe the greatest debt. Work on this book took up a great many evenings and weekends, and I am immensely grateful to my family for their tolerance. Without the help and support of my wife, completion of this book for the REF deadline would not have been possible, and I lovingly dedicate the book to her.

ABBREVIATIONS

Early Christian and Other Ancient Sources

Ap. Trad.	*Apostolic Tradition*
Apuleius	
Apol.	*Apologia*
Met.	*Metamorphoses*
Cicero	
Fin.	*De finibus*
Flac.	*pro Flacco*
CIL	Corpus Inscriptionum Latinarum
Clement of Alexandria	
Paed.	*Paedagogus*
Protrep.	*Protrepticus*
Strom.	*Stromateis*
1 Clem.	*1 Clement*
The Pseudo-Clementines	
Hom.	*Homilies*
Rec.	*Recognitions*
Cyprian	
ad Demetr.	*ad Demetrianum*
Ep.	*Epistles*
Did.	*Didache*
Didascal.	*Didascalia Apostolorum*
Dio Chrysostom	
Or.	*Orationes*
Epictetus	
Diss.	*Dissertationes*
Epiphanius	
Pan.	*Panarion*
Eusebius	
H.E.	*Historia Ecclesiastica*
VC	*Vita Constantini*
Homer	
Od.	*Odyssey*
Horace	
Ep.	*Epistles*
Ignatius	
Eph.	*Epistle to the Ephesians*
Mag.	*Epistle to the Magnesians*
Phld.	*Epistle to the Philadelphians*
Pol.	*Epistle to Polycarp*

Smyrn.	*Epistle to the Smyrnaeans*
Trall.	*Epistle to the Trallians*
Irenaeus	
Adv. Haer.	*Adversus Haereses*
Josephus	
Ant.	*Antiquities of the Jews*
War	*Jewish War*
Justin	
Apol. 1.	*First Apology*
Trypho	*Dialogue with Trypho*
Lactantius	
De mort. pers.	*De mortibus persecutorum*
Libanius	
Or.	*Orations*
Lucretius	
de rerum	*de rerum natura*
Martial	
Ep.	*Epigrams*
Minucius Felix	
Oct.	*Octavius*
Origen	
C. Cels.	*Contra Celsum*
De Orat.	*De Oratione*
P. Oxy.	Oxyrhynchus Papyri
Petronius	
Satyr.	*Satyricon*
Philo	
Flacc.	*In Flaccum*
Mos.	*De vita Mosis*
Mut.	*De mutatione nominum*
Opif.	*De opificio mundi*
Somn.	*De somniis*
Spec. Leg.	*De specialibus legibus*
Philostratus	
Vit. Soph.	*Vitae Sophistarum*
Plato	
Rep.	*The Republic*
Pliny the Elder	
Nat. His.	*Naturalis Historia*
Pliny the Younger	
Ep.	*Epistles*
Plutarch	
Maxime cum princ.	*Maxime cum principibus philosopho esse disserendum*
De Recta Rat.	*De Recta Ratione Audiendi*
Sull.	*Life of Sulla*
Seneca	
Ep.	*Epistulae morales*

S.H.A.	*Scriptores Historiae Augustae*
Comm.	*Commodus*
Firmus, Sat.	*Firmus, Saturninus, Proclus and Bonosus*
Had.	*Hadrian*
Sev. Alex.	*Severus Alexander*
Tac.	*Tacitus*
Verus	*Lucius Verus*

Shepherd of Hermas
Man.	*Mandates*
Sim.	*Similitudes*
Vis.	*Visions*

Suetonius
Gramm.	*De Illustribus Grammaticis*
Claud.	*Life of Claudius*
Nero	*Life of Nero*
Tib.	*Life of Tiberius*
Taan.	*Taanith*

Tacitus
| *Ann.* | *Annales* |

Tertullian
Apol.	*Apology*
De Bapt.	*De Baptismo*
De Corona	*De Corona Militis*
De Idol.	*De Idololatria*
De Ieiunio	*De Ieiunio Adversus Psychicos*
De Monog.	*De Monogamia*
De Pud.	*De Pudicitia*

Xenophon
Mem.	*Memorabilia*
Oecon.	*Oeconomicus*

Abbreviations of Periodicals and Series

AB	Anchor Bible
AJA	*American Journal of Archaeology*
AJP	*American Journal of Philology*
ANRW	Hildegard Temporini and Wolfgang Haase (eds.), *Aufstieg und Niedergang der römischen Welt: Geschichte und Kultur Roms im Spiegel der neueren Forschung* (Berlin: W. de Gruyter, 1972–)
BAIAS	*Bulletin of the Anglo-Israel Archaeological Society*
BARev	*Biblical Archaeology Review*
BECNT	Baker Exegetical Commentary on the New Testament
BNTC	Black's New Testament Commentaries
BR	*Bible Review*
CBQ	*Catholic Biblical Quarterly*
CIL	Corpus inscriptionum latinarum
ECC	Eerdman's Critical Commentary
ExpTim	*Expository Times*
HTR	*Harvard Theological Review*

ICC	International Critical Commentary
JBL	*Journal of Biblical Literature*
JECS	*Journal of Early Christian Studies*
JEH	*Journal of Ecclesiastical History*
JRA	*Journal of Roman Archaeology*
JRH	*Journal of Religious History*
JRS	*Journal of Roman Studies*
JSJ	*Journal for the Study of Judaism in the Persian, Hellenistic and Roman Period*
JSNT	*Journal for the Study of the New Testament*
JSNTSup	Journal for the Study of the New Testament, Supplement Series
JSOT	*Journal for the Study of the Old Testament*
JTS	*Journal of Theological Studies*
LCL	Loeb Classical Library
LNTS	Library of New Testament Studies
NICNT	New International Commentary on the New Testament
NIGTC	The New International Greek Testament Commentary
NovT	*Novum Testamentum*
NovTSup	*Supplements to Novum Testamentum*
NTS	*New Testament Studies*
SBLDS	Society of Biblical Literature Dissertation Series
SBS	Stuttgarter Bibelstudien
SNTSMS	Society for New Testament Studies Monograph Series
SNTW	Studies of the New Testament in its World
TNTC	Tyndale New Testament Commentaries
VC	*Vigiliae christianae*
WBC	Word Biblical Commentary
WUNT	Wissenschaftliche Untersuchungen zum Neuen Testament
ZNW	*Zeitschrift für die neutestamentliche Wissenschaft*

Other Abbreviations

BDAG	W.F. Bauer, F.W. Danker, W.F. Arndt and W.F. Gingrich, *A Greek–English Lexicon of the New Testament and Other Early Christian Literature* (Chicago: University of Chicago Press, 3rd edn, 2000)
CBCR	*Corpus Basilicarum Christianarum Romae* (R. Krautheimer; 5 vols.; Vatican: Pontifical Gregorian Institute, 1937–77)
LSJ	H. Liddle, R. Scott, H.S. Jones and R. McKenzie, *A Greek–English Lexicon* (Oxford: Clarendon, 9th edn with supplement, 1996)
LXX	Septuagint
NIDNNT	*New International Dictionary of New Testament Theology* (ed. C. Brown; 4 vols.; Exeter: Paternoster, 1975–8)
NRSV	New Revised Standard Version
OLD	*Oxford Latin Dictionary* (ed. P.G.W. Glare; Oxford: Clarendon, combined edition, 1982)
TDNT	*Theological Dictionary of the New Testament* (eds. G. Kittel and G.Friedrich; trans. G.W.Bromiley; 10 vols.; Grand Rapids: Eerdmans, 1964–76)

UPDATE

Since the publication of this book in 2013, a number of reviews have appeared in academic journals. Reactions have been generally positive. Paul Foster in his review in *The Expository Times* (126.3 [2014], pp. 143–44) finds the monograph 'stimulating and rich'. While in his view it illustrates how little we actually know about early Christian meeting practices and places, it nevertheless clearly shows 'that the evidence is more varied than has typically been recognized'. He thinks that my study helps us 'to reconceptualise the meaning of domestic spaces where Christians may have met'. Thus, it is no longer possible to focus only on large elite villas. Rather, 'one must think in terms of mixed spaces such as the workshop-dwelling place'. Eric Meyers in a review in *Strata* (32 [2014], pp. 142–44) applauds the effort I have undertaken and believes that my work 'has wide implications for a variety of fields within Early Christian Studies and offers a new way of evaluating the data on Christian assembly, worship, and the material culture associated with it'. David Allen, writing in *Reviews in Religion & Theology* (21.3 [2014], pp. 297–99), gives a fine summary of the book's contents and argument. He regards my analysis of the evidence as 'fair and consistent', in that where there is clear testimony to the house as meeting location (as in the book of Acts), I acknowledge and affirm it. He clearly appreciates that my problem is not with the notion of houses being early Christian meeting places but rather the assumption that Christians met nearly always in houses.

Richard Last, reviewing the book in *Religious Studies Review* (41.1 [2015], pp. 22–23), thinks that I would have benefited from having a typology of gatherings and clarifying what kinds of meetings are most relevant to the scholarship with which I am engaging. Most proponents of the AEH consensus, he notes, are primarily interested in 'church' meetings. Thus, it is not certain whether my evidence relating to teaching in open spaces and baptisms beside water bodies actually affects the majority view that 'church' meetings happened almost exclusively in houses. It does seem to me, though, that AEH advocates tend to view the house as the sole setting for the full range of activities that mark 'church' gatherings: evangelism; teaching; prayer; fellowship; the communal meal (e.g. Klauck 1981: 36–39; Gehring 2004: 27; according to Stowers 1984, Paul and other early Christian leaders eschewed teaching in open spaces). Baptism, to be sure, is regarded as the exception (Branick 1989: 112; Gehring 2004: 290), but my argument about watersides is not just that they would have served baptismal purposes but that they would have been suitable as Christian meeting places more generally. While the evidence I cite admittedly majors on the baptismal usage of watersides, I do also draw attention to literary evidence for watersides as settings for Christian prayer, teaching and dining (see pp. 186–88). Despite this slight demurral, Last considers that I have provided 'a wealth of evidence' counterbalancing the current place of houses in the social history of early Christianity.

Carolyn Osiek's lovely review in *Biblical Theology Bulletin* (45 [2015], pp. 185–86) is particularly pleasing, since as she acknowledges at the outset, she is among those who have 'enthusiastically embraced the "house church"'. She states that I have offered 'an alternative view that is a healthy balance'. Somewhat like Last, she thinks that it would have been helpful for me 'to make some distinctions among different kinds of meetings: meal, baptism, instruction, etc.'. While one can envisage baptism happening in a bathhouse, it is less easy to imagine a meal taking place there. In assessing the adequacy of a given space for Christian meeting, I actually do distinguish between different kinds of meetings (see pp. 12, 145–46, 149, etc.), but perhaps, going forward, more along this line would prove helpful. I have argued that a meal meeting in a bathhouse is indeed quite imaginable (p. 179), but perhaps more needs to be done to establish this scenario. Unsurprisingly, Osiek resists my call for the term 'house church' to be dropped from the study of earliest Christianity. For her, there is more to be considered about the family basis of early church life before the abandonment of the category 'house church' can be contemplated. But in my view, familial dynamics in early Christianity are better accounted for without the unhelpful connotations of the 'house church' label getting in the way. Overall, Osiek finds much of my argument sound, though she feels that sometimes I push it too far. Yet, 'a good case has been made here to exercise caution and to consider the widest possible alternatives for early Christian meeting places'. I am grateful to these reviewers for their serious consideration of this book and for their appreciative and constructive feedback.

A few items of relevant research that have appeared since my book was finished may be noted. In a co-authored article published in 2014 ('Accounting Practices in *P.Tebt.* III/2 894 and Pauline Groups', *Early*

Christianity 5 [2014], pp. 441–474), Richard Last and Sarah Rollens give detailed attention to a fragmentary papyrus document containing the financial records of an association in Tebtunis. The papyrus dates to around 114 BCE and is the most extensive club financial account yet discovered. Of particular interest is the fact that the club meeting place seems to have rotated, with shops and workshops among the venues. In his forthcoming monograph, *The Pauline Church and the Corinthian Ekklēsia* (SNTS 164; Cambridge: Cambridge University Press, 2015), Last argues that the meeting locale of the Corinthian church (he thinks that the church was quite small) similarly rotated. Last offers independent confirmation of my view that Romans 16.23 is unlikely to mean that Gaius accommodated the Corinthian congregation in his house (while giving a new interpretation of his own).

   In his new book, *The Cross Before Constantine: The Early Life of a Christian Symbol* (Minneapolis: Fortress Press, 2015), Bruce Longenecker attacks the firmly held assumption that the cross was not a Christian symbol until Constantine. He devotes a chapter to the cross-shaped bas-relief found in the bakery shop at VI.6.20, Pompeii (the shop is pictured on the front cover of my book), arguing that it was indeed a Christian cross (though 'styled to reference the Egyptian Ankh, a primary symbol within the popular Isis cult.' p. 142). He takes the cross figure as evidence of Jesus-devotion within the bakery.

   Jennifer Cianca's PhD thesis, 'Sacred Ritual, Profane Space: The Roman House as Early Christian Meeting Place' (University of Toronto, 2013) is a study of pre-Constantinian Christian meeting places in terms of sacred space. Although she operates within the general 'house church' paradigm of which I am critical, she defines 'house church' in quite broad terms 'to indicate any unrenovated, inhabited living space used by the Christians for worship, including not only houses, but apartments, shops, tenement blocks and rural or farm estates' (p. 4). This means that there is a good deal of common ground between her view of pre-Constantinian ecclesial space and mine. She makes a major new contribution to our understanding of how domestic spaces used for Christian meetings would have been considered sacred.

   Ecclesial space in early Christianity is a research area with great potential for fresh scholarly work. I remain convinced that the way forward is to consider the fullest range of spaces available to early Christians for gathering, and I reiterate my hope that this book will serve as a stimulus for new research in this direction.

INTRODUCTION

> On one point nearly all NT scholars presently agree: early Christians met almost exclusively in the homes of individual members of the congregation. For nearly three hundred years – until the fourth century, when Constantine began building the first basilicas throughout the Roman Empire – Christians gathered in private houses built initially for domestic use, not in church buildings originally constructed for the sole purpose of public worship.[1]

So writes Roger Gehring in the introduction to his study of the New Testament 'house church' and its missional significance. There can be little doubt about the accuracy of Gehring's representation of scholarly opinion: it is commonly accepted within New Testament and Early Christian studies that early Christians groups gathered for worship nearly always in the houses of church members.[2]

1. *Early Christian Meeting Places: Almost Exclusively Houses*

The view that the earliest Christian meeting places were 'almost exclusively' houses is a longstanding one. As Gehring has shown, it has been dominant in scholarship since at least the early nineteenth century.[3]

---

1 Gehring 2004: 1.

2 See, for example, the following statements. '[I]t can be stated that the earliest locations used by Christians for their gatherings were private houses, in most cases house of comparatively richer Christians' (Alikin 2010: 57). 'The earliest churches met in private households, and this remained true for the first two or three centuries' (Cox 1998: 75). 'Almost all churches met in private homes for the first two centuries of Christianity's existence' (Dunn 1996: 284; cf. Dunn 2009: 602–3). '[T]he primary meeting place for early Christian groups was the "house" until at least 150 CE' (MacDonald 2011: 69). 'Homes were frequently the settings in which the gospel was first preached…and for generations they remained the places where Christian met for worship' (Malherbe 1993: 293). 'Pauline churches, likely virtually all early Christian groups, tended to be house churches' (Smith 2003: 177). '[F]or the first two centuries at least, Christians met not in separate church buildings but in homes' (Verbrugge 1998: 13).

3 Gehring 2004: 1–2.

The consensus opinion on early Christian meeting places has been foundational for the study of the social formation of the early churches over the past few decades. According to the household model, which is the prevailing model of early ecclesial formation, the household unit – understood as an extended social body that included not only immediate family members but also slaves, freedmen and other dependants – provided the nucleus of a congregation, while the material house provided the congregational meeting place.[4] The household is thus understood to be 'the basic context' in which the early churches were set,[5] shaping their identity (as households or families of faith),[6] providing their primary leadership structure (in the form of household heads),[7] and enabling the active participation of women in ecclesial life.[8]

Since the early 1980s, the early 'house church' has become a major focus of scholarly attention.[9] The trend began with the appearance of Robert Banks' *Paul's Idea of Community: The Early House Churches in their Historical Setting* and then Hans-Josef Klauck's *Hausgemeinde und Hauskirche im frühen Christentum*.[10] There followed, among other studies, Victor Branick's work on 'house churches' in Pauline Christianity,[11] Bradley Blue's long essay on the 'house church' in Acts,[12] and

4   Meeks 1983: 75–6. The prevailing idea that the extended family was the norm in the Roman world has been challenged. In a groundbreaking study, Saller and Shaw (1984) showed that the nuclear family comes to the fore in funerary inscriptions.

5   Meeks 1983: 84. Cf. Ascough 1998: 5–9; J.H. Elliott 1981: 189–200; Judge 1960: 30–9; Stegemann and Stegemann 1999: 277–80; Tidball 1983: 79–86.

6   Osiek and Balch 1997.

7   Campbell 1994. Cf. J.H. Elliott 1981: 189–92; Holmberg 1978: 104–7; Maier 1991; Meeks 1983: 76.

8   Shüssler Fiorenza 1983: 175–84. Cf. Osiek and MacDonald 2006; Torjesen 1995.

9   For a review of scholarship on the early 'house church' up till the time of publication, see Gehring 2004: 1–16. Within scholarship on the early 'house church', the term 'house church' is mainly used in a social/ecclesial sense, denoting a group of believers meeting in a house, but sometimes it is used in an architectural sense, with reference to a house in which believers meet (e.g. Blue 1994: 188–9). I place the expression 'house church/churches' in inverted commas throughout the study because I believe it to be problematic. In the Conclusion, I will suggest that the use of the term for early churches should be abandoned.

10   Banks 1980; Klauck 1981. The appearance of Filson's (1939) article, 'The Significance of the Early House Churches', marked the beginning of research interest in 'house churches' within New Testament scholarship, but it was not until the early 1980s that research on the topic really took off. That the modern house church movement was in full swing at this time is not coincidental.

11   Branick 1989.

12   Blue 1994.

Gehring's book on the 'house church' and early Christian mission. More recently, we have seen Carolyn Osiek and Margaret MacDonald's investigation of women and 'house churches' in early Christianity,[13] and David Balch's book, *Roman Domestic Art and Early House Churches*.[14] That the earliest churches were almost invariably 'house churches' is intrinsic to all this research.

The conviction that the early Christians consistently worshipped in houses has been influential within scholarship on the origins and early development of ecclesiastical architecture. For many years, the leading theory of the origins of the Christian basilica postulated its derivation from the architecture of the houses (*domus*) in which the early Christians were assumed to have gathered.[15] That theory can no longer be sustained, but a process by which Christians met at first in private houses and then in renovated houses and eventually in larger halls until Constantine introduced basilican buildings is widely recognized. The most comprehensive and important account of that process is that of L. Michael White in his two-volume work, *The Social Origins of Christian Architecture*.[16] Taking up and modifying a scheme proposed by Richard Krautheimer,[17] White identifies three phases in the pre-Constantinian development.[18] The first phase was the 'house church' phase, when Christians met in ordinary, unaltered homes belonging to church members. The second phase was typified by the *domus ecclesiae*, literally 'house of the church', a term with a long pedigree in scholarship on early church architecture[19] and by which White means 'any building specifically adapted or renovated' for Christian use.[20] Despite the wide definition, it is clear that White has adapted *houses* mainly in mind. One *domus ecclesiae*, known from archaeology, is the Christian building at Dura Europos, modern Syria, discovered in 1931, which is generally accepted as the earliest archaeologically identifiable Christian place of worship.[21] The building is a

13 Osiek and MacDonald 2006.
14 Balch 2008. Despite its main title, *Christliche Hauskirche und Neues Testament*, Mell's 2010 monograph is mainly a study of the iconology of the baptistery in the Christian building at Dura Europos.
15 White 1990: 11–25; cf. Swift 1951: 12–30.
16 White 1990, 1997. This immensely impressive work of scholarship derives from White's 1982 Yale University PhD thesis.
17 Krautheimer 1986: 23–38.
18 White 1990: 102–39; summarized in White 2000.
19 On the history of the term in modern scholarship, see Sessa 2009: 92–6.
20 White 1990: 21.
21 Though the excavator of the Megiddo Prayer Hall, discovered in 2005, claims that this structure predates the Christianizing renovation of the Dura building: Tepper and Di Segni 2006: 50. See further in Chapter 4.

renovated domestic structure, and its conversion to a dedicated church building is dated to the 240s CE. In the third phase, larger halls, such as the rectangular hall underlying the Church of S. Crisogono at Rome,[22] were constructed. For this development, White coins the term, *aula ecclesiae*, meaning 'hall of the church'. Finally, after the Edict of Peace issued in 313 CE, the church at large adopted the basilican style of architecture, modeled on the civic basilica, a long rectangular building with colonnaded aisles. White, following Krautheimer and J.B. Ward-Perkins, maintains that basilican architecture was a Constantinian revolution and not a natural development out of the *domus ecclesiae* and the *aula ecclesiae*.[23] Once the basilica appeared, the earlier forms did not immediately disappear but continued in use long after the introduction of basilican churches. According to White, in using houses for meeting places and adapting and then renovating them for religious use, the early Christians were following a well-established pattern in the Graeco-Roman world, exemplified by private cults and other associations and also by Diaspora Jewish communities.[24] For White, the whole development from 'house church' to *domus ecclesiae* to *aula ecclesiae* requires that Christians of the pre-Constantinian era 'had access to higher socioeconomic strata'.[25]

The belief that the earliest Christian meeting places were virtually only houses has also been fundamental to study of the early liturgy. In his epochal book, *The Shape of the Liturgy*, published in 1945, Gregory Dix argued that the house setting of assembly gave rise to the distinctive shape of Christian liturgy.[26] Though few today would accept his reconstruction of early 'house-church' worship,[27] a link between the houses in

22   See White 1997: 233–40, largely following Krautheimer in *CBCR* 1.144–64. The hall was constructed around 310 CE. White believes that it was erected *de novo* as a church building. Not all scholars, though, agree that the hall was built or functioned as an ecclesiastical building. Sande (1999: 17), for example, wonders whether the basilica was built over the pre-existing edifice simply because of its dimensions and because its foundations were good.

23   White 1990: 18; cf. Ward-Perkins 1954. The first Christian basilica built under Constantine's patronage was the Church of St John Lateran in Rome, built from an imperial palace donated in 314 CE, and completed around 320. A structure discovered in the late 1990s in Aqaba, Jordan has been identified as a possible early fourth-century, pre-Constantinian basilica: see Parker 1999.

24   White 2000: 696–707.

25   White 1990: 142. Contrast Krautheimer 1986: 24: 'congregations were recruited by and large from the lower and middle classes, their houses would have been typical cheap houses'.

26   Dix 2005.

27   As White (1990: 16–17) points out, Dix was projecting later liturgical practice and church organization back onto the early assemblies.

which the early Christians are thought to have met and the shape of early church worship is still generally acknowledged, insofar as the habit of meeting in the house, and the *triclinium* in particular (with meeting sometimes spilling over into the atrium or peristyle), is understood as making (or helping to make) the communal meal the central act of worship.[28] Correspondingly, the relegation or abandonment of the worship meal (due to the detachment of the Eucharist from it) is linked with the shift away from ordinary houses as meeting places to dedicated church buildings.[29]

The view that the early Christians met almost always in church members' houses is thus one of the strongest consensuses in New Testament and Early Christian studies. It has been foundational for a great deal of work and has rarely been explicitly challenged.[30] However, the 'almost exclusively houses' – AEH for short – consensus has begun to be undermined by new thinking about the kinds of domestic spaces that might have constituted early Christian meeting places.[31]

2. Shops and Workshops as 'House Church' Settings

When envisaging the setting of an early 'house church', scholars have traditionally thought of a large Roman *domus*, or atrium house,[32] provided by a wealthy member of the congregation. Jerome Murphy-O'Connor, in his book *St Paul's Corinth*, first published in 1983, uses the Anaploga Villa in the environs of ancient Corinth to illustrate the type, picturing it as Gaius's house (cf. Rom. 16.23) and as the location of the Corinthian Eucharistic assembly.[33] However, prompted in part by a reassessment of the social level of the Christians, there has been

---

28   White 1990: 109.

29   Thus Bradshaw (2004: 66) writes: 'The *terminus ad quem* for this development [the giving up or severe curtailment of the meal] has to be the end of the use of private homes and their replacement by specially adapted buildings that would accommodate larger congregations'. Cf. Doig 2008: 4.

30   I have found only one scholar, Sande (1999), who explicitly dissents from the consensus: see below.

31   My label for the consensus viewpoint is derived from the statement by Gehring cited at the beginning of this Introduction; cf. Klauck 1981: 66.

32   An atrium house is a house comprising of rooms around a central open-roofed front hall. Often an atrium house would have a colonnaded garden or peristyle (hence it is called an atrium-peristyle house). See Allison 2007; Brothers 1996: 33–49.

33   Murphy-O'Connor 2002: 178–85. See further Chapter 1.

increasing doubt about whether large *domus* can be regarded as typical
locales for 'house churches'. David Horrell has been critical of Murphy-
O'Connor's appeal to the Anaploga Villa.[34] Persuaded to a certain extent
by Justin Meggitt's critique of the 'new consensus' view that early
Christian congregations contained some members of the wealthy elite,[35]
Horrell doubts that any member of the Corinthian congregation could
have owned a plush residence like this. He thinks that non-elite upper-
floor living space is a more likely setting for the Corinthian Eucharistic
assembly.[36]

Some scholars have suggested shops and workshops as domestic
locales for early Christian meetings.[37] Robert Jewett argues that most
Christians in large cities such as Rome would have lived in *insulae*,
multi-storey apartment blocks, rather than in private villas.[38] He posits
that in them 'tenement churches' would have thrived. A tenement church,
he believes, would have been more egalitarian than a 'house church',
since it would not have been dependent on a wealthy homeowner, and
would have met either in living space in the higher floors or in 'one of
the workshop areas on the ground floor'.[39] Balch, having previously
insisted that *domus* were the primary meeting places for early churches,
in an article published in 2004, acknowledges large apartment blocks
and rentable shops as 'typical' spaces for Pauline 'house churches'.[40]
Shops, he observes, often took up the street level of *insulae* and sometimes fronted wealthy *domus*. He envisages Chloe's people at Corinth
worshipping 'in a shop in her *insula* that they as her slaves managed'.[41]
Peter Oakes, in his book, *Reading Romans in Pompeii*, appearing in
2009, situates his imagined 'model craftworker house church' in Rome

34   Horrell 2004.
35   See esp. Meggitt 1998.
36   Horrell 2004: 359. For Horrell's own reconstruction, see Chapter 1. Horrell
(369) urges scholars to 'pay more attention to the varieties of domestic space in the
urban setting of Corinth and other cities of the Roman empire, and consider these as
possible settings for early Christian meetings'. For a similar appeal, see P. Richardson 2004b: 62–4.
37   A workshop is taken by Murphy-O'Connor (1992) and Lampe (2003: 192–3)
as the most likely setting of the 'house church' hosted by Prisca and Aquila first in
Ephesus (1 Cor. 16.19) and then in Rome (Rom. 16.5). See further Chapter 1.
Murphy-O'Connor (2002: 192–8) also contends that the couple also hosted a 'house
church' in their workshop at Corinth.
38   Jewett 1993: 26.
39   Jewett 1993: 26; cf. 2007: 65.
40   Balch 2004.
41   Balch 2004: 40.

in a 45 square metre *insula* street-level workshop, with the host and his family living either higher up in the same block or in a flat in another block.[42] He tries to visualize meeting conditions:

> dark if the doors were closed, open to the street if they were open; in a very noisy environment; heavily encumbered with materials, tools and work in progress (although in this particular case, some might have been able to be sat on!); lacking in the cooking facilities and latrine that were available in the house… However, the amount of space would presumably allow, say, 30 people to gather.[43]

The growing acceptance of shops and workshops[44] as typical 'house church' (or in Jewett's case 'tenement church') settings seems anomalous, since we would not normally regard such places as 'houses'.[45] To be fair, shops and small workshops containing sleeping areas (at the rear or in a mezzanine) can legitimately be classed as 'dwellings' (and could come under the referential embrace of the Greek words οἶκος and οἰκία). But as Penelope Allison, an expert on Roman housing, states, 'Not all dwellings…can be considered "houses"'.[46] For Allison, shops and small workshops with accommodation attached – *taberna*-dwellings – cannot be regarded as 'houses' in the strict sense. Clarity is served by following Allison's lead and reserving the word 'house' for a building designed and used exclusively or primarily for residential purposes (whether *domus* or tenement flat) and not applying it to structures such as shops and workshops which were primarily commercial and industrial units that secondarily functioned as living quarters for (some of) those who worked in them. More correctly as understood as 'non-house' spaces, the recent inclusion of shops and workshops among typical spaces for early church gatherings undermines the consensus view that the early Christians met almost always in houses.[47]

In a very recent contribution, Balch further destabilizes the AEH consensus by recognizing that inns and gardens attached to inns could

42 Oakes 2009: 94.
43 Oakes 2009: 94–5.
44 Shops and small workshops – *tabernae* – could be found in other architectural settings as well as in *insulae*. See further in Chapter 6.
45 For Jewett, tenements are architecturally 'houses' ('multi-story tenement houses', Jewett 2007: 53).
46 Allison 2007: 277.
47 It might be argued that the adverb 'almost' in the AEH consensus allows for the possibility that non-house settings were also used, but 'almost exclusively' implies that other settings were highly exceptional, and Jewett, Balch and Oakes are claiming that shops/workshops should be regarded as 'typical' and 'model' settings for church meetings, not exceptional possibilities.

have served as Christian gathering places.[48] He tries to show that the idea
of Christians meeting in an inn is consistent with the understanding of
early Christian meeting places as houses by pointing out that Pompeian
taverns were sometimes *domus* converted into taverns. He states: 'They
became "taverns" and were also "houses," where their owners may have
lived with their slaves'.[49] But the prior form and function of a converted
property does not define its subsequent use. *Domus* turned into inns were
commercial hospitality properties, serving business ends, even if staff
(usually slaves) stayed on site (owners rarely did). Balch does accept,
though, that some Pompeian inns, such as the *caupona* of Euxinus, completely resist architectural classification as houses.[50] In so doing, he
seems more overtly to move beyond the AEH paradigm.[51]

3. *Reassessing Early Christian Meeting Places*

The recent expansion of early 'house church' scenarios to include what
were really *non-house* settings calls for a reconsideration of the AEH
perspective. There are two further reasons for reexamining the assumption that early Christians met almost only in houses.

First, if Jewett is right that most Christians in large cities tended to live
in large apartment blocks,[52] their homes – aside from the ground-floor
tabernae – would have been difficult as meeting places. Tenement flats
were typically small and were used mainly for sleeping. According to
Siri Sande, in a Norwegian-language article published in 1999, Christians
housed in such conditions must have gathered for worship elsewhere:
shops and workshops, rented premises and other non-house settings.[53]

Jewett thinks that more space could have been created for meetings by
removing partition walls between flats, but such partition walls, Gehring
points out, were constructed with tufa blocks or wood and were not
portable.[54] The idea that they could be cleared away once or week or so
to make room for Christian meetings, he insists, is not supported by

---

48   Balch 2012.
49   Balch 2012: 232.
50   Balch 2012: 232.
51   It is also interesting to note that he drops the terminology of 'house church'
in this piece.
52   Jewett's claim needs to be treated with some caution. Horrell (2004: 361)
points out that there is no archaeological evidence for multi-storey apartment blocks
in Corinth.
53   Sande 1999.
54   Gehring 2004: 149.

archaeology. Oakes emphasizes that spaces within apartment blocks were varied and often contained 'fairly opulent apartments' on the level above the street.[55] However, these more lavish apartments were normally occupied by members of the elite and thus might be considered doubtful as the homes of Christians.[56] Typical *insula* flats would not have been impossible as assembly venues. If they averaged about ten square metres, as Jewett claims,[57] they could have accommodated groups of up to about ten people.[58] In Acts 20.7-11, Luke pictures a Christian meeting in a cramped upper-floor *insula* dwelling. Yet, it is not easy to see how groups at the higher end of estimated sizes of early 'house churches' (thirty or more people)[59] could have gathered in standard tenement spaces or in some other forms of non-elite urban housing.[60]

Second, other places of meeting are explicitly indicated in the early literature. This has not gone unnoticed and unacknowledged by White and others,[61] but it is quickly passed over. The evidence for non-house meeting places has not been investigated systematically and, aside from Sande's article, it has not really figured in discussion of early Christian meeting places. The entrenched opinion that the early Christians met almost only in houses has largely precluded serious engagement with these data.

There is thus a need for a re-investigation of the topic of the earliest Christian meeting places, scrutinizing the literary, archaeological and ancient comparative evidence for the consensus AEH view and examining the evidence and possibilities for non-house venues.

55　Oakes 2009: 91.

56　Meggitt 1998: 63.

57　Jewett 1993: 26.

58　Applying the formula given by Osiek and Balch (1997: 201): 'one half square meter per person and an equal half square for furniture'. I use this formula in Part II of the book in estimating the number of people a given built space-type could reasonably contain.

59　Estimates of how many people comprised a house church vary somewhat. Banks (1980: 42) takes forty to forty-five persons as the upper limit, with the average size of a 'house church' being around thirty people. Klauck (1981: 100) thinks that 'house churches' would have consisted of ten to thirty persons. Gehring (2004: 290) believes that 'house churches' averaged between twenty to forty persons, though in rare cases, the number could have reached 'up to a hundred'. Oakes (2009: 69–97) works with numbers of thirty and forty in constructing his 'model craftworker house church'.

60　Such as lean-tos and shanties: see Meggitt 1998: 62–7; cf. Scobie 1986.

61　White 2000: 710. Cf. Kraeling 1967: 129; G.F. Snyder 2003: 128.

4. *The Aims, Approach and Structure of the Book*

This book has two main aims: (1) to show that while there is indeed good evidence for houses as meeting places, it is not as extensive, or as excluding of other possibilities, as is usually thought;[62] (2) to identify, on the basis of explicit literary evidence and sometimes archaeological evidence, a variety of other types of spaces that could plausibly have served as early Christian meeting places. Moving beyond the AEH consensus, I seek to make the case that during the first two centuries, the alleged era of the 'house church',[63] Christians could credibly have met in a diversity of places and not almost invariably houses.

To be absolutely clear, I am not denying that houses acted as early Christian meeting spaces; my objection is to the notion that they did so 'almost exclusively'.[64]

My 'thesis' is not unprecedented. Sande, in the aforementioned article, has made a similar argument. Although her essay is not well known outside of Norwegian scholarship, it is a pioneering study to which I can point for scholarly support.[65]

The book divides into two parts, corresponding to my main objectives. Part I, embracing Chapters 1 to 5, deals with 'Evidence for Houses as Christian Meeting Places', and examines the literary, archaeological and comparative evidence for early Christian use of houses as assembly places. Although my primary period of interest is the first two centuries, it is necessary to deal with data relating to the whole *ante-pacem* era (till 313 CE). This is because some of the post-New Testament literary evidence commonly cited for ordinary houses as meeting places (e.g. passages in the Pseudo-Clementines) is post-200 CE.[66] Also, claimed and potential evidence for adapted houses as church buildings is later

62　Dix (2005: 18), for instance, speaks of 'those "house-churches" which meet us everywhere in the N.T. and in the 2nd century'.

63　For the period up to 200 CE as the era of the house church, see, e.g., Dunn 1996: 28; Krautheimer 1986: 24; Smith 2012: 18.

64　As noted above, I think that small groups of believers could have met in tenement flats. Also, as Oakes (2009: 69–89) has demonstrated, modestly sized *domus* would have been quite possible as Christian meeting places in smaller urban centres like Pompeii.

65　Given the brevity of the piece, Sande does not cover the full range of evidence and possibilities for non-house meeting places discussed here.

66　Some literary evidence, in particular legends linking Rome's titular churches with pre-Constantinian 'house churches', is even later (see p.68 n.2, below). But I do not go beyond the writings of Eusebius.

than 200 CE. It is important to take account of possible literary and archaeological evidence for domestic *domus ecclesiae*[67] since a well-documented phase of meeting in modified houses would tend to imply a prior phase gathering in unaltered houses. Chapters 1 and 2 consider the New Testament evidence. Chapter 1 treats the epistles, especially the Pauline epistles, and Chapter 2 takes in the Gospels and Acts. Chapter 3 assesses the literary (including papyrological) evidence outside and beyond the New Testament, covering (more or less) the period 100 to 313 CE. From written evidence I turn in Chapter 4 to archaeological evidence, discussing the Christian building at Dura Europos and other alleged instances of *ante-pacem* domestic *domus ecclesiae*. Chapter 5 deals with comparative evidence, which is the evidence constituted by seeming parallels in the Roman world to the Christian use of houses as gathering places. I discuss the practice of 'domestic religion' in the house; the usage of houses for scholastic activities; the use of houses and renovated houses as collegial meeting places; 'house synagogues'.

Part II, comprising Chapters 6 to 8, deals with 'Evidence and Possibilities for Non-House Meeting Places'. In Chapters 6 to 8, I identify a number of non-house spaces that could plausibly have served as meeting sites for the early Christians. I do so precisely on the basis of literary and archaeological evidence. All the space-types discussed are explicitly indicated or suggested as Christian meeting places in literary sources and/or relevant ecclesiastical archaeology. None stems from sheer speculation. Chapter 6 covers retail, industrial and storage spaces, and looks at shops and workshops, barns and warehouses. Chapter 7 focuses on leisure and hospitality spaces and considers hotels and inns, rented dining rooms and bathhouses. Chapter 8 discusses outdoor spaces and burial places and gives attention to gardens, watersides, urban open spaces and tombsides.[68]

In discussing each space-type I generally take a three-step approach. First, I set out or recap the evidence for use of the given space-type as a venue for early Christian meeting. Second, I offer a description of the space-type using archaeological and other data. I draw particularly on the rich resources of Pompeii and Ostia for archaeological illustration. These two sites contain some of the best-preserved Roman ruins available

---

67   Given White's notionally wide definition of a *domus ecclesiae*, I add the qualification 'domestic' to specify a *house* adapted for church use.

68   Scobie (1986: 402–3) points out that the poor sometimes slept in urban public space, tombs, cheap hotels and probably even in and around public baths. That they could function as 'dwellings' of a basic kind does not, though, make them 'houses'.

to us dating to the first and second centuries (Pompeii reflecting the first century CE, and Ostia the second), and offer 'typical' examples of many Roman built-forms. When dealing with certain outdoor spaces (watersides and urban open space), I omit this second step, since internal building space is not in view. Third, I endeavour to establish the plausibility of the space-type as a setting for Christian meeting applying the criteria of availability, analogous usage, adequacy and advantageousness (not necessarily all four in each instance). By *availability* I mean the general accessibility of the space-type to Christians. In determining availability, two judgments are made in advance: first, that Christians of the first two centuries were predominantly urbanites;[69] second, that they were generally non-elites and thus, as a rule, would not have had access to elite strata (*contra* White).[70] By *analogous usage* is meant the use of the given space-type for similar purposes (private religion, teaching, dining) or by analogous groups (schools, associations or Jewish groups). *Adequacy* has to do with the fitness or basic suitability of the space-type for Christian meetings, which were mainly meal meetings,[71] though Christians could also meet on separate occasions for communal prayer, worship and instruction.[72] By *advantageousness* I mean the possession of some feature that would make the space-type preferable, in some circumstances, to house space as meeting space (especially the capacity to accommodate a larger amount of people). Envisioning various non-house space-types as Christian meeting space requires a large degree of 'disciplined imagination',[73] but the same goes for envisioning Christian meetings in residential space.

69   On early Christianity as primarily an urban phenomenon, see Meeks 1983.

70   While 'new consensus' scholarship, typified by White, has maintained that emerging Christianity was to a significant extent dependent on wealthy elites, as Smith (2012: 7) notes, 'recent scholarship has emphasized the extent to which earliest Christianity would have been a movement among non-elites'. See Friesen 2004, 2010; Horrell 2004: 56–9; Longenecker 2009, 2010; Meggitt 1998; Oakes 2009: 46–80.

71   It is generally accepted that the communal meal was the main Christian meeting in the first two centuries. As Alikin (2010) shows, Christian meal meetings incorporated a range of activities, including the celebration of the Eucharist, the reading out of authoritative texts, prophecies and revelations, preaching, singing and prayer.

72   For prayer meetings, see Acts 1.14; 12.12; 21.5. For worship meetings, distinct from the communal meal, see Pliny the Younger, *Ep.* 10.96. For large preaching/teaching meetings, see *Acts of Paul* 11.1.

73   To take up Horrell's (2004: 367) phrase; cf. Meggitt 2001: 93.

The discussion of non-house possibilities for Christian meeting in Chapters 6 to 8 takes place at an intentionally general level. The aim is to identify a number of settings that could sometimes have served as meeting places for Christians in the Roman world over the course of the first two centuries; I certainly do not claim that these places were always accessible to, and able to be used by, every Christian group in every locality. I also discuss the non-house options for meeting, for the most part, in a deliberately abstract manner, i.e., without any reference to specific localities. In Appendix 1, though, I draw on local archaeology to illuminate a possible setting for Corinthian communal meal (as reflected in 1 Cor. 11–14).

A consequence of the abstract treatment of non-house possibilities for Christian gathering in Part II is that I do not take into account Christian experience of persecution, since until the Decian persecution of 250–251 CE, the persecution of Christians was sporadic and local and not constant and empire-wide. Certainly, by the second century, Christians were subject to widespread social prejudice (though opinions probably varied), which constituted a potentially deadly threat for them.[74] However, outbreaks of violence were irregular, sudden and localized. As Judith Lieu points out, 'The very suddenness of the persecution and the lack of any clear cause presuppose earlier, more "normal", co-existence'.[75] The *Epistula ecclesiarum apud Lugdunum et Viennam*, preserved by Eusebius, describing the persecution of Christians at Lyons and Vienne in Gaul, indicates that the persecution began with believers being 'excluded from houses and baths and markets' (*H.E.* 5.1.5). As Lieu notes, this action presupposes believers' 'normal association in these places' beforehand.[76] During spells of persecution, or intense harassment, to be sure, inns, restaurants, bathhouses, etc., are not really plausible as meeting places, but in such periods, even meeting in houses would have been difficult.[77]

74   Holloway 2009: 41–66, esp. 65–6.
75   Lieu 2009: 55.
76   Lieu 2009: 55.
77   Note that the Gallic Christians were 'excluded from houses' as well as baths and marketplaces. According to Gehring (2004: 290), the 'architectural anonymity' of the private house could have provided a degree of protection in times of persecution. However, the regular use of a private house as a Christian meeting place could not have escaped the notice of people living in the vicinity. A house that served as a Christian meeting venue would have been well known within the immediate neighbourhood and would thus have been easy for the authorities to locate when persecution struck. Gehring himself concedes that the anonymity of the house would not always have been possible to maintain (291).

A conclusion summarizes the case made in the preceding chapters and considers, albeit briefly, its implications for study of early ecclesial formation, the origins and early development of ecclesiastical architecture, and early Christian worship, and also for scholarship on the early 'house church'.

Part I

EVIDENCE FOR HOUSES AS MEETING PLACES

Chapter 1

NEW TESTAMENT EVIDENCE: EPISTLES

This chapter and the next assess the claimed New Testament evidence for the use of houses as Christian meeting places. The present chapter takes up the evidence in the New Testament epistles, especially the Pauline epistles; the chapter that follows is concerned with the data in the Synoptic Gospels and the book of Acts.[1]

Respecting the scholarly distinction between the undisputed and disputed Pauline letters, we look first at the undisputed Paulines, which are generally regarded as the earliest writings in the New Testament, and then at the so-called deutero-Pauline letters.[2] For the sake of convenience Col. 4.15, from a disputed letter, is treated along with other references to the 'church at the home' in the undisputed epistles.[3] After considering the data in the Pauline corpus, we turn to relevant material in the 'General' or 'Catholic' epistles, a number of which are thought, at least by some, to exhibit a 'house church' setting.

1. *The Undisputed Pauline Letters*

There is general agreement that the Pauline churches met in houses.[4] It is widely held that a Pauline community in a given location was composed

---

1 Aune (1997: 203) assumes an audience situation for Revelation in which Christian communities were made up of 'house churches', but he offers no evidence for it. The same goes for Balch (2008: 139).

2 The undisputed epistles are Romans, 1 and 2 Corinthians, Galatians, Philippians, 1 Thessalonians and Philemon.

3 Following Gehring 2004: 119–21, 154–5. While the authorship of Colossians is disputed, many critics, especially in Anglophone New Testament scholarship, regard it as genuine.

4 The terms 'Pauline churches', 'Pauline Christianity', etc., are used here for communities established or addressed by Paul. The terminology is problematic (see Horrell 2008) but expedient.

of multiple house churches.⁵ Corinth and Rome are taken as exempli-
fying the pattern; Gehring finds it in other localities too.

The main lexical evidence for 'house churches' in Pauline Christianity
is the so-called house church formula,⁶ ἡ κατ' οἶκον ἐκκλησία. We look
first at this expression and then consider more broadly household and
family terminology, which has been claimed as bearing more general
witness to the use of houses as meeting space. There next follows a
discussion of the evidence for 'house churches' at specific locations,
concentrating first on Corinth and Rome, the two localities for which we
are best informed, and then broadening out to other places.

1.1. *'The Church at the Home'*
According to Dennis Smith, 'Paul frequently mentions the church meeting at someone's house'.⁷ However, in the entire Pauline corpus (all
thirteen letters), there are only four occurrences of the formula ἡ κατ'
οἶκον (+ personal pronoun) ἐκκλησία, and all four are within epistolary
greetings.⁸ In 1 Cor. 16.19, Paul, writing from Ephesus (cf. 16.8),
extends to his readers warm greetings from Aquila and Prisca together
with τῇ κατ' οἶκον αὐτῶν ἐκκλησία. In Rom. 16.3-5, Paul greets Prisca
and Aquila, who are evidently now in Rome, and τὴν κατ' οἶκον αὐτῶν
ἐκκλησίαν (16.5). At the beginning of his shortest extant letter, Paul gives
greetings to Philemon and τῇ κατ' οἶκόν σου ἐκκλησίᾳ. Finally, in Col.
4.15, Nympha is greeted along with τὴν κατ' οἶκον αὐτῆς ἐκκλησίαν.⁹

The term οἶκος, within the larger expression, could refer to a social
unit, 'household', or a material habitation, whether a 'house' proper or
a 'dwelling' more broadly.¹⁰ If οἶκος is understood to mean 'household',
ἡ κατ' οἶκον ἐκκλησία would refer to a household unit that forms a
Christian congregation. However, the churches of Prisca and Aquila at

---

5   So Banks 1980: 37–42; Branick 1989: 22–7; Button and Van Rensburg 2003;
Gehring 2004: 155–65; Klauck 1981: 33–42; Meeks 1983: 75–7.

6   As Button and Van Rensburg (2003: 1) call it.

7   Smith 2003: 177.

8   The precise Greek formulation has no parallel outside of Christian literature.
A set of inscriptions refers to a *collegium quod est in domo Sergiae Paullinae* (CIL
6.9148, 9149, 10260–4), which is sometimes taken as a Latin counterpart to the
Pauline expression. Indeed, it has been contended that the *collegium* was a 'house
church' (Sordi 1986: 185–6), but, as White (1990: 47) points out, there is no warrant
for such speculation. I refer to these inscriptions again in Chapter 5.

9   Ancient manuscripts vary at Col. 4.15b, but the reading accepted above
(taking Νύμφα as a feminine noun) is to be preferred: Metzger 1994: 560.

10   BDAG 698–9; LSJ 1204–5. Other possible senses of οἶκος ('room'; 'building'; 'temple'; 'clan'; 'nation') are not applicable.

Ephesus and Rome do not appear to have been constituted by their household.[11] There is no indication in the Pauline letters or the book of Acts that Prisca and Aquila had children or slaves;[12] they simply appear as a 'missionary couple'.[13] We never read of 'the household of Prisca and Aquila', especially when such an expression could have been used, as in 2 Tim. 4.19 where Prisca and Aquila are greeted alongside 'the household of Onesiphorus.[14] Their churches were likely composed of converts made by them. Philemon's church probably revolved around his family, but it was not co-extensive with his household since we know of at least one member of that household who was not a believer (Onesimus, who did not convert until his encounter with Paul). We can be fairly sure, then, that the word οἶκος within the expression ἡ κατ' οἶκον ἐκκλησία denotes a habitation. Most exegetes agree that οἶκος within ἡ κατ' οἶκον ἐκκλησία means 'house' or 'home'.[15]

Papyrological evidence shows that κατ' οἶκον was equivalent to ἐν οἴκῳ (cf. 1 Cor. 11.34; 14.35) in Koine Greek.[16] As such, the expression means 'at home'.[17] The formulation ἡ κατ' οἶκον (+ personal pronoun) ἐκκλησία, therefore, has the meaning 'the church at the home of so-and-so'. It thus indicates the use of a believer's home as a gathering site. It is important to emphasize, though, that the words οἶκος and οἰκία, largely overlapping in meaning in the New Testament period (Paul uses them

11   Banks 1980: 38.
12   As Lampe (2003: 193) points out, Paul is their only verifiable employee.
13   Osiek and MacDonald 2006: 32.
14   Lampe 2003: 193.
15   As Button and van Rensberg (2003: 10) emphasize.
16   Gielen 1986: 111–12. Some maintain that the preposition κατά within the wider expression functions distributively: 'of a whole divided into parts'. Thus, according to Button and van Rensberg (2003: 9), 'The noun ἐκκλησία refers to the entire local church, and the preposition κατά indicates that the members of this body were conceived of as being distributed into οἶκοι, specifically the οἶκοι of the people named each time the phrase is used'. On this understanding, the very formulation ἡ κατ' οἶκον ἐκκλησία itself implies a situation in which a local church is made up of a number of home-based groups. However, as Gielen (pp.122–4) argues, a distributive interpretation is not an option in the context of a greeting where only one, specifically identified, οἶκος is mentioned (cf. Gehring 2004: 156). Grammatically, κατ' οἶκον in 1 Cor. 16.19, etc., must be understood in a locational sense (so also Gehring 2004: 159). To insist on the locational meaning of κατ' οἶκον within the expression ἡ κατ' οἶκον ἐκκλησία, however, is not to deny that in three of the passages in which the formulation occurs, a larger local community of believers is indicated beyond the κατ' οἶκον ἐκκλησία mentioned, though as will be seen, there is no necessary implication in any of these texts that that wider community is a collection of 'house churches'.
17   Lampe 2003: 193.

interchangeably: 1 Cor. 1.16; 16.15), can refer to a wide variety of dwellings, and not only 'houses' strictly understood.[18] The variety includes a dwelling arrangement such as a shop or workshop with living quarters attached, i.e., a *taberna*-dwelling.[19] Thus, οἶκος within the formula ἡ κατ' οἶκον ἐκκλησία need not refer to a 'house' in the sense of a building used mainly or solely for domestic purposes. Philemon's οἶκος may well have been a 'house' in the strict sense (since in Philem. 22 Paul refers to a ξενία or 'guest room'),[20] though not necessarily a house of relatively large proportions. Jewett (somewhat surprisingly in view of his emphasis on 'tenement churches') locates the οἶκος of Prisca and Aquila in Rome 'in the elegant Aventine quarter' of the city,[21] on the site of the *Titulus Priscae*/Church of S. Prisca.[22] Excavations underneath the church building reveal large elite residences dating from the time that Paul wrote Romans. One of these houses contains a mithraeum,[23] and Jewett wonders whether this was the house of Prisca, and whether the presence of a mithraeum in it 'indicates that her house had been confiscated and put to non-Christian use'.[24] However, the existence of the *Titulus Priscae* is first documented in the late fifth century, and the identity of the Prisca whose name the *titulus* bears is very uncertain.[25] While one tradition identifies her with the Prisca/Priscilla of the New Testament, another links her with a different Prisca, an early Christian virgin-martyr. Moreover, the house with the mithraeum was constructed no earlier than 95 CE, and so could not have been the οἶκος of Prisca and Aquila at the time of the letter of the Romans.[26] It is extremely unlikely that Prisca and Aquila could have lived in an aristocratic house on the Aventine anyway, since, according Acts 18.3, they earned their living by making tents.[27] As

18   LSJ 1204–5. Button and Van Rensburg 2003: 10–11; Gehring 2004: 135; Horrell 2004: 359 n. 51; Jewett 1993: 24; Klauck 1981: 15–20. As Button and Van Rensburg (2003: 10) point out, the Cyclops' cave is called an οἶκος in Homer, *Od.* 9.478, and the tents of Jacob and Leah are called οἶκοι in Gen. 31.33 LXX.

19   Gehring 2004: 135. Luke, though, seems to use the terminology more narrowly for 'houses' proper. See the next chapter.

20   Though Paul may be using the term in the more abstract sense of 'hospitable reception' (Barth and Blanke 2000: 493).

21   Jewett 2007: 957.

22   Jewett 2007: 63.

23   On which see Vermaseren and Van Essen 1965.

24   Jewett 2007: 63.

25   *CBCR* 3.274–5; Petersen 1973: 279.

26   Vermaseren and Van Essen 1965: 107. See further the discussion in Chapter 4, below.

27   The clause, 'for they were tentmakers', ἦσαν γὰρ σκηνοποιοί, could be interpreted as referring to Paul and Aquila (so Barrett 1998: 863). However, it is

Murphy-O'Connor and Lampe have argued, given their occupation, the οἶκοι in which their churches met, both at Ephesus and Rome, were most likely workshop (*taberna*) dwellings.[28] The genitive case of the personal pronoun within the formulation ἡ κατ᾽ οἶκον (+ personal pronoun) ἐκκλησία does not necessarily indicate that the building was owned by the person or persons mentioned.[29] If we are right in thinking that Prisca and Aquila's οἶκοι were *tabernae*, they were probably rented workshops (given the mobility of the couple).

The four occurrences of the expression ἡ κατ᾽ οἶκον ἐκκλησία thus provide hard textual evidence for the use of believers' homes as ecclesial meeting places, but two caveats must be added. First, in at least two instances *taberna*-dwellings rather than 'houses' (strictly defined) may be in view. Second, four references to a κατ᾽ οἶκον ἐκκλησία do not on their own point to an *extensive* practice of meeting in houses (or even 'homes' broadly understood).[30]

1.2. Household and Family Terminology

Branick finds evidence for 'house churches' in the Pauline mission in Paul's frequent and pervasive use of household and family terminology.[31] According to Branick, Paul's application of this language to the believing community reflects the practice of gathering in houses, Paul's theological understanding of the Christian community as a family and household blending with '[t]he practical necessity of meeting in private homes'.[32]

Although Branick discusses them together, and although they are obviously interrelated, family language based on organic relationships (parent–child; sibling) and household language should be taken, as least notionally, as discrete semantic fields. Language of brother/sisterhood need not reflect the ideal of the hierarchically structured household.[33]

As Horrell has shown, household language is not very prominent in the undisputed Pauline letters.[34] The term οἶκος occurs only six times.

much more natural to take it as referring to Priscilla (i.e. Prisca) and Aquila, with the plural picking up the previous αὐτοῖς, which indubitably refers to the couple (so Murphy-O'Connor 1992: 44).

28   Murphy-O'Connor 1992: 49; cf. 2002: 195; Lampe 2003: 192–3. On *tabernae* as possible Christian meeting places, see Chapter 6.

29   Lampe 2003: 193; Murphy-O'Connor 1992: 49.

30   Especially bearing in mind that the word ἐκκλησία is used some 62 times in the Pauline corpus.

31   Branick 1989: 16–17.

32   Branick 1989: 17.

33   So Horrell 2001: 295–6.

34   Horrell 2001: 299–304.

Aside from its use in within the formula ἡ κατ' οἶκον ἐκκλησία, it is applied to an actual household, that of Stephanas, in 1 Cor. 1.16 (see below), and to actual houses/dwellings in 1 Cor. 11.34 and 14.35 (see below). There are only five occurrences of the word οἰκία. It is used of the household of Stephanas in 1 Cor. 16.15 (see below) and the emperor's household in Phil. 4.22.[35] Actual houses/dwellings are in view in 1 Cor. 11.22 (see below), and in 2 Cor. 5.1, Paul uses οἰκία in articulating the contrast between the earthly dwelling (the physical body) and the heavenly dwelling not made with hands. The terms οἶκος and οἰκία are never used in the undisputed letters to designate metaphorically the believing community as a household.

Branick treats as household language in Paul the terms οἰκοδομή, οἰκονομία and οἰκονόμος.[36] True, these lexemes are etymologically related to οἶκος, but both in terms of standard Greek usage and in terms of Paul's utilisation of them, it is misleading to classify these words as household language.[37] The word οἰκοδομή denotes either the process of building something or a built structure.[38] It is not restricted to the building of domiciles or to domiciles as buildings (e.g. in Mk 13.1-2, it refers to the temple buildings). Paul mainly uses οἰκοδομή, and also the cognate verb οἰκοδομέω, in a figurative sense with regard to the building up of believers individually and especially communally.[39] The metaphorical usage carries no necessary implication of the church as a household.[40] In 1 Cor. 3.9, Paul calls the Corinthian congregation 'God's building', but the context makes clear that the building in view is a temple and not a

35   The phrase οἱ ἐκ τῆς Καίσαρος οἰκίας 'refers not to Caesar's relatives but rather to the large number of imperial clients, friends and civil servants, predominantly slaves and freed slaves, who were directly subject to the Emperor' (Bockmuehl 1997: 269).

36   Branick 1989: 16. Even Paul's self-designation, 'master builder', σοφὸς ἀρχιτέκτων (1 Cor. 3.10), claims Branick, 'belongs to this linguistic context of housebuilding'. But ἀρχιτέκτων meaning master builder or director of works belongs to the wider sphere of construction and not only house-building: see, e.g., Philo, *Opif.* 24; *Spec. Leg.* 3.95; *Mut.* 30; *Somn.* 2.8. Cf. BDAG 139.

37   Branick commits the 'etymological fallacy', assuming that the meaning of a word is determined by its etymology. On the etymological fallacy, see Cotterell and Turner 1989: 129–31. They give the example of 'greenhouse'. To take the component 'house' as an indicator of the meaning of 'greenhouse' would be a mistake, since 'a greenhouse is not a house' (130), though like a house it is a building.

38   BDAG 696–7.

39   οἰκοδομή: Rom. 14.19; 15.2; 1 Cor. 3.9; 14.3, 5, 12, 26; 2 Cor. 10.8; 12.19; 13.10; οἰκοδομέω: Rom. 15.20; 1 Cor. 8.1, 10; 10.23; 14.4, 17; Gal. 2.18; 1 Thess. 5.11.

40   Cf. Horrell 2001: 304.

domestic structure (1 Cor. 3.16-17).[41] The word οἰκονομία originally referred to the management of a household, but it came to be used of the administration of a state and then of any kind of activity that stems from holding an office.[42] In 1 Cor. 9.17, Paul uses it with regard to his apostolic 'commission' to preach the gospel. The term οἰκονόμος refers in the first place to a household manager or estate manager, but it could also be used for the holder of a civic office, as in Rom. 16.23, with regard to Erastus, who is designated, ὁ οἰκονόμος τῆς πόλεως,[43] or more generally for someone entrusted with management. In 1 Cor. 4.1-2, Paul describes himself and his co-workers as οἰκονόμοι of the mysteries of God. John Goodrich has recently argued that Paul's metaphor 'should be interpreted in the context of private commercial administration'.[44] According to Goodrich, Paul employs the metaphor 'to emphasise the servility *and* authority of apostles in order to eliminate partisanship and to defend himself against critics'.[45] Only twice in the undisputed letters does Paul's employment of an οἶκος-related word suggest the idea of the Christian community as a household: in Rom. 14.4, where he calls a believer an οἰκέτης ('household slave') of the Lord, and in Gal. 6.10, where he refers to community members as οἰκεῖοι τῆς πίστεως, members of the household of faith. In neither passage, though, is the notion of the church as household developed. As Horrell states, there is 'little evidence of the household image providing a structuring model for relationships ἐν ἐκκλησίᾳ'.[46] In the undisputed letters, other images (body, temple) are preferred as metaphors for the local church.[47] Even if household language were more prevalent, the application of such imagery to the church need not imply the house as meeting place, a point I will expand on below.

---

41   In 2 Cor. 5.1, οἰκοδομή is used of the everlasting building that replaces the earthly tent, which is the physical body.

42   BDAG 697–9; *NIDNNT* 2.253.

43   The precise nature of the office held by Erastus is highly debated. While some think that he occupied a significant civic position, such as *quaestor* (so Theissen 1982: 82–3; Goodrich 2010), Meggitt (1998: 139) thinks that his role could have been a relatively menial one. The debate is bound up with whether the Erastus of Rom. 16.23 is to be identified with the famous 'Erastus' mentioned in a Corinthian inscription. For recent contributions to that question, see Friesen 2010; Goodrich 2011.

44   Goodrich 2012: 200.

45   Goodrich 2012: 202.

46   Horrell 2001: 304.

47   Barton 1986: 239. Økland (2004: 152–9) argues that Paul uses cultic language in the Corinthians letters to define ecclesial space as 'sanctuary' (i.e. temple) space.

In contrast to household parlance, family language is used widely in the undisputed letters.[48] Believers are called 'children of God' (υἱοί: Rom. 8.14, 19; Gal. 3.26; τέκνα: Rom. 8.16, 21; 9.8; Phil. 2.15). Paul identifies himself as a 'father' to communities founded by him (1 Cor. 4.15; 1 Thess. 2.11) and refers to members of these churches as his 'children' (1 Cor. 4.14; 2 Cor. 6.13; 12.14; Gal. 4.19). Most significantly, community members are designated ἀδελφοί (and Paul refers to individual believers as an ἀδελφός or ἀδελφή). As Banks notes, the term ἀδελφοί is 'far and away Paul's favorite way of referring to the members of the communities to whom he is writing'.[49] On Horrell's count, Paul uses ἀδελφοί with reference to community members 122 times in the letters commonly regarded as authentic.[50] One can agree with Branick and Banks[51] that the application of family language to the Pauline churches would fit with the use of houses as meeting places. However, applying family language to church members does not necessitate a situation of gathering in houses. As Philip Harland has shown, familial language, particularly 'brothers' and (less frequently) 'sisters', but also 'mothers' and 'fathers', is attested for members of associations.[52] While some associations met in private houses, as we will see, many did not, gathering in their own collegial halls, or in other places such as temple dining rooms, inns and restaurants.[53] The language of familial relation is not, therefore, inextricably tied to a house setting. Paul himself never draws any connection between the family character of the believing community and meeting in houses.

1.3. *The Church at Corinth*
Having considered the relevant terminological data in the undisputed Pauline letters, we turn now to locational evidence in them: evidence for the use of houses as meeting places at specific locations, beginning with Corinth. In 1 Cor. 14.23, Paul speaks of 'the whole church' coming together (cf. 11.20). The statement implies that at other times, probably more frequently, the believers in Corinth gathered in smaller groups.

48   See, e.g., Meeks 1983: 87.
49   Banks 1980: 50–1.
50   Horrell 2001: 299–303.
51   Banks (1980: 61) states: 'Given the family character of the Christian community, the homes of its members provided the most conducive atmosphere in which they could give expression to the bond they had in common'.
52   Harland 2009: 63–96.
53   See further in Chapter 5.

1.3.1. Subgroup Gatherings. It is normally assumed that the Corinthian subgroups were 'house churches'. Branick attempts to identify these 'house churches' by identifying socially prominent individuals, such as Stephanas, Gaius, Erastus and Phoebe, who as householders could have hosted them.[54] However, there is no explicit indication of 'house churches', or home churches, at Corinth, since the formula ἡ κατ' οἶκον ἐκκλησία is not attested anywhere in Paul's letters for this location.[55]

From 1 Cor. 11.22, 34, we know that the Corinthians had οἶκοι/οἰκίαι in which to eat and drink (see further below). However, some of these homes were evidently occupied by 'mixed' households (households consisting of believers and non-believers; cf. 7.12-16) and presumably would not have been suitable as meeting places, though a group of believing slaves (Chloe's people mentioned in 1.11?) could have worshipped in the property of an unbelieving master/mistress. Moreover, the οἶκοι/οἰκίαι need not all have been 'houses'. If, as seems likely, some of the Corinthians were 'small traders and business folk',[56] their dwellings may have been shop/workshop dwellings rather than 'houses' proper.[57]

1 Corinthians bears witness to at least one believing household: the household of Stephanas (1 Cor. 1.16; 16.15).[58] We cannot assume, though, that a believing household necessarily constituted for Paul a κατ' οἶκον ἐκκλησία.[59] The κατ' οἶκον ἐκκλησίαι of Prisca and Aquila, as we have seen, were probably not Christian families. Paul never calls

54   Branick 1989: 59–66.
55   A line of interpretation going back at least to Filson (1939: 110) sees the problem of factionalism addressed in 1 Cor. 1–4 as rooted in a situation of multiple house congregations at Corinth. However, the allegiances expressed in these verses may not have coincided at all with the subgroups in which the Corinthians met.
56   Horrell 2004: 367.
57   At Corinth, numerous *tabernae* have been excavated that date to the first-century city. These include: the North Market Shops, a series of 44 *tabernae* arranged round a colonnaded courtyard (Murphy-O'Connor 2002: 194); the West Shops, two groups of six *tabernae* opening onto a portico (J.R. Wiseman 1979: 518); a series of 16 shops that formed the basement level of the Lechaeum Road Basilica (J.R. Wiseman 1979: 520). There would have been other *tabernae* in streets further away from the centre. Murphy-O'Connor (195) thinks that between ten and fifteen believers could have assembled in one of the North Market Shops in Corinth. Lampe (2003: 192–3) opines that around twenty people could have assembled in the one of the somewhat larger West Shops. The West Shops, though, were evidently high-end boutiques and probably not the places we should expect to find early Christian meetings.
58   The household of Crispus is mentioned in Acts 18.8 (cf. 1 Cor. 1.14).
59   *Contra* Button and van Rensburg 2003: 14.

Stephanas's household a 'church in the home'. The household of Stephanas is nevertheless a strong candidate for one of the Corinthian sub-gatherings, not because it is a believing household but because Paul himself, in 1 Cor. 16.15, treats it as a distinct collective entity within the Corinthian Christian community. Again, Stephanas and his dependents need not have lived and worshipped in an actual 'house' but perhaps in a *taberna*-dwelling.[60]

In sum, while 1 Cor. 14.23 implies the existence of subgroup gatherings at Corinth, it does not imply that subgroup meetings took place in private houses. Some groups may well have worshipped in houses, but others may have met in shops, workshops and perhaps other non-house settings.[61]

1.3.2. *The Whole-Church Gathering*. When Paul speaks in 1 Cor. 14.23 of the 'whole church' coming together for worship,[62] 'it is reasonable to assume that he is talking about the same gathering that began with the meal in chapter 11'.[63] As scholars such as Smith have shown, the order

60   As Button and van Rensburg (2003: 20–2) show, none of Paul's statements about Stephanas indicate that he was necessarily a well-to-do individual. Furthermore, there is no indication that his household was especially large (so Horrell 2004: 359 n. 51).

61   1 Cor. 8.10 might suggest that some of the Corinthians gathered as a group in a temple dining room (despite the singular σὲ...κατακείμενον). Each of the three dining rooms linked to the Asclepion at Corinth, which may have been operational at the time, could have accommodated eleven persons reclining on couches: Fotopoulous 2003: 61; Murphy-O'Connor 2002: 189.

62   The larger gatherings were probably less frequent, perhaps once a month: so Banks 1980: 41.

63   Smith 2003: 200. Gehring (2004: 173–9) thinks that two distinct meetings are in view: the celebration of communion in 1 Cor. 11, and the service of the word in 1 Cor. 14. But the distinction he makes is clearly anachronistic. Exegetically, that the same communal meeting is in mind in both chapters is strongly suggested by the fact that similar wording appears in the two passages. The verb 'come together', συνέρχομαι, is used in 11.17, 18, 20, 33 and 34, and also in 14.23 and 26. The language of 'giving thanks' (εὐχαριστέω, εὐχαριστία) is used in 11.24 and also 14.16-18. Also, the word 'body' is used for the congregation in 11.29, and it is used with that meaning throughout ch. 12. For Gehring (178), the presence of unbelievers as mentioned in 14.23-25 seems to tell against the concomitance of the two meetings, since the Lord's Supper was a more exclusive affair (11.27-32). But on the pattern of the Graeco-Roman dinner party, new guests could arrive after the meal (cf. Lampe 1994: 38). It is feasible, therefore, to imagine the meal itself being a more restricted event (members only), and the plenary worship being accessible to others who might for some reason drop in or be in attendance. Maintaining a distinction between an

of meal followed by plenary worship, as indicated in 1 Corinthians 11–14, fits the standard pattern of the Graeco-Roman dinner party in which the meal was followed by learned conversation or entertainments.[64]

It is generally supposed that the whole-church gathering took place in a house. The most influential reconstruction of the house setting of the whole-church meeting is that of Murphy-O'Connor,[65] who, as noted in the Introduction, imagines the Corinthians assembling in a traditional Roman house like the Anaploga Villa. He argues that the spatial limitations of such a setting help to explain the 'divisions' (σχίσματα) of which Paul speaks in 1 Cor. 11.18. The host would have had to make a social distinction between his guests, inviting better-off believers to dine in comfort in the *triclinium* while assigning the rest to the atrium, which would have been cold and over-crowded.[66] Horrell, as we have seen, is critical of Murphy-O'Connor's reconstruction. He argues that the Eucharistic assembly is more likely to have occurred in non-elite domestic space, such as the hypothesized upper levels of buildings 1 and 3 on Corinth's East Theatre Street.[67] At ground level, these buildings served as premises for the preparation and sale of cooked meats. Thus the (conjectured) flats above constitute the kind of domestic spaces that might be occupied by people running a small business.[68]

Murphy-O'Connor and others find specific exegetical evidence for a house as the setting of the Corinthian communal assembly in Rom. 16.23, where Paul states that Gaius is 'host to me and to the whole church' (ὁ ξένος μου καὶ ὅλης τῆς ἐκκλησίας).[69] Gaius here is almost certainly the same Gaius mentioned in 1 Cor. 1.14, as one of Paul's first converts at Corinth. His hosting of 'the whole church' is taken to mean that he made available his house for gatherings of the whole church *at Corinth*. However, it is interesting to note that the majority of commentators on Romans take καὶ ὅλης τῆς ἐκκλησίας in Rom. 16.23 as implying that Gaius was renowned for extending hospitality to travelling

exclusive meal and accessible plenary worship might have been more difficult, though not impossible, if the whole-church gathering sometimes took place in an outdoor setting. See Appendix 1.

64 Smith 2003: 188–214; cf. Lampe 1994: 37–8; Osiek and Balch 1997: 203. According to Smith (2003: 188), the taking of the cup after supper (μετὰ τὸ δειπνῆσαι, 11.25) signals the transition from *deipnon* to symposium.

65 Murphy-O'Connor 2002: 178–85.

66 Murphy-O'Connor 2002: 183–4.

67 Horrell 2004.

68 Horrell 2004: 367.

69 Murphy-O'Connor 2002: 182.

Christians from all over.[70] The majority view of Rom. 16.23 does seem to be the more likely interpretation. The word ξένος, in the sense of 'host', refers to someone who gives hospitality to guests,[71] not (as far as I can tell) to someone acting as the patron of a *collegium* or group in his home.[72] There is no doubt that when Paul says that Gaius is 'host to me' he means that Gaius is giving him lodgings at the time of writing. It is natural, then, to infer that the words 'and to the whole church' continue the same thought and indicate that Gaius has provided food and shelter for many other Christian travellers. The phrase 'the whole church', on this interpretation, must thus be viewed as hyperbolic, but making hyperbolic statements is hardly alien to Paul. Earlier in the same chapter, he speaks hyperbolically of Prisca and Aquila eliciting the thanksgiving of 'all the churches of the Gentiles' (Rom. 16.4).[73]

James Dunn makes four objections to the majority interpretation of καὶ ὅλης τῆς ἐκκλησίας in Rom. 16.23.[74] First, nowhere else in the undisputed letters does Paul use ἐκκλησία of the universal church, only of churches in particular cities or regions. Second, the phrase 'the whole church' is similar to the expression πᾶσα ἡ ἐκκλησία, which occurs frequently in the LXX for actual gatherings of Israel's representatives. Third, to speak of Gaius as host of the universal church, even in a hyperbolic way, would set his hospitality above that of others mentioned, such as Phoebe and Prisca and Aquila, 'in a wholly invidious (and indeed unpauline) manner'. Fourth, where the universality of the gospel was under dispute, as in Rome, to speak of the universal church would be unrealistic or factional. But none of these objections holds up. First, the claim that Paul does not use ἐκκλησία of the universal church is contradicted by 1 Cor. 10.32 and Gal. 1.13. Second, the point about πᾶσα ἡ ἐκκλησία is not really relevant since Paul never uses that phrase (one might argue that he deliberately avoids it because of its 'Israel' connotations). Third, it would be no more 'invidious' to speak of the excelling hospitality of Gaius than to speak, as the apostle does, of the universal esteem in which Prisca and Aquila are held (Rom. 16.4). That Paul makes mention of the special service of some does not devalue the contribution of others, nor does it undermine the Pauline principle of

70   See the list of commentators in Dunn 1988: 910.

71   Jewett 2007: 980; *TDNT* 5.20.

72   The word does not appear in the index of Greek titles for officers of associations in Kloppenborg and Ascough 2011: 438–42.

73   See also Rom. 1.8, where Paul tells his Roman readers that their 'faith is proclaimed throughout the whole world', by which he means that their progress in the faith is widely reported.

74   Dunn 1988: 910.

divine impartiality (Gal. 2.6). Fourth, in a situation where the universality of the gospel is under dispute it would hardly be any more controversial to speak of the universal church than to speak of the universality of sin and redemption, which Paul does at some length in Romans. As Jewett notes, a reference to the ecumenical scope of Gauis's hospitality, extending to both Jewish and Gentile Christians, is fully consonant with the theology and ethics of the epistle.[75] It might be argued that the use of the phrase 'the whole church' in 1 Cor. 14.23 for the Corinthian Christian community stands in favour of the expression bearing the same meaning in Rom. 16.23, but the application of a word or phrase in one context does not necessarily determine its meaning in another. As we have just noted, the broader meaning of 'the whole church' fits both its immediate and wider context in Romans.

If Rom. 16.23 cannot be taken as certain proof of the thesis that a believer's home functioned as the venue of the whole-church assembly at Corinth, then 1 Cor. 11.22 and 34 tell strongly against it. In 1 Cor. 11.22, Paul asks rhetorically, 'Do you not have homes (οἰκίας) to eat and drink in? Or do you show contempt for the church of God...?' In 11.34, he issues the instruction: 'If you are hungry, eat at home (ἐν οἴκῳ), so that when you come together, it will not be for your condemnation'. The rhetorical questions of 11.22 and the injunction of 11.34 would have less persuasive value if some of the congregants (the host and his family) *were* eating in their own house. Surprisingly, few interpreters have been alert to the negating consequences of these verses for the alleged domestic setting of the community meal at Corinth. One scholar who has keenly sensed the problem is Jorrun Økland.[76] She notes that 1 Cor. 11.22 seems to be 'declaring that the *space of the assembly is not identical with the space of the household*'.[77] Yet, such a declaration would contradict the assumption, which Økland shares, that the earliest Christians met in houses. Økland, therefore, offers another reading of the verse. Drawing on David Harvey's notions of multidimensional space, she argues that the differentiation that Paul is making here is between 'alternative representations of space', i.e., household and *ekklesia*, both of which occupy the same 'material space of a Christian household's *villa* or *insula*'.[78] It seems unlikely, however, that such a distinction, informed as it is by modern spatial theory, could have been consciously

---

75   Jewett 2007: 981.

76   Finney (2011: 63–8) is another.

77   Økland 2004: 141.

78   Økland 2004: 142–3. Similarly, Thiselton (2000: 865) thinks that Paul is contrasting domestic and ecclesial uses of the same space, i.e., the house

intended by Paul.[79] By οἰκίας in this verse (and οἶκος in 11.34), the apostle clearly has in mind physical dwellings of some sort, and not the 'households' that inhabit them. The natural historical inference to be drawn from 11.22 (if we assume that Paul is accurately mirroring the situation at Corinth) is that none of the homes of the Corinthian believers, whatever physical form these domiciles took (including shop/workshop dwellings), served as the material space of the whole-church gathering.

The distinction between 'the space of the *oikos* and that of the *ekklesia*' is repeated in 14.34-35,[80] the notorious passage in which wives or women are commanded to be silent in church. Verse 35 states: 'If there is anything they desire to know, let them ask their husbands at home (ἐν οἴκῳ). For it is shameful for a woman [or wife] to speak in church (ἐν ἐκκλησίᾳ)'. Many interpreters regard this passage as an interpolation, since it appears to contradict the permission granted in 11.5 that women can pray (audibly) and prophesy so long as their heads are covered.[81] We cannot here enter into the debate about the authenticity of these verses, but if they are genuinely from Paul, addressing a local problem, they lend support to our view that the whole-church meeting at Corinth did not occur in someone's home.

If the whole-church gathering of 1 Cor. 11–14 did not take place in a believer's home, where then did it happen? One possibility is rented dining space, exemplified possibly by Corinth's Roman Cellar Building; other possibilities include a barn and large garden (see Appendix 1).

1.4. *The Christian Community at Rome*
A 'church at the home' is clearly documented for Rome in the form of the church at the home of Prisca and Aquila (Rom. 16.5). Their 'home', as previously noted, is likely to have been a workshop dwelling and thus not a 'house' proper (i.e. a building or unit used exclusively or primary as a residence).[82] Paul greets the couple and the church they host in the

---

79   This is not to deny the great value of Økland's analysis of 1 Cor. 11–14 in terms of modern spatial categories. She is correct that for Paul 'the material space where the *ekklesia* gathers is rather irrelevant' (2004: 142). Paul is much more interested in what, from an etic perspective, can be called 'ritually constructed space'.

80   Økland 2004: 151.

81   For arguments in favour of interpolation, see Horrell 1996: 184–95. Økland (2004: 149–52) finds the arguments unconvincing. The lack of textual evidence for the verses being a later insertion along with important connections between these verses and preceding ones point, for her, to the genuineness of the passage.

82   The ground-floor *tabernae* of the *Insula Aracoeli* of the Capitoline Hill provide local instantiation of the space-type. See further p.141 n.30, below.

long list of greetings at the end of Romans.[83] In addition to the church at the home of Prisca and Aquila, Paul mentions four other groups in Rome in this section:

> Those who belong to Aristobulus (16.10)
> Those who belong to Narcissus (16.11)
> Asyncritus, Phlegon, Hermes, Patrobas and Hermas, and the brothers with them (16.14)
> Philologus, Julia, Nereus and his sister, and Olympas, and all the saints with them (16.15)

These groups are often labelled 'house churches' or 'house communities'[84] despite the fact that Paul does not refer to any of them as a κατ' οἶκον ἐκκλησία. They appear to be distinct groups of believers meeting separately. As Banks observes,[85] unlike in 1 Corinthians, there is no indication that these distinct groups ever came together to meet as a 'whole church' in one place. Gehring points out that Paul nowhere in the letter calls the Roman Christians in their entirety an ἐκκλησία, which suggests that the community of believers in Rome did not have a 'physical center'.[86]

The group referred to as οἱ ἐκ τῶν 'Αριστοβούλου was probably a group of slaves or freedmen of Aristobulus. This person was not himself a believer, or else Paul would have greeted him personally. Some commentators have suggested that the Aristobulus mentioned here is the grandson of Herod the Great,[87] who lived in Rome and was a friend of the Emperor Claudius. Although he was dead by the time Paul wrote (he died around 45 CE), his household may have continued and retained its identity. But the Aristobulus of Rom. 16.10 may have been an otherwise unknown person bearing this name.[88] As Peter Lampe points

83   As a result of the text-critical work of Gamble (1977), there can be little doubt now that Rom. 16 is an integral part of the letter to the Romans and thus can be used as evidence for Christianity at Rome.

84   E.g. Finger 2007; Lampe 2003: 360. According to Lampe (2003: 359–60), if it can be assumed that the 14 other people named in Rom. 16 are not attached to any of these groups, and that all of these individuals did not belong to just one other circle, then Rom. 16 bears witness to 'at least seven separate islands of Christianity', each of which 'can be referred to as a house community'. Jewett (2007: 62) thinks that there could have been dozens of Christian groups in Rome at the time that Paul wrote.

85   Banks 1980: 39.

86   Gehring 2004: 146. But *Acts of Paul* 11.1 might reflect an occasion or occasions in which a large number of believers in Rome did come together.

87   E.g. Jewett 2007: 966.

88   Dunn 1988: 896.

out, Paul's formulation indicates that not all members of the household were Christians (οἱ ἐκ τῶν ᾽Αριστοβούλου not οἱ ᾽Αριστοβούλου).[89] The believing members of the household may have come together for worship in the master's house. But equally, they might have worshipped in a large workshop owned by Aristobulus in which they lived and worked.[90]

The group specified as 'those of Narcissus', οἱ ἐκ τῶν Ναρκίσσου, similarly appears to have been a group of slaves and dependents. Since Narcissus is not greeted, it is likely that he was not a believer. Again, Paul's wording distinguishes the members of Narcissus's household who were believers from those who were not (the partitive genitive is reinforced by the words ὄντας ἐν κυρίῳ). Some think that the Narcissus mentioned here may have been the Narcissus who served as one of Claudius's aides.[91] Although he was forced to take his own life shortly after Nero's accession (54 CE), his household may have persisted, keeping his name. But the name Narcissus was common, especially among slaves and freedmen,[92] so a prominent individual need not be in view. Like 'those of Aristobulus', this group of believers may have worshipped in the master's house or in his business premises.

The background of the names Asyncritus, Phlegon, Hermes, Patrobas and Hermas (all of which are of slave origin) suggests that these individuals were of low social status.[93] Jewett takes these men and those with them to be an egalitarian 'tenement church' since no patron is identified.[94] However, even a group meeting in rented accommodation in a multi-storey apartment block, whether an upper apartment or ground-floor *taberna*, would have required a host.[95] The lack of reference to a host (or hosting couple) suggests that this, possibly all-male, group did not meet in the dwelling of a believer. Possible locations for this group would include some of the options discussed in Part II (e.g. a room in a warehouse, dining space in an inn or *popina*).

Again, the names Philologus, Julia, Nereus and Olympas are of slave origin, suggesting a group of relatively low social standing.[96] Jewett

---

89   Lampe 2003: 165
90   For this kind of scenario, see pp.141–2, below.
91   Accepting that this is the Narcissus referred to in Rom. 16.11, Jewett (2007: 968) thinks that this slave group would have been 'well educated and comfortably maintained'.
92   Dunn 1988: 896.
93   Jewett 2007: 971.
94   Jewett 2007: 971.
95   Cf. Oakes 2009: 92.
96   Jewett 2007: 971–2.

again thinks that this group fits the profile of a 'tenement church'.[97] However, the lack of a patron would suggest that this group, like the previously mentioned one, did not meet in someone's home.

In sum, then, although the five groups referred to in Romans 16 are often called 'house churches', only one is actually designated a 'church at the home' and the home in this case is likely to have been a workshop dwelling. The groups mentioned in Rom. 16.10-11 may have worshipped in houses, but they could also have worshipped in commercial/industrial premises owned by their non-Christian masters. The two units referred to in Rom. 16.14-15 (in my view) are liable to have gathered in non-house circumstances.

1.5. *Other Locations*
In addition to Corinth and Rome, Gehring identifies Philippi, Thessalonica, Cenchreae, Ephesus, Colossae and Laodicea as 'cities with demonstrable house churches'.[98] In so doing, he draws on the evidence of Acts as well as Paul's epistles. Here, we only consider the locational evidence he derives from Paul's letters.[99] The Acts data are dealt with in the next chapter.

For Gehring, the fact that Paul mentions several ἐπίσκοποι in Phil. 1.1 shows that 'there were several house churches in Philippi at the time'.[100] But Gehring's reasoning is circular: since Paul's churches were 'house churches', leadership would have been provided by 'house church' hosts; the reference to plural leadership in Phil. 1.1 thus points to a plurality of 'house churches' at Philippi. The house as meeting place is assumed not demonstrated. The word ἐπίσκοπος, 'overseer', is not drawn from the sphere of the household and bears no necessary connotations of household leadership.[101] The reference to ἐπίσκοποι thus offers no explicit evidence of 'house churches', nor does it necessarily imply them. This is not to deny the use of houses as meeting places at Philippi (as we will see in the next chapter, in Acts 16.40, Paul speaks to believers who have gathered in Lydia's house); it is simply to say that the epistle offers no direct evidence for the phenomenon.

In similar fashion, Gehring finds multiple 'house churches' in Thessalonica indicated in 1 Thess. 5.12, where Paul refers to 'those who labor among you, and have charge (προϊσταμένους) of you in the Lord'.[102] But

97   Jewett 2007: 972.
98   Gehring 2004: 130–55.
99   I discuss the locations in the order that Gehring treats them.
100 Gehring 2004: 132.
101 BDAG 379–80; *TDNT* 2.608–15.
102 Gehring 2004: 133.

again, a reference to plural leadership does not necessarily imply a situation in which there were several 'house churches'. Although the verb προΐστημι is used in connection with household management in 1 Tim. 3.5, it is the object of the verb that expresses that connection not the verb itself. The verb does not in and of itself connote household leadership.[103] 1 Thessalonians does not provide clear and direct information about the meeting circumstances of Christians at Thessalonica. However, the likelihood that it was composed of artisans and manual-workers (cf. 1 Thess. 4.11) would in turn make it likely that the Thessalonian believers met in a workshop or workshops.[104]

For Gehring, a 'house church' at Cenchreae can be deduced from Paul's designation of Phoebe in Rom. 16.2 as προστάτις, meaning a female 'patron' or 'benefactor'.[105] In Gehring's view, this means that 'she played the role of hostess to the local church in Cenchreae'.[106] However, she is actually described as 'a benefactor of many and of myself as well', a role that seems to be over and above her status as a διάκονος of the church at Cenchreae (16.1). The wording of Rom. 16.2 does not exclude the possibility that Phoebe offered her home as a meeting place for the church at Cenchreae, but neither does it positively indicate this scenario. Gehring's deduction that Phoebe hosted the local church in her home is a speculative inference, a deduction that goes beyond what we are explicitly told.

1 Corinthians 16.19 clearly indicates the existence of a 'church at the home' in Ephesus at the time of writing. As previously stated, this was likely a group meeting in Prisca and Aquila's workshop dwelling. According to Gehring, the greeting from 'all the brothers' in 1 Cor. 16.20 points to a plurality of 'house churches' in Ephesus,[107] but all it indicates is the existence of a larger number of Christians beyond those meeting with Prisca and Aquila. Whether these other believers also met in houses or dwellings is not specified.

A 'church at the home' in or near Colossae can be established from the letter to Philemon, when read in connection with the epistle to the Colossians. Onesimus and Archippus are both mentioned in Colossians (in 4.9 and 17 respectively), suggesting that Philemon's home church was in Colossae or its vicinity.

---

103   BDAG 870.
104   So De Vos 1999: 154. Jewett (1993: 33–42) thinks that 2 Thess. 3.10 implies a 'tenement church'.
105   BDAG 885. Meggitt (1998: 146–8) rightly cautions against presuming that she was a member of the wealthy elite.
106   Gehring 2004: 143.
107   Gehring 2004: 144.

The church in Nympha's home mentioned in Col. 4.15 was evidently located in or near Laodicea (about ten miles from Colossae), since it is mentioned in association with the 'brothers in Laodicea'. In the next verse (4.16), Paul refers to 'the church of the Laodiceans' (Λαοδικέων ἐκκλησία). Nympha's home church was thus evidently part of the larger church at Laodicea.[108] On this basis, Dunn thinks that 'we have to assume at least one other house church in Laodicea itself'.[109] However, all we have to assume is that there were believers in Laodicea beyond those that belonged to Nympha's congregation. Whether they also met in an οἶκος or in οἶκοι is not indicated.

To sum up: the use of a believer's home as a congregational meeting venue can be ascertained for Ephesus (while Prisca and Aquila were there), in or around Colossae, and in or around Laodicea, but only on the basis of the formula ἡ κατ' οἶκον ἐκκλησία in 1 Cor. 16.19, Philemon 2 and Col. 4.15, and not any other data. There is no explicit evidence from Paul's letters for 'house churches' at Philippi, Thessalonica and Cenchreae. Of course, this is not to deny that believers in these places ever gathered in houses. What I am saying is that Paul's letters offer no proof that they did so.

2. *The Deutero-Pauline Letters*

We turn now to the 'deutero-Pauline' letters, dealing first with Colossians and Ephesians, which tend to be taken together because they display an exceptionally close literary relationship, and then with the Pastoral Epistles.[110]

2.1. *Colossians and Ephesians*
In Colossians, there is growing emphasis on the universal church. The dominant image of the church is that of the body with Christ as its head (Col. 1.18, 24; cf. 2.19). Building imagery appears only once in the letter (Col. 2.7); the metaphorical understanding of the church as a household does not figure at all.[111]

---

108   It is only in Col. 4.15 that a κατ' οἶκον ἐκκλησία is presented as part of the wider local ἐκκλησία.

109   Dunn 1996: 284.

110   Colossians and Ephesians tend to be viewed in critical scholarship as reflecting second-generation Pauline Christianity, while the Pastorals are taken as representing the third generation of Pauline churches. See, e.g., MacDonald 1988: 3–4.

111   The word οἰκονομία occurs in Col. 1.25, but as in 1 Cor. 9.17, the word means 'commission' and has no necessary household connotations.

A key feature of Colossians (not found in the undisputed letters) is the so-called household code of 3.18–4.1.[112] This is sometimes thought to reflect the alleged 'house-church' setting of early Christianity.[113] In this section, advice is given to wives and husbands, children and fathers, and slaves and masters. According to Gehring, 'With the Colossian household code we encounter for the first time a model that is intended as a set of rules within a Christian household community'. The readers are addressed as 'all members in all households and all house churches'.[114] However, as R. Alistair Campbell observes, 'The fact that all Christians are addressed by these codes does not mean they are addressed as members of house churches, but only as Christians needing to live out their faith in the own natural families'.[115] The code is concerned with how believers behave in the actual households to which they belong. It does not assume an equivalence of household and ἐκκλησία; nor does it presume that all those addressed belong to 'Christian' households. The instruction given to slaves (3.22-23) to obey their 'earthly' (κατὰ σάρκα) masters is applicable to slaves in a non-believing house or workplace.[116] Similarly, the command to masters to treat their slaves justly and fairly (4.1) could apply to the treatment of non-believing slaves. The domestic paranaesis of Colossians is not dependent on a practice of worshipping in houses, and nowhere is it suggested or hinted at that the conduct enjoined is especially appropriate because the house is characteristically where gathering takes place. The material context in which believers meet does not come into the picture at all.

The only evidence for the house as Christian meeting place in Colossians is the reference to the church in Nympha's home in 4.15, which we have already noted.[117]

112   The background to the household codes of Col. 3.18–4.1, Eph. 5.21–6.9 and 1 Pet. 2.18–3.7, it is now generally recognized, is the Greaco-Roman philosophical tradition, going back to Aristotle, concerning the management of the household. See Balch 1981: 29–61.

113   E.g. MacDonald 1988: 112.

114   Gehring 2004: 258.

115   Campbell 2007: 670.

116   Contrast 1 Tim. 6.2, 'Those who have believing masters must not be disrespectful to them on the ground that they are members of the church; rather they must serve them all the more, since those who benefit by their service are believers and beloved'.

117   I have no wish to undermine the significance of this verse as evidence of female leadership in the early church. As Dunn (1996: 285) states, 'as the householder and the only one named in connection with the church in her home, Nympha was probably the leader of the church there, or at least she acted as host for the gathering and for the fellowship meal'.

In Ephesians, the word ἐκκλησία is used exclusively with reference to the universal church (1.22; 3.10, 21; etc).[118] Despite the words 'in Ephesus' in 1.1 (which are not present in the earliest manuscripts), no particular church is addressed or specific situation reflected. As in Colossians, the idea of Christ as head of the church is given prominence (4.15; 5.23). The image of the church as a household appears only once in the letter, in 2.19, where believers are called 'members of the household of God' (οἰκεῖοι τοῦ θεοῦ; cf. Gal. 6.10). The thought progresses into a building metaphor (2.20), with Christ as the cornerstone, and it becomes clear that the building in mind is a temple (2.20-21) and not a domestic structure.[119]

Like Colossians, Ephesians contains household teaching (5.21–6.9) with instructions given to wives and husbands, children and fathers, and slaves and masters. The Ephesian household code seems to envisage a 'Christian' household.[120] Yet, as John Muddiman points out, it is quite possible 'that the slaves and masters addressed do not necessarily belong to the same households'. He continues: 'Only Christians are addressed, of course, but the possibility that they lived in mixed households is not excluded by the apparently reciprocal form'.[121] In any case, as with the Colossian version of the code, the household paranaesis neither requires nor envisions a house environment of meeting. Ephesians offers no direct evidence of gathering in houses.

2.2. *The Pastoral Epistles*
The word οἶκος is found eight times in the Pastoral epistles (1 Tim. 3.4, 5, 12, 15; 5.4; 2 Tim. 1.16; 4.19; Tit. 1.11), always with the sense 'household'. The word οἰκία occurs three times (1 Tim. 5.13; 2 Tim. 2.20; 3.6), twice clearly meaning 'house' or 'dwelling' (1 Tim. 5.13; 2 Tim. 2.20). Other household terms also appear (οἰκεῖος, 1 Tim. 5.8; οἰκοδεσποτέω, 1 Tim. 5.14; οἰκουργός, Tit. 2.5).

In 1 Tim. 3.15, the church is designated 'household of God' (οἶκος θεοῦ). This is the central ecclesiological image in all three letters.[122] Church members are to see themselves as utensils in a 'large house'

118 MacDonald 1988: 87.
119 The word οἰκονομία occurs three times in the letter but with no household connotations. In 3.2, it refers to Paul's apostolic 'commission'. In 1.10 and 3.9, the word denotes God's universal/cosmic plan.
120 As Barclay (1997: 76) points out, there appears here, for the first time in Christian literature, an instruction about 'the Christian socialisation of children' (6.4).
121 Muddiman 2001: 278.
122 Gehring 2004: 260. Cf. Verner 1983: 127.

(μεγάλη οἰκία), 'dedicated and useful to the owner of the house' (δεσπότης), who is God (2 Tim. 2.20-21). They are to relate to each other as members of a household (1 Tim. 5.1-2).[123] The ἐπίσκοπος is expected to be a householder (1 Tim. 3.4) and to exercise that function in the church (1 Tim. 3.5); similarly, διάκονοι must 'manage their children and their households well' (1 Tim. 3.12).[124] There thus emerges in the Pastorals an *'oikos* ecclesiology',[125] in which the institution of the household serves as the model for social relations within the church and for the social ordering of it.[126]

The Pastorals also exhibit a concern for actual households. Emphasis is laid on household responsibilities, not just on the part of those seeking leadership. The children and grandchildren of a widow should make some recompense to her, fulfilling 'their religious duty to their own household' (οἶκος, 1 Tim. 5.4). Older women are to encourage young women to be 'good managers of the household' (οἰκουργοὺς ἀγαθάς, Tit. 2.5). Younger widows should 'manage their households' (οἰκοδεσ-ποτεῖν, 1 Tim. 5.13-14). Every believer must meet her/his family obligations: 'whoever does not provide for relatives, and especially for household members (οἰκείων), has denied the faith and is worse than an unbeliever' (1 Tim. 5.8).

There is some anxiety that households are becoming 'seedbeds of heresy'.[127] False teachers are said to 'make their way into households (ἐνδύνοντες εἰς τὰς οἰκίας) and captivate silly women' (2 Tim. 3.6). Rebellious people are said to be 'upsetting whole households' (οἵτινες ὅλους οἴκους ἀνατρέπουσιν) by their erroneous teaching (Tit. 1.11). These households are plainly assumed to be Christian. One believing household receives explicit mention: that of Onesiphorus (2 Tim. 1.16; 4.19), which is set forth as a model household.

According to Gehring the *'oikos* ecclesiology' that comes to the fore in the Pastoral Epistles is best explained by assuming a 'house-church' setting in which 'private domestic houses belonging to a few wealthy members of the congregation served as gathering places for the

---

123   This is a case where organic family language merges with household language, since these are family roles (father, mother, brothers, sisters) within a hierarchically structured household.

124   As Horrell (2001: 308) puts it, 'Competent leadership of the human household is an essential prerequisite for competent leadership of God's household, and only those who are in a position to do the former can legitimately undertake the latter'.

125   Gehring 2004: 263.

126   Cf. MacDonald 1988: 207–14.

127   Branick 1989: 128.

church'.[128] However, the characterization of the church as the household of God is a metaphor. Of course, the metaphor would carry additional potency if congregations were meeting in houses, but the designation of the church as 'household of God' no more *requires* the house as actual meeting place than the depiction of the church as the temple (1 Cor. 3.16, 17; Eph. 2.21) requires the Jerusalem temple as the actual venue for assembly. It is clear that the leadership instructions of 1 Tim. 3.1-13 invoke a parallel between household and church (3.5). But it is also clear from this passage that οἶκος and ἐκκλησία are discrete spheres; they are not coextensive. As Branick puts it,

> Although a link to the household is thus maintained, in effect a clear distinction is made between the household and the church. The household is the proving ground for work in the church.

A church leader's role as ἐπίσκοπος or διάκονος is 'over and above his role as head of the household'.[129] According to Campbell, the Pastoral Epistles were written to legitimate the recognition of a single ἐπίσκοπος in a town or city from among those were already 'house-church' leaders.[130] If this is correct, it is surprising that nothing is said in 1 Tim. 3.1-7 about a prospective ἐπίσκοπος managing the *church* in his home well.[131] There is no indication at all in this passage that the households over which aspiring ἐπίσκοποι have authority have been functioning as ἐκκλησίαι. Indeed, there is no explicit evidence of 'house churches' in the Pastorals. The formulation ἡ κατ' οἶκον ἐκκλησία does not occur anywhere in them.

The emphasis on acting responsibly towards one's own household is probably partly a reaction against an emerging asceticism that threatens to destroy family life (1 Tim. 4.3).[132] The approbation of the institution of the household, central to Graeco-Roman society, may also partly relate to a desire to reduce tension with society at large.[133]

It is important to emphasize that I am not saying that the original recipients of the Pastoral Epistles did not at all meet in houses (or homes broadly understood). My point is that the use of houses as meeting places cannot be independently verified from these letters.

128   Gehring 2004: 264.
129   Branick 1989: 126.
130   Campbell 1994: 196.
131   1 Tim. 5.17–18 seems to envisage the remuneration of elders for their work. Here the elder looks less like the patron of a 'house church' and more like a 'dedicated professional'. So Branick 1989: 127.
132   Cf. Barclay 1997: 77; MacDonald 1988: 180.
133   Cf. MacDonald 1988: 211.

3. *The General Epistles*

William Lane takes the epistle to the Hebrews 'to be addressed to the members of a house church' in Rome, sometime between 64 and 69 CE.[134] The 'house-church' setting of early Roman Christianity is apparent, Lane assumes, from Romans 16, which 'indicates the existence of several house churches in Rome'.[135] It is reasonable to believe, therefore, that Christians in Rome continued to assemble in private houses in the imperial capital only a decade after the writing of the epistle to the Romans. Lane finds internal evidence of the domestic context of meeting in Hebrews' description of the church as God's οἶκος (3.6; 10.21), which he thinks may be an 'implied reference to the gathering of the house church'.[136] The household setting of Roman Christianity at this time is also presupposed, he maintains, in the catechetical precepts of Heb. 13.1-6.[137]

However, as we saw above, while Romans 16 testifies to the existence of scattered congregations in Rome, only one of them is explicitly said to be located in someone's home, which is liable to have been a workshop dwelling, and at least two of the others referred to likely met in non-house locales. Talk of the church as God's house, we have seen, need not imply that the meeting venue of the addressees was an actual house (in 10.21, the 'house' is probably the true temple). The admonition to 'show hospitality to strangers' (φιλοξενία) in Heb. 13.2 has to do with welcoming and entertaining strangers and guests, probably travelling Christians.[138] The instruction presupposes that (some of) the readers have homes (of some sort), but it does not prove that believers' homes were the meeting places of the Roman churches. The appeals to brotherly love (13.1), to remember those in prison (13.3), to marital faithfulness (13.4) and to be content with what one has (13.5) are hardly contingent on a household setting. There is nothing in the pastoral precepts of 13.1-6 that demands the house as meeting place. This is not to rule out the possibility that the original readers of Hebrews gathered and worshipped domestically; it is simply to note that the letter offers no explicit indication of such a scenario.

---

134   Lane 1998: 217.
135   Lane 1998: 208.
136   Lane 1998: 218.
137   Lane 1998: 219.
138   Cf. Rom. 12.13. On φιλοξενία, see BDAG 1058.

In Jas. 2.2-4, the author refers literally to 'your synagogue' and seems to envisage the setting of meeting:

> For if a person with gold rings and in fine clothes comes into συναγωγὴν ὑμῶν, and if a poor person in dirty clothes also comes in, and if you take notice of the one wearing the fine clothes and say, 'Have a seat here, please', while to the one who is poor you say, 'Stand there', or, 'Sit at my feet', have you not made distinctions among yourselves, and become judges with evil thoughts? (Jas. 2.2-4).

A strand of interpretation takes συναγωγὴν ὑμῶν to be the domestic house (or the room in the house) in which Christians assembled.[139] A recent advocate of this line is Scot McKnight who thinks that someone's home is 'far more likely' than a dedicated synagogue building, pointing out that 'We should not think of a synagogue always as a building constructed exclusively for public worship, instruction, and prayer'.[140] Whether the word συναγωγή in 2.2 refers to a gathering of people, i.e., an 'assembly', or to a place of gathering is much debated. Most commentators take συναγωγή to mean an 'assembly' (the NRSV translates συναγωγὴν ὑμῶν as 'your assembly'). I am inclined to agree with McKnight that the word refers in context to a meeting place rather than a gathering, since when the writer refers to the believing community, he uses ἐκκλησία (5.14).[141] That a house is in mind, though, seems to me less probable. McKnight is influenced by the view that synagogue buildings in this period were often the plain houses of members of the Jewish community, but as we will see (in Chapter 5), firm evidence for this view is lacking. What is said in v. 3 would fit with the place of meeting being a synagogue building of the kind attested for Palestine in the first century CE,[142] with stone benches around the walls of the main assembly area. On this understanding, the assembly venue would be a local synagogue that has passed into 'Jewish-Christian' use.[143] Of course, a house context cannot be ruled out.[144] Even so, it is safe to say that Jas. 2.2-3 cannot be

---

139   E.g. MacKnight 1810: 354.
140   McKnight 2011: 182.
141   McKnight 2011: 183. Talk of 'entering' and 'sitting' might also point to a place of meeting, but as Catto (2007: 46) correctly points out, 'it is also possible to enter a "gathering" and take a seat there, for example, on wooden furniture'.
142   So also Riesner 1995: 207. On the characteristics of first-century Palestinian synagogues, see Catto 2007: 103–4, and see further the discussion of synagogues in Chapter 5.
143   Cf. Riesner 1995: 207.
144   Though if a house is in mind, the setting would not be a traditional *triclinium* since the honoured visitor is invited to 'sit' rather than 'recline'.

taken as definite evidence for houses as meeting places. The epistle offers no other potential evidence for 'house churches'.

Twice in 1 Peter, the readers are designated an οἶκος. In 2.5, they are said to be an οἶκος πνευματικὸς, and in 4.17, they are called ὁ οἶκος τοῦ θεοῦ. John Elliot argues that the word οἶκος in both instances means 'house(hold)'.[145] He contends that the 'household of God' functions as 'the root metaphor and organizing ecclesial image in 1 Peter'.[146] The explicit labelling of readers as God's household in 2.5 and 4.17 is supported by an extensive use of '*oikos*-related terminology' and familial language, such as the terms ἀδελφότης, 'brotherhood' (2.17; 5.9), and φιλάδελφος, 'love of one's brother' (3.8), and by the employment of the household management tradition in 2.13–3.7. For Elliott, the symbolization of the community as God's household fits with the historical reality of the house/household as the 'social locus, basis, and focus' of Christian mission.[147]

However, the idea of the church as God's house/household may not be as dominant within 1 Peter as Elliott believes. The notion of the believing community (surprisingly, the word ἐκκλησία never occurs in 1 Peter) as God's household is clearly expressed in 4.17, but in 2.5, it is probably the temple, as God's spiritual house, to which the readers are being compared.[148] Not all the terms Elliot takes as οἶκος-related words actually belong to the realm of the household,[149] and familial language, especially language of brotherhood, as we have seen, does not necessarily express the ideal of the hierarchically ordered household. Moreover, as has been emphasized, the application of the image of the household to the community of faith is not dependent on an actual practice of meeting in houses and does not provide exegetical proof of such a custom. Elliot seems to think that 'house churches' were formed out of existing households, but it is clear from the domestic paranaesis that conversion to Christ divided some existing households (2.18-20; 3.1-6). 1 Peter conveys no direct information about the material setting of assembly.

According to Gehring, in the second and third epistles of John, 'the vital importance of the house church for early Christian missional

---

145   J.H. Elliott 2000: 414–18, 798–800.

146   J.H. Elliott 2000: 113.

147   J.H. Elliott 2000: 114.

148   Achtemeier 1996: 155–6. Horrell (1998: 40) thinks that the meaning of οἶκος πνευματικὸς in 2.5 is ambiguous.

149   παροικία (1.17), which J.H. Elliott (2000: 354) translates as 'residence as aliens', and πάροικος (2.11), translated by Elliott (p.456) as 'resident aliens', have nothing to do with the household.

outreach is unambiguously confirmed'.[150] White, drawing on Abraham Malherbe's reconstruction,[151] posits an underlying situation in which Diotrephes, the patron of a 'house church', had refused to give hospitality to travelling believers from another congregation (3 Jn 9–10).[152] In addition, he finds in 2 Jn 10–11 a 'prohibition against admitting heretics to the house of assembly'.[153]

2 John 10 states: 'Do not receive into the house (εἰς οἰκίαν) or welcome anyone who comes to you and does not bring this teaching'. The injunction most obviously denotes 'the refusal of any domestic hospitality'[154] to someone seeking actively to share a different message from the accepted 'teaching of Christ' (cf. 2 Jn 9). It may further be understood as a warning against receiving a false teacher into the congregational meeting place, but only if a practice of meeting in houses is presumed to lie in the background. The text itself does not independently witness to such a phenomenon. In 3 Jn 9–10, Diotrephes is censured for refusing to welcome 'the friends' and for preventing other believers from providing them with hospitality. Diotrephes is very clearly a significant authority figure within the ἐκκλησία addressed, but that the church was a 'house church' and that he was its patron go beyond what we are told.

I do not disagree that the second and third letters of John read well against a 'house-church' background, but to claim that they offer unambiguous confirmation of 'house churches' is to exceed the bounds of these texts. Neither document overtly speaks of the house as meeting place.

In sum, then, while 'house churches' might be inferred from or illuminatingly read into passages in the General Epistles (especially 2 and 3 John), these letters do not *explicitly* testify to the use of houses as Christian meeting venues.

4. *Conclusion*

To conclude: much of the claimed evidence in the New Testament epistles for houses as meeting places (the metaphorical use of house/household language for the believing community, references to plural leadership, domestic paranaesis, etc.) falls well short of firm evidence.

---

150   Gehring 2004: 281.
151   Malherbe 1977.
152   White 1997: 24.
153   White 1997: 24.
154   Lieu 2008: 259.

The only explicit evidence within this body of New Testament literature for believers' οἶκοι as church meeting places is the fourfold occurrence of the Pauline formula ἡ κατ᾽ οἶκον ἐκκλησία. However, these four references hardly bear witness to a widespread practice of gathering in houses in the early church, and in two instances (1 Cor. 16.19; Rom. 16.5), the οἶκος in question is likely to have been a workshop dwelling, which is more commercial/industrial space than 'house' space (strictly understood). Moreover, there is evidence that some groups of believers did not meet in a believer's house (Rom. 16.14-15; 1 Cor. 11.22, 34). In short, the evidence in the New Testament epistles does not justify the AEH consensus.

Chapter 2

NEW TESTAMENT EVIDENCE: GOSPELS AND ACTS

The book of Acts is widely seen as reflecting, whether generally or with some degree of historical accuracy, the 'house-church' phase of early Christian assembly.[1] Some scholars also find the assumed house environment of early Christianity mirrored in the house settings of Jesus' ministry and the mission charge regarding houses in the Synoptic Gospels. This chapter evaluates the evidence that the Synoptic Gospels and especially Acts are thought to offer for the use of houses as the early church's meeting places.

1. *The Synoptic Gospels*

According to Branick, the Synoptic evangelists closely link the missions of Jesus and his disciples with homes. Jesus is often to be found in houses, and, especially in Mark's Gospel, he frequently gives special teaching 'at home'. In his missionary instructions to his disciples, found in all three Synoptics, he tells them to enter a house. Luke's version of this instruction 'implies a full incorporation into the household'. The key to their mission would be acceptance by a household. Branick comments:

> The stress that this link between mission and home receives in the gospels...indicates a similar link in the communities producing these gospels. From the number of times especially in the Gospel of Mark that we see Jesus giving special instructions at home, we can conclude that the catechetical practices of the Marcan church in particular developed in and around home life.[2]

---

1   Blue 1994: 121.
2   Branick 1989: 20

Others also see a connection between the house locales of Jesus' ministry, in particular his teaching and his table fellowship, in the Synoptic Gospels, especially Mark, and the settings in which early Christians gathered.[3] For Gehring, the Synoptic data show that 'house churches' have their origin in Jesus' missionary use of houses.[4]

1.1. *House Settings of Jesus' Ministry*
In the Synoptic Gospels, we repeatedly read of Jesus ministering in an οἶκος or οἰκία. As pointed out in the previous chapter, when used with reference to a habitation, the words οἶκος and οἰκία can denote either a 'house' proper or any kind of dwelling. Archaeology has registered a wide range of dwelling-types in Palestine dating to the Roman period, including shops and workshops with living quarters.[5] The οἶκοι and οἰκίαι of the Synoptic Gospels are hardly ever described (the details provided in Mk 2.1-4 are exceptional), but let us assume, for the sake of argument, that houses proper (i.e. buildings used exclusively or primarily as residences) are generally in view. The judgment seems justified at least in the case of Luke's Gospel: the evangelist's comment in Lk. 8.27 ('he [the Gerasene demoniac] did not live in a house (ἐν οἰκίᾳ) but in the tombs') appears to indicate that for him οἰκίαι, and thus presumably also οἶκοι, are actual houses rather than dwellings more broadly understood.

Klauck points out that in Mark's Gospel, Jesus is frequently depicted as dining (or, in one case, trying to dine) in a house.[6] Jesus receives domestic hospitality in the house of Peter, after healing his mother-in-law (1.29-31). He has a meal in the house of Levi (2.15). Following the appointment of the twelve, Jesus enters into an unspecified house to dine (3.19b-20) but is prevented from doing so by the sudden appearance of a crowd. At Bethany, he dines in the house of Simon the leper (14.3), where a company is gathered. In the domicile, a woman anoints his head with oil (14.3-9). Finally, Jesus holds his Last Supper in the upper room of a house (14.14).[7] Moreover, Jesus is often shown in Mark as giving private teaching in a house (7.17-23; 9.28-99, 33-50; 10.10-12).[8] Mark's

---

3   Best 1981: 226–7; Crosby 1998: 21–48; Gehring 2004: 28–48; Klauck 1981: 56–62.

4   Gehring 2004: 46–8.

5   See Guijarro 1997; P. Richardson 2004b. The number of *tabera*-dwellings found across Palestine suggests that this was a very common type of living arrangement: so Guijarro 1997: 54–5.

6   Klauck 1981: 60–1.

7   Klauck (1981: 61) observes that Luke shows Jesus as a dinner guest in a house on other occasions as well (7.36-38; 14.1; 19.5-6; cf. 10.38-42).

8   Klauck 1981: 61.

domestic scenes, Klauck argues, reflect a setting in Mark's community in which church members gathered in houses to participate in worship that revolved around 'Wort und Mahl' (word and meal).[9]

The connection that Klauck posits between Mark's domestic settings and 'house churches' in Mark's community, it must be emphasized, is conjectural. The house settings of Jesus' table fellowship and teaching in Mark and the other Synoptic Gospels cannot be claimed as direct evidence of the use of houses as meeting places in early Christianity since the Gospels are ostensibly narratives about Jesus and not the post-Easter church. Having said that, it is not unreasonable to see some sort of correlation between the narrative settings of Jesus' ministry in the Gospels and the physical settings in which readers of the Gospels gathered.[10] In this respect, the domestic scenes in Mark and the other Synoptics may offer indirect evidence of houses as Christian meeting places. However, it is important to recognize that houses are not the only settings in which Jesus teaches in the Gospels. In Mark's Gospel, Jesus often teaches by the sea (2.13; 3.9; 4.1); on one occasion, he instructs his disciples privately in a boat (8.13-21).[11] He teaches in synagogues (1.21-29, 39; 6.1-2),[12] gives private teaching on mountains (9.9; 13.3) and imparts important information on discipleship 'on the road' (8.27; 9.33; 10.32).[13] In Jerusalem, he teaches in the temple 'day after day' (14.49). Nor are houses the only settings of meals in Mark. Jesus hosts a meal for five thousand in a 'deserted place', located near the sea (6.32-45). Another outdoor banquet hosted by Jesus is also set in a 'wilderness' location near the sea (8.1-10). The upstairs room (ἀνάγαιον, 14.15) in which the Last Supper takes place is evidently part of a domestic property (cf. the

---

9 Klauck 1981: 62.

10 Whether one understands the Gospels as intended for particular Christian communities or, as Bauckham (1998: 45) argues, for 'any or every church of the late first century'.

11 The sea, θάλασσα, is mentioned 17 times between Mk 1.16 and 7.31. Shiner (2003: 52) opines that 'the constant presence of the sea in the first half of the Gospel is a result of its being composed for performance in such a setting'.

12 The word συναγωγή may mean a gathering (as argued by Kee 1990), but Mark and the other Synoptists probably use the word with reference to a place of meeting, i.e., a synagogue building: see Binder 1999: 93–9. A synagogue building is definitely indicated in Mk 12.39 (cf. Binder 1999: 97–8). In an inscription from Bernice dating to 55 CE, the word συναγωγή is clearly used of the building in which the Jewish congregation gathers (see Binder 1999: 109–10; Catto 2007: 81–2). Archaeological evidence shows that there were at least some formal synagogue buildings in Palestine before 70 CE. See further in Chapter 5.

13 As observed by Hooker (1991: 245).

mention of the οἰκοδεσπότης, 'householder', in 14.14),[14] but the room is also called a κατάλυμα (14.14),[15] a word meaning 'lodging' or 'inn',[16] which is suggestive of commercial hospitality space. It could be that Mark wants us to think of a room that forms part of a house but which functions as a separate unit, perhaps a rentable dining room. Upper rooms were often built on existing flat-rooftop houses and rented out for various purposes.[17] Guestrooms equipped for dining would have been needed by families and other groups coming as pilgrims to Jerusalem so that they could celebrate the Passover in the customary way.[18]

Matthew and Luke follow Mark in depicting Jesus as ministering in a range of settings.[19] In John's Gospel, houses hardly figure as explicit narrative locations;[20] non-house settings dominate the narrative. Interestingly, the garden (κῆπος) in which Jesus is arrested (Jn 18.1, 26) is said by the evangelist to be a place where Jesus met often with his disciples (18.2).[21]

14   That the structure on Mt. Zion known as the Cenacle was the actual site of the Last Supper lacks credible archaeological support: see Taylor 1993: 207–20.

15   Cf. Lk. 22.11.

16   LSJ 899.

17   Le Cornu and Shulam 2003: 30.

18   According to Le Cornu and Shulam (2003: 31), 'Rabbinic texts indicate that pilgrims were not charged for accommodation throughout the feasts'.

19   Matthew: seaside/boat (13.1-3); synagogues (4.23; 9.35; 12.9; 13.54); deserted place (14.13-21); mountains (5.1; 15.29-31; 17.1; 24.3; 28.16-20); roadside (21.19-22); the temple (21.12-17; 21.23–24.1). Luke: lakesides (5.1-11); synagogues (4.15-30, 33-38, 44; 6.6; 13.10); deserted places (4.42; 9.10-17); mountains (6.12; 9.28); roads/roadsides (9.57; 24.13-35, esp. vv. 32, 35); the temple (2.22-38, 41-51; 19.45-47; 20.1–21.38; 24.53); κατάλυμα (22.11).

20   The οἶκος/οἰκία terminology is used very sparingly in this Gospel. Excluding the use in 7.53, in the Pericope Adulterae, the word οἶκος occurs only four times (2.16 [×2], 17; 11.20), and in three of these occurrences (2.16 [×2], 17), the reference is to the temple. The word οἰκία appears five times (4.53; 8.35; 11.31; 12.3; 14.2), twice meaning 'household' (4.53; 8.35), and once (14.2) with reference to heaven ('my Father's house'). An οἶκος/οἰκία is mentioned in the story of the raising of Lazarus (11.20, 31), but the main action takes place away from the house. Only in the account of Mary's anointing is narrative action explicitly located in a house (12.1, 3).

21   In Mk 14.32 and Mt. 26.36, the place of Jesus' arrest is called Gethsemane (meaning 'oil press'). Taylor (2003) argues that Gethsemane itself was a cave, which she identifies with the holy site known as the Gethsemane Cave (under the control of the Franciscan Custody of the Holy Land). The cave, she thinks, was 'probably securely located in a pleasant, cultivated enclosure' (2003: 33). This would fit with John's reference to a κῆπος. Luke speaks more vaguely of a 'place' (τόπος) on the Mount of Olives (Lk. 22.40). Like John, he indicates that Jesus was in the habit of visiting the location (Lk. 22.39).

If the settings in which Jesus ministers in the Gospels bear any relation to the gathering places of early Christians, then these texts support a wider view of early Christian meeting places than the AEH consensus allows. Now, of course, not all the contexts in which Jesus teaches, dines or meets privately with his disciples in the Gospels (mountains, boats) can be considered as credible sites of assembly for urban Christian groups outside of Palestine, but, as we will see in Part II, it is quite plausible to imagine early Christians gathering at watersides, in commercially available dining rooms and in gardens.

1.2. *The House Missional Rule*
All three Synoptic Gospels contain at least one set of missionary instructions given to the disciples (Mk 6.7-13; Mt. 10.5-42; Lk. 9.1-6; 10.1-12), among which is an instruction regarding entering a house (Mk 6.10; Mt. 10.11-13; Lk. 9.4; 10.5-7). The version of the discourse in Lk. 10.1-12 is taken by Gehring to be the most original.[22] The so-called house missional rule (or *Hausmissionsregel*) within it reads:

> Whatever house you enter, first say, 'Peace to this house!' And if anyone is there who shares in peace, your peace will rest on that person; but if not, it will return to you. Remain in the same house, eating and drinking whatever they provide, for the laborer deserves to be paid. Do not move about from house to house (Lk. 10.5-7).

The 'rule' plainly articulates a house/household mission and thus seems to connect with household evangelism in the early church. David Matson argues that Lk. 10.5-7 functions as a prefiguration of the household conversions narrated in Acts.[23] He finds the 'taxonomy' of household evangelism outlined in Lk. 10.5-7 – entering the house, preaching salvation to the household, and staying in the house for purposes of inclusive table-fellowship – present in the account of the conversion of Cornelius and his household in Acts 10.23-48.[24]

Gehring is confident that the house missional rule goes back to the historical Jesus. He further maintains that it encapsulates Jesus' own approach to mission. According to Gehring, summary statements such as Mk 6.6, in which we read that Jesus 'went about among the villages teaching', indicate that Jesus undertook village-to-village missional

---

22 Gehring 2004: 49.
23 Matson 1996: 26–52.
24 Matson 1996: 86–134. He struggles, though, to find the pattern replicated in subsequent household conversions in Acts (1996: 135–83); see below, pp.58–9, on the Philippian jailer and his household.

outreach in Galilee.[25] During his itinerant mission, Gehring reasons, he would surely have stayed as a guest in people's homes. His village-to-village mission, therefore, was also implicitly a 'house-to-house' mission.[26] The homes in which Jesus stayed, along with the homes of many of those who came to faith through his itinerant preaching, would have become small 'house communities',[27] precursors of the more developed post-Easter 'house churches'.

Gehring's reconstruction is not implausible; it is, however, almost entirely speculative. He concedes that there are no overt references in the Gospels to houses in which Jesus stayed as a guest (though he thinks that the house in Tyre mentioned in Mk 7.24 may have been one such house),[28] and he admits that the existence of house groups formed as a result of Jesus' evangelization 'can only be assumed; they cannot be documented in our texts'.[29]

It is clear from the Pauline Epistles (1 Cor. 1.16; 16.15) and Acts that household evangelism was an element of early Christian mission. However, household conversion was not, as has been claimed, 'the natural or even necessary way of establishing the new cult in unfamiliar surroundings'.[30] The book of Acts presents conversion as a variegated phenomenon: within the narrative of Acts household conversion is only one of the ways in which the church expands.[31] As we have seen, conversion often cut across existing households (1 Cor. 7.12-16; Col. 3.22-23; 1 Pet. 2.18-20; 3.1-6). There is a lot of material in the Synoptic Gospels indicating that discipleship divides and brings discord into households (Mk 10.29-30; 13.12; Mt. 8.21-22; 10.34-38; Lk. 9.61-62; 14.26).[32]

---

25   Gehring 2004: 42.
26   Gehring 2004: 43.
27   Gehring 2004: 44–5.
28   Gehring 2004: 42.
29   Gehring 2004: 46. Gehring (2004: 37–42, 46–7) argues that the house of Peter functioned as a kind of proto-'house church', but his proposal involves speculation and eisegesis.
30   Cf. Judge 1960: 36.
31   We also read of mass conversions (e.g. 2.37-42), group conversions (19.1-7) and the conversion of individuals (e.g. 8.9-13, 26-39; 9.1-30).
32   See further Barton 1994; Barclay 1997: 73–5. It is true, as Gehring (2004: 61) notes, that the winning of households and the renunciation of them may be seen as complementary aspects of a singular missionary strategy in which those summoned to leave their families and occupations and engage in itinerant evangelism become dependent on the domestic hospitality of others. However, the radical subordination of family loyalties demanded in some of these texts (esp. Mt. 10.34-38; Lk. 14.26) cannot be restricted in their application only to those called to be itinerant missionaries.

That the house missional rule envisages the formation of house communities or embryonic 'house churches', as Gehring thinks,[33] seems rather doubtful. It is not clear that Lk. 10.5-7 pictures a wholesale conversion of the house's occupants. Certainly, nothing is said about the house becoming an 'assembly place'.[34]

2. *The Book of Acts*

The words οἶκος and οἰκία frequently appear in Acts, often with reference to a habitation or habitations.[35] As in his Gospel, in Acts when Luke uses οἶκος or οἰκία to denote a habitation, he seems to have in mind a house proper.[36] It is striking that Luke does not apply either term to the dwelling of Aquila and Priscilla (18.1-3), which (as noted in the previous chapter), given their occupations, was likely to have been a workshop dwelling. Luke even avoids using οἶκος and οἰκία when describing the upper-level apartment in 20.7-12, suggesting that he does not even regard a tenement flat as an οἶκος/οἰκία![37] It may be, though, that the expression κατ' οἶκον, meaning 'at home',[38] has a broader range of reference, taking in dwellings in general (2.46; 5.42). The phrase κατ' οἴκους in 20.20 may also embrace dwellings generally.

The book of Acts offers the clearest and fullest New Testament documentation of the use of houses as Christian meeting places. But not all the evidence scholars derive from Acts for 'house churches' is exegetically convincing. References to 'house churches' have been found in

33 Gehring 2004: 56.
34 *Contra* Gehring 2004: 56.
35 The term οἶκος appears 25 times in Acts. In 13 instances (2.2, 46; 5.42; 8.3; 10.22, 30; 11.12, 13; 16.15, 34; 19.16; 20.20; 21.8) it refers to a habitation. The word οἰκία occurs 12 times (4.34; 9.11, 17; 10.6, 17, 32; 11.11; 12.12; 16.32; 17.5; 18.7 [×2]), always with reference to a house or dwelling.
36 See the discussion in Ascough 2009: 29–35 (with particular reference to the kind of house in which Lydia dwelt). Several of the houses we encounter in Acts seem to be of some size. The house of Simon in Joppa and that of Mary in Jerusalem both have a πυλών (10.17; 12.13), meaning gate or porch, which implies that they are large buildings. The house of Cornelius is able to accommodate a large gathering (10.27). If a house, the οἶκος of 2.2 would be extremely large; see the discussion on pp.56–7, below.
37 The οἶκος/οἰκία terminology is not applied to Paul's rented accommodation in Rome (28.23, 30).
38 The expression κατ' οἶκον could have a distributive sense, 'in their various houses', but the use of the singular οἶκον and the contrast with 'in the temple' (ἐν τῷ ἱερῷ) in both verses weigh in favour of a locational meaning.

stories of the conversion of a household,[39] in mentions of someone's
house[40] and in mentions of some person or persons offering hospitality[41]
(these overlap with each other to some extent). But such data are not
sufficient in themselves to establish textual evidence of 'house churches';
needed are more explicit indications in the passages concerned that the
converted household forms a distinct and ongoing ecclesial unit, or that
the named householder opens up her/his home to a group of believers, or
that a house in which Peter or Paul stays functions also as a church
meeting place.

    In what follows, we examine passages in Acts which have been taken
as indicating house meetings and 'house churches', making the following
distinctions: texts that unambiguously speak of or instantiate meeting in
a house or houses; passages in which the claimed reference to a house
meeting or house as meeting place is more debatable; texts in which the
alleged reference to the house as meeting place is no more than a speculative inference. After discussing these texts, we look, more briefly, at
other settings of mission and meeting in the narrative of Acts.

2.1. House Meetings and Houses as Meeting Places: Unambiguous Texts
The summary statement of Acts 2.46 reports that members of the believing community in Jerusalem gather both in the temple and 'at home'
(κατ' οἶκον). It is in their dwellings that believers 'break bread', by
which Luke probably means that they celebrate the Lord's Supper, taken
as part of a common meal ('ate their food with glad and generous hearts';
cf. 2.42).[42] In 5.42, Luke tells us that the apostles ceaselessly teach and
preach Jesus as the Messiah 'in the temple and at home' (κατ' οἶκον).[43]
The use of believers' dwellings as meeting places by the fledgling Jerusalem church is thus clearly and indisputably indicated. In both verses,

---

39   E.g. Klauck 1981: 51–6.
40   Klauck 1981: 51; Blue 1994: 177.
41   Various named individuals host Christian missionaries: Simon the Tanner
(9.43; 10.6, 18, 32) and Cornelius (10.48) offer Peter a place to stay; Lydia (16.15),
Aquila and Priscilla (18.3), Philip (21.8, 10), Mnason (21.16) and Publius (28.7) put
up/entertain Paul. According to Blue (1994: 188), 'For Luke, the mention of these
people (and their hospitality and homes) has little to do with their invitation to Paul
to enjoy a warm bed for the night or two. These are likely the people who opened
their homes to the local Christian community.'
42   Luke may thus be projecting a later practice back onto the early Jerusalem
community.
43   In 4.34, we read that 'as many as owned lands or houses sold them and
brought the proceeds of what was sold' to the apostles. Evidently, some dwellings
remain at the community's disposal.

Luke underlines the regularity of meeting and receiving instruction at home ('day by day', 2.46; 'every day', 5.42).

In 10.24-48 (cf. 11.12), the house of Cornelius in Caesarea is the scene of a powerful evangelistic sermon by Peter. Peter preaches to a large company gathered in the house consisting of Cornelius's family and close friends (10.24). After he preaches, the Holy Spirit falls on the Gentiles assembled, and they speak in tongues and praise God (10.44-46). Peter orders them to be baptized (we are not told where the baptism is carried out), and he is invited to stay in Cornelius' house (10.48). Klauck interprets this episode as a report of a foundation of a 'house church',[44] but as Gehring rightly points out, 'the text does not inform us of further developments regarding the house of Cornelius'.[45]

In 12.12-17, we read of a meeting in the house of Mary, the mother of John Mark, in Jerusalem. After his miraculous escape from prison (12.6-11), Peter goes straight to Mary's house (not hitherto mentioned in the narrative),[46] where many have gathered for prayer (12.12). When he is eventually allowed in, he reports how the Lord has delivered him. Mary's house appears to be a regular meeting place in Jerusalem (at least within the narrative world of Acts) since Peter heads directly to this house after escaping from prison, apparently expecting believers to be gathered there.[47]

Acts 16.40 relates a gathering in the house of Lydia in Philippi, whose conversion is recounted earlier in the narrative (16.13-16). She was one of the women gathered at the 'place of prayer' (see further below). Lydia is a trader, dealing in purple cloth (πορφυρόπωλις), and has charge over a household (16.15).[48] The lack of reference to a husband would indicate that she is unmarried (perhaps divorced or widowed).[49] She responded to Paul's message, and she and her household were baptized. Subsequently, she persuaded Paul and his colleagues to stay at her οἶκος.[50] Paul and

44 Klauck 1981: 56.
45 Gehring 2004: 108.
46 There is no indication that Mary's house is the upper room of 1.13 or the οἶκος of 2.2.
47 In addition to the company gathered at Mary's house, the text makes reference to a second group: 'James and the brothers' (12.17). Gehring (2004: 70–3) takes this to be another 'house church' in Jerusalem, which he thinks may have been located in the upper room mentioned in 1.13, but this is pure eisegesis.
48 Her name is not Jewish, but she appears to be a Jewish sympathizer (though this is doubted, unnecessarily, by Ascough [2009: 83–90]).
49 Ascough 2009: 45.
50 Her capacity to accommodate the missionary group suggests that the οἶκος is more than a modest dwelling.

Silas make their way to Lydia after leaving the prison, having received an apology from the Philippian magistrates for wrongful punishment (16.39). The Greek construction in v. 40, εἰσῆλθον πρὸς τὴν Λυδίαν, is almost certainly to be understood as be a shorthand for εἰσῆλθον τὸν οἶκον τῆς Λυδιάς, 'they went into Lydia's house'.[51] There, we are told, they 'encouraged the brothers', παρεκάλεσαν τοὺς ἀδελφοὺς, which effectively means that Paul preached to an assembled company.[52] Lydia's house thus appears to have become the meeting place of a group of believers (beyond her own household).[53] This is the only instance in Acts of a household conversion explicitly leading to the transformation of house space into ecclesial space.

In 20.7-12, Luke describes a gathering of believers in Troas on the first day of the week.[54] The central feature of the episode is the raising of Eutychus, who, becoming drowsy while Paul preaches, falls out of the window on which he is perched, and is 'picked up dead' on the street below (v. 9). The believers have gathered to 'break bread' (v. 7) and to receive teaching from Paul. The meeting begins in the evening, when workers, and even some slaves, would have been free from their duties, and takes places in a 'room upstairs' (ὑπερῷον, v. 8). That Eutychus falls ἀπὸ τοῦ τριστέγου, 'from the third storey', which in British English is the second floor, indicates that the room is in an *insula*, or apartment-block, with at least three storeys. Thus, we have here a meeting in a tenement flat, presumably the home of one of the believers. The room is crowded, as evidenced by the fact that Eutychus has to sit in the window, and illuminated by 'many lamps'. The fatal fall of Eutychus interrupts the meeting. After restoring Eutychus to life, the apostle returns to the upper room, resumes the meal, and continues teaching until dawn.

Paul's address to the Ephesian elders at Miletus in 20.18-35 begins by recalling his ministry in Ephesus. In v. 20, he states: 'I did not shrink from doing anything helpful, proclaiming the message to you and teaching you publicly and at home' (κατ' οἴκους).[55] A regular practice of conducting teaching and proclamation in believers' homes during his mission in Ephesus is thus signalled.

51   Barrett 1998: 805.
52   The verb παρακάλεω is often used of preaching in Acts (2.40; 11.23; etc), as noted by Gehring (2004: 131); cf. Barrett 1994: 156.
53   The reference to the 'brothers' indicates a larger group than Lydia's household.
54   How the church came to be in existence is not explained by Luke.
55   NRSV, 'from house to house'.

When Paul arrives in Rome, he is allowed to stay on his own under guard (28.16). In 28.30, we read that Paul lives ἐν ἰδίῳ μισθώματι, which may mean 'at his own expense', but more likely means 'in his own hired house'.[56] In 28.17-28, Luke narrates two meetings of Paul with the local Jewish leaders. The second meeting clearly takes place in Paul's lodgings (εἰς τὴν ξενίαν, v. 23),[57] and the first presumably occurs there also. In vv. 30-31, the conclusion to the book of Acts, Luke tells of Paul's continued witness in Rome over a two-year period, welcoming into his lodgings 'all who came to him' and 'proclaiming the kingdom of God and teaching about the Lord Jesus Christ'. It seems reasonable to assume that the 'all' of v. 31 includes fellow believers or those who would become believers, and so to deduce that Paul's accommodation in Rome functions as a teaching centre for Christians as well as a place of evangelistic activity. It is perhaps going too far, though, to deduce, as Gehring and Lampe do,[58] that Paul becomes the host of his own 'house church'.

From these passages, we get clear and repeated witness to the use of houses (perhaps dwellings more broadly in 2.46, 5.42 and 20.20) as meeting places in the nascent church. Houses are used for sacral eating (2.46; 20.7-12), corporate prayer (12.12-17), evangelistic preaching and witness (10.24-48; 28.17-31), and preaching to and teaching believers (5.42; 16.40; 20.7-12, 20; 28.30-31).

2.2. *House Meetings and Houses as Meeting Places: Debatable Texts*
While the passages discussed above provide incontrovertible textual evidence for a practice of meeting in houses, other passages in Acts often or sometimes taken as illustrative of the house as meeting place are more open to debate.

In 1.15-26, Luke narrates the meeting to appoint Judas's successor. It is usually presumed that the 'room upstairs' (τὸ ὑπερῷον) to which the disciples return after the ascension is the location of this meeting.[59] This upper room is described in 1.13 as 'where they were staying' (οὗ ἦσαν καταμένοντες), which probably means that it is their lodgings,[60] but the

56   Barrett 1998: 1252.
57   Barrett 1998: 1243.
58   Gehring 2004: 146 n. 155; Lampe 2003: 359.
59   As Barrett (1994: 86) states, Luke 'does not go out of his way' to equate this room with the room in which the Last Supper was held. That Luke uses a different word here (ὑπερῷον as opposed to ἀνάγαιον in Lk. 22.12) suggests that he makes a distinction between them. Cf. Bock 2007: 77.
60   Barrett (1994: 87) thinks that ἦσαν καταμένοντες must mean that they habitually met in this room, rather than they were residing in it. But the verb κατα-

text does not demand that the room be understood as the setting of the meeting Luke goes on describe in 1.15-26.[61] An upper-room locale is difficult to square with the number of people said to be present at this gathering: 'about one hundred twenty persons' (1.15). Another unspecified location makes better sense.[62]

Acts 2.1-4 recounts the outpouring of the Spirit upon the gathered company of believers on the day of Pentecost. The event takes place in the οἶκος 'where they were sitting' (2.2). Luke does not identify the οἶκος with the 'upper room' mentioned in 1.13, and the change in terminology makes it more likely that he intended to distinguish them. By the word οἶκος a domestic residence is usually understood, but there are two problems involved in this interpretation. First, there is great difficulty in imagining 120 people meeting in the room of a house.[63] Blue attempts to show that houses in Jerusalem could hold groups of such numbers by drawing attention to the remains of the so-called Palatial Mansion (destroyed in 70 CE) in the south-eastern quarter.[64] This grand house contained a large reception hall, measuring 11 × 6.5 m, and three connected rooms.[65] Taken together, the hall and these rooms, he points out, would easily have accommodated some 100 people. But the Palatial Mansion was one of the very largest and most splendid residences in the city. According to Yizhar Hirschfeld, the owner must have been 'an important personage in the city's political or religious establishment before the destruction of the Second Temple'.[66] That the early believing community in Jerusalem had access to a house like this is extremely

μένω means 'to live', or 'to stay', and not 'to gather' (cf. BDAG 522; LSJ 901). *Contra* Barrett, it is not unreasonable to imagine a group of eleven men residing in one room. The ὑπερῷον is best understood as rented domestic quarters; this would form a nice *inclusio* with the reference to Paul's hired house in 28.30.

61   The upper room is normally understood to be the place in which the disciples and others are 'constantly devoting themselves to prayer' (1.14): so, e.g., Bock 2007: 76. However, the text does not demand this, and they could be meeting for prayer within the temple (cf. Lk. 24.53).

62   The words 'in those days' in 1.15, and elsewhere in Acts (cf. 6.1; 9.37; 11.27), function as a transition to a new section. A switch to a different location would fit with the narrative transition.

63   It might be argued that by 'all', in 2.1, Luke means a more restricted group than the 120 of 1.15 (note the addition of the words οἱ ἀπόστολοι in some manuscripts). However, a reference to a more limited number than the 120 is at odds with the inclusiveness of the Pentecost event (2.17, 18).

64   Blue 1994: 140–4

65   Blue 1994. See also Hirschfeld 1995: 59–62. See further in Chapter 8.

66   Hirschfeld 1995: 62.

improbable. Assuming the basic historicity of the event described (which is of course debated), if one takes οἶκος as meaning 'house', one would surely have to conclude that Luke has greatly exaggerated the number of those involved. Balch raises the possibility that the meeting happens in a spacious garden linked to a house or inn.[67] He highlights hospitality gardens in Pompeii, some of which could accommodate a large number of people.[68] This interpretation is attractive, but it seems to stretch the meaning of οἶκος (denoting 'habitation') beyond Luke's restricted use of the word. Moreover, Luke could simply have used κῆπος if a garden setting were in view. The second problem with taking οἶκος to mean a house is that a public place is definitely in view in 2.6 when a massive crowd gathers. We thus have to assume that Peter and the other apostles leave the house and speak to the crowd (numbering 3000 people by the time Peter finishes preaching, 2.41) in a large, open public area, even though no shift in location is narrated. It has occasionally been suggested that by οἶκος in 2.2 the Jerusalem temple is meant.[69] Blue objects to this suggestion on the grounds that 'when Luke refers to the Temple he uses τὸ ἱερόν'.[70] But his observation is not strictly correct. Luke can use οἶκος of the temple (cf. Acts 7.47, 49). Indeed, he can use ὁ οἶκος without qualification with reference to it (Lk. 11.51). A setting in the wider temple or perhaps, as C.K. Barrett suggests, a room within the temple precincts[71] coheres with the sudden appearance of a multitude in v. 6. As Ben Witherington notes, the temple precinct is 'the only place such a crowd could or would likely be congregated'.[72]

In 4.23-31, Peter and John, after their release by the authorities, go to οἱ ἴδιοι, literally 'their own', and report their experiences, immediately after which the whole gathered company offers prayer. After prayer is complete, 'the place in which they were gathered' (ὁ τόπος ἐν ᾧ ἦσαν συνηγμένοι) trembles, and all are filled with the Spirit (4.31). According to Richard Pervo, Luke in this passage 'envisions the entire community gathered…in a house'.[73] But the location is unspecified, and if the assembled company is the believing community as a whole, or a signi-ficant representation of them, rather than just the other apostles, a house

---

67   Balch 2012: 230–1.
68   Balch 2012: 226–8. See further pp.183–4, below.
69   Holtzmann 1901: 31; Schneider 1980: 247–8; cf. Bruce 1951: 81.
70   Blue 1994: 134 n. 53. So also Bock 2007: 94.
71   Barrett 1994: 114. Barrett points out that Josephus, in *Ant.* 8.65, employs οἶκος both for the temple itself and for chambers within it.
72   Witherington 1998: 132.
73   Pervo 2009: 122. Gehring (2004: 66 n. 29) thinks that the locale is the upper room of 1.13, but this has no textual warrant.

setting would be out of the question. There is nothing in Luke's wording that requires a domestic venue. The 'place' could be enclosed outdoor space (a garden)[74] or a space within the temple (such as Solomon's Portico, on which see below).

In 8.3, we are told that Saul was 'ravaging the church by entering house after house; dragging off both men and women' (κατὰ τοὺς οἴκους εἰσπορευόμενος, σύρων τε ἄνδρας καὶ γυναῖκας) and taking them into custody. According to Gehring, Saul targeted 'precisely the houses in which he suspected Christian assemblies, in hopes of catching them in flagrante delicto'.[75] But on the most obvious reading of the text, Saul is conducting a general house-to-house search with a view to uncovering believers, not a limited search of the houses of known or suspected Christians. The words κατὰ τοὺς οἴκους εἰσπορευόμενος may be understood as serving to underscore the extent and intensity of Paul's quest,[76] not as drawing attention to the role of houses as Christian meeting places.

For Matson, the account of the conversion of the Philippian jailer and his household, given in 16.25-34, illustrates 'the "conversion" of household space', by which he means 'the transformation of the house from private domestic space to the "public" space of the church, the locus for the inclusive act of "eating and drinking"'.[77] On Matson's reading of the passage, the jailer's house is the setting of the evangelization of the jailer and his family, as well as of a shared meal, which Matson regards as 'eucharistic in nature'.[78] Luke does not expressly narrate an entry into the jailer's house until v. 34 ('He brought them up into the house'), which comes after the evangelization and baptism of the jailer and his kin, but Matson thinks that entry into the house is presupposed in v. 32, where we are told that Paul and Silas 'spoke the word of the Lord to him and to all who were in his house (πᾶσιν τοῖς ἐν τῇ οἰκίᾳ αὐτοῦ)'.[79] According to Matson, πᾶσιν τοῖς ἐν τῇ οἰκίᾳ αὐτοῦ cannot simply denote the members of the jailer's household: 'nowhere in Luke or Acts does οἰκία stand for the personified house, only a house in an architectural sense'.[80] We are meant to infer from the phrase that all the members of the family 'gather in the house to hear the word of the Lord', as in the story of Cornelius.

74   As in Lk. 22.40 (cf. Mk 14.32).
75   Gehring 2004: 88.
76   Bock 2007: 320.
77   Matson 1996: 191–2 n. 27.
78   Matson 1996: 154–68.
79   Matson 1996: 160.
80   Matson 1996: 160.

Acts 16.34 thus narrates 'a re-entry into the house'.[81] One may readily acknowledge Matson's point that οἰκία in 16.32 means the physical 'house' and not the social 'household', but the larger phrase, πᾶσιν τοῖς ἐν τῇ οἰκίᾳ αὐτοῦ, clearly foregrounds the *occupants* of the house and is thus equivalent to οἶκος (meaning 'household') in v. 31 and πανοικεί in v. 34. The wording does not require us to presume that the jailer and his family are actually in the house when Paul and Silas preach to them in v. 32. Matson's reading over-complicates a relatively clear sequence in vv. 30-34: Paul and Silas are brought 'outside' (ἔξω) the jail (v. 30); outside, Paul and Silas speak the word of the Lord to the jailer and members of his household (vv. 30-32); the jailer takes Paul and Silas somewhere to wash their wounds; the jailer and his family receive baptism (v. 33); the jailer brings Paul and Silas into the house and sets food before them (v. 34). Matson takes the meal eaten in the jailer's house to be Eucharistic on the basis of the unusually late hour during which the meal takes place (vv. 25, 33), the language of (lit.) 'setting a table', παρατίθημι τράπεζαν (v. 34), and the note of rejoicing (ἠγαλλιάσατο).[82] However, the unusual timing of the meal simply follows from the timing of the earthquake, and παρατίθημι τράπεζαν is an old and common Greek expression for preparing a meal and carries no necessary Eucharistic connotations.[83] The verb ἀγαλλιάω similarly need not carry a Eucharistic nuance.[84] Had Luke wanted to indicate that the meal is a celebration of the Lord's Supper, he could have done so with talk of 'breaking bread'.[85] The most obvious way of taking v. 34 is simply to read it in terms of the jailer entertaining men 'who had been wronged, whom he revered, and to whom he was indebted' and rejoicing to do so.[86] The jailer's house is thus a setting for hospitality but probably no more than that. For Gehring, the story of the conversion of the jailer and his family is a '"church origins" report of a house church in Philippi whose nucleus consisted of an *oikos* (house and household)',[87] but we are not told by Luke whether the jailer's household becomes a 'house church'. Taking v. 40 into account, we might infer that the jailer and his dependents join with the 'brothers' meeting in Lydia's house.

81   Matson 1996: 162 n. 125.
82   Matson 1996: 163-4.
83   Barrett 1998: 799.
84   The verb occurs elsewhere in Luke-Acts without a Eucharistic tint (Lk. 1.47; 10.21; Acts 2.26). The cognate noun ἀγαλλίασις, though, occurs in 2.46, in connection with the 'breaking of bread'.
85   Barrett 1998: 799.
86   Barrett 1998: 799.
87   Gehring 2004: 124.

In 17.5-9, Luke tells how hostile Jews along with some thugs from the marketplace set upon the house of Jason (17.5) seeking Paul and Silas. Unable to find them there, they haul Jason and some brothers before the city authorities (17.6). The house of Jason, who appears to be a convert,[88] is plainly Paul and Silas's lodgings in Thessalonica. This is made clear in v. 7, in the accusation that 'Jason welcomed them into his house' (οὓς ὑποδέδεκται 'Ιάσων).[89] Blue contends that the house is also a meeting place for Thessalonian believers.[90] He thinks that a meeting is in progress in the house at the very time that the troublemakers arrive.[91] This is not an unreasonable deduction, but we are not explicitly informed by Luke that Jason's house is an assembly venue. Nor are we told that the brothers are actually inside the house when the mob descends; perhaps they arrive on the scene to support Jason, or perhaps they are hunted down by the mob as other suspected or known believers. Luke's text can support various scenarios.

In 18.7, relating to Paul's mission in Corinth, we read in the NRSV that Paul 'left the synagogue and went to the house of a man named Titius Justus, a worshipper of God; his house was next door to the synagogue'. The Greek text, however, states that Paul left (lit.) 'from there', ἐκεῖθεν, leaving the antecedent of ἐκεῖθεν unspecified. The reference could be, as the NRSV takes it, to the synagogue to which Paul has just lost access (18.4). If the synagogue is meant, the point would be that Paul transfers his base of operations from the synagogue to Titius Justus's house, using the latter as his new 'preaching centre',[92] having been 'proclaiming the word' at the synagogue next door. However, ἐκεῖθεν could be pointing back to the dwelling of Aquila and Priscilla, where Paul has been staying in Corinth up to this point.[93] The editor of the Western text took the words to mean that Paul left Aquila.[94] If the reference is to Aquila and Priscilla's quarters, the point would be that Paul no longer lodges with them but with Titius Justus, with no *necessary* thought of Titius Justus's house functioning as a venue for Paul's preaching and teaching.[95] On

88   However, the wording does not make this a certainty; cf. Barrett 1998: 813.
89   The word ὑποδέχομαι bears the sense, 'to welcome into one's house' (cf. Lk. 10.38; 19.6).
90   Blue 1994: 187.
91   Blue 1994: 187.
92   Barrett 1998: 867.
93   Fitzmyer 1998: 627.
94   Adding ἀπὸ 'Ακύλα.
95   Since Luke does not indicate that Paul used the quarters of Aquila and Priscilla as a teaching locale; see below in the main text.

balance, ἐκεῖθεν probably refers to the synagogue, but it is difficult to be certain.

Acts 21.8-14 concerns Paul's visit to Philip the evangelist at Caesarea. During his visit, Paul receives a prophecy from Agabus (21.10-14). The acted prophecy takes places in gathered company: Paul's travel companions together with οἱ ἐντόπιοι, the local Christian residents (21.12).[96] The setting could be Philip's house (vv. 8, 10) as Neyrey thinks,[97] or it could be another unspecified location. Luke's wording in v. 10, ἐπι-μενόντων δὲ ἡμέρας πλείους, indicates that the event happens while Paul and his friends are staying with Philip but not specifically that it occurs in Philip's house.

In all these passages, the alleged reference to a house meeting or the house as meeting place is subject to debate. In some passages (17.5; 18.7; 21.8-14), the reference is possible but not certain due to a lack of clarity. In others (1.15-26; 2.1-4; 4.23-31; 8.3; 16.25-34), the reference is possible but (in my view) unlikely because of some countervailing factor (the number of persons said to be or implied as being present at the gathering; a more convincing alternative reading; the locational information provided). We turn now to passages in which the claimed reference to the house as meeting place is simply a speculative inference.

2.3. *Houses as Meeting Places: Speculative Inferences*
In Acts 9.11 and 17, reference is made to the house of Judas. Located on the street called Straight (9.11, 17), this house is Saul's residence in Damascus in the days immediately following his dramatic encounter with Jesus. It is in this locale that Ananias lays hands on Saul to restore his sight and that Saul receives the filling of the Spirit (9.17).[98] Gehring infers that Judas's house is the meeting place of a 'house church' in Damascus. He writes:

> Concrete memories of the conversion of Paul before Damascus, the disciple by the name of Ananias (9:10-19a), the explicit mention of the house of Judas on Straight Street (9:11), and the large number of disciples in Damascus (9:2, 12) are all reasons to believe that a fairly large congregation might have existed there that could have met in the house of Judas.[99]

---

96 Barrett 1998: 996.
97 Neyrey 2003: 90.
98 That Paul's baptism occurs in the house is unlikely; cf. 8.36.
99 Gehring 2004: 107.

But these data hardly provide support for such a conclusion. Luke gives no indication that Judas is a believer let alone a 'house-church' host. While Ananias is introduced as 'a disciple', no such descriptor is applied to Judas. As Barrett states, 'Paul's residence with him may have been on a purely commercial basis'.[100] The manner in which Ananias is directed to Judas's house suggests that the two are not known to each other. Were Judas the implied host of such a large congregation, one might expect Ananias to find reassurance in the fact that he is hosting Saul. But the information that Saul is to be found in Judas's house does nothing to alleviate Ananias's trepidation at the prospect of meeting the persecutor. Judas may have gone on to become a convert to 'the Way' and his house may have become a meeting place for believers in Damascus, but of such developments Luke tells us nothing.

In Acts 9.43, we learn that in Joppa Peter lodges with a certain Simon who is the proprietor of a tannery business (10.6).[101] It is in Simon's residence that Peter sees his heavenly vision and receives the messengers from Cornelius (10.9-16). For Gehring, we have here 'clear evidence' of a householder providing hospitality to Peter and supporting his missionary work in the area.[102] Gehring thinks it likely that Simon's house was the meeting locale of a 'house church'.[103] However, it is not even certain that Simon is a believer (though we would presume that he is) let alone a 'house-church' host. Luke gives no indication that Simon's house serves as a place of assembly.

Acts 18.2-3 tells how Paul lodges with Aquila and Priscilla in Corinth and works with them in their tentmaking business. While (as noted above) Luke does not refer to the οἶκος or οἰκία of Aquila and Priscilla, the formulation ἔμενεν παρ' αὐτοῖς implies that they control a dwelling (probably, as we have seen, a *taberna*-dwelling). It seems reasonable to suppose that 'at Corinth Prisca and Aquila did what they subsequently did at Ephesus and Rome, where we hear of "a church in their house"'[104] (1 Cor. 16.19; Rom. 16.5). However, the fact is that Luke does not actually mention here a church in their home.

---

100   Barrett 1994: 453.

101   That he lives in a house with a πυλών implies that he is a relatively wealthy businessman (Ascough 2009: 30). The house does not appear to be his place of business. Presumably, the tannery is located close by (a seaside location, 10.6, 32, is an apt one for a tannery). In Pompeii, the fullonica of Marcus Vesonius Primus occupied the building next door to his house (see Chapter 6).

102   Gehring 2004: 107.

103   Gehring 2004: 107 n. 248.

104   Murphy-O'Connor 1992.

Acts 18.8 narrates the conversion of Crispus, the Corinthian synagogue official, 'together with all his household' (σὺν ὅλῳ τῷ οἴκῳ
αὐτοῦ). Blue takes it for granted that Crispus had 'a house which would
have accommodated a group of Christian believers'.[105] Crispus, whom
Paul mentions in 1 Cor. 1.14, may well have hosted a group of believers
in his home, but Luke does not tell us that, and there is no indication in
the narrative that his house (which is never actually mentioned) functions
as a church meeting place during Paul's time in Corinth, or that it goes
on to do so after Paul leaves.

In 21.16, we read that when Paul and his companions reach Jerusalem, they are taken to Mnason, with whom they are to lodge (παρ' ᾧ
ξενισθῶμεν).[106] Mnason is described as a Cypriot and as a disciple of long
standing. According to Blue, 'there is no reason to believe that his
[Mnason's] home was not one of the numerous places in Jerusalem
where part of the Christian community gathered'.[107] Mnason's house
could well have been the meeting place of a group of believers in
Jerusalem, but Luke does not tell us so, and to deduce that it was is to
speculate beyond the text.

In all these texts, the 'reference' to the house as meeting place is not
present in the given content but is a speculative addition to it. Such
speculative inferences cannot be regarded as textual evidence for the
practice of gathering in houses.

2.4. *Other Settings of Mission and Meeting*

Houses are by no means the only explicit settings of missionary/
evangelistic speech in the book of Acts. The most prominent setting of
missionary proclamation in the early chapters of Acts is the Jerusalem
temple. The temple is the explicit locale of Peter's second major speech
(3.1–4.3), and, as we have seen, it is most likely the location of his first
speech too. Peter's second speech is set in Solomon's Portico (3.11),
which Josephus locates on the east side of the temple.[108] Porticoes or
colonnades were traditional teaching sites for philosophers and teachers
of higher education (see further in Chapter 8). The most consistently
mentioned location of Paul's missionary preaching is the synagogue.[109]

105   Blue 1994: 176.
106   The Western text places him in an unnamed village on the way to Jerusalem; see Barrett 1998: 1004. It seems more likely, though, that Luke would name
Paul's host in Jerusalem than his host on the way (cf. Marshall 1980: 341–2).
107   Blue 1994: 188.
108   Josephus, *War* 5.184–85; *Ant.* 15.396-401.
109   Generally in Acts συναγωγή refers to a building (of some kind), though on
one occasion (13.43), Luke uses the term for a gathering (cf. Catto 2007: 191).

Soon after his baptism, Paul is found preaching in the synagogues in Damascus (9.20), and in most of the cities he visits in his mission, he preaches first in the synagogue (13.5, 14-43; 14.1; 17.1-3, 10, 17; 18.4, 19; 19.8). He is usually forced out (13.44-48; 14.2; 17.5, 13; 18.5-7; 19.9) but not without some initial success. Paul also engages in evangelistic speech at other locales too. At Lystra, he preaches to a crowd at the city gates (14.13-18).[110] At Philippi, on a Sabbath day, he speaks to a group of women (who are either Jews or Jewish sympathizers) gathered at a προσευχή outside the city gate by the river (16.13). While some scholars think that by προσευχή in 16.13, 16, a synagogue building is meant,[111] the fact that elsewhere in Acts Luke uses συναγωγή to denote synagogue buildings (including Diaspora synagogue buildings) tells against that meaning here. The word προσευχή probably means 'place of prayer' (as NRSV),[112] i.e., a spot where prayers can be made[113] (for watersides as Jewish meeting places, see further in Chapter 5). It is noteworthy that Paul and his companions continue to go to the riverside 'place of prayer' even after Lydia makes her house available to them (16.15-16). In Athens, in a manner reminiscent of Socrates,[114] Paul argues 'every day' in the marketplace or agora (ἐν τῇ ἀγορᾷ) with those who happen to be present (17.17). On one occasion, an exchange with Stoics and Epicureans in the agora leads to the apostle being taken to the Areopagus, where he delivers his famous speech (17.22-31). In Ephesus, when Paul withdraws from the synagogue (after three months spent teaching there), he relocates to the σχολή or 'school' of Tyrannus (19.9), where, over a period of two years, 'all the residents of Asia, both Jews and Greeks' get to hear God's word (19.10).[115] The range of spaces in which missionary speech occurs shows that the progress of the gospel in the books of Acts is not simply, as Elliott claims, 'from house to house'.[116]

---

110   The 'gates' in 14.13 could be the gates of the temple of Zeus, but the phrase ἐπὶ τοὺς πυλῶνας probably relates to the preceding πρὸ τῆς πόλεως; thus the city gates are meant.

111   E.g. Hengel 1971: 175. As Binder notes (1999: 117), by at least the first century BCE, the word προσευχή 'became the common term for synagogue buildings throughout the diaspora'. See his discussion of the term in 1999: 111–18.

112   Shorthand for τόπος προσευχῆς (1 Macc. 3.36; *3 Macc.* 7.20).

113   Catto 2007: 186–90.

114   Xenophon, *Mem.* 1.1.10.

115   Paul's forensic speeches (22.1-21; 23.6-10; 24.10-21; 26.1-29), as Neyrey (2003: 102 n. 78) points out, are delivered in public or in public forums, such as the Jerusalem temple (22.1-21) and the 'audience hall' (ἀκροατήριον) in Caesarea (25.23). As a prisoner on a ship being pounded by a violent storm (27.18), Paul speaks to the ship's company of God's protection and (lit.) 'salvation' (27.34).

116   J.H. Elliott 1991: 226.

Houses are certainly the most oft-mentioned meeting places of believers in Acts. But Christians assemble in other places too. In the early days of the Jerusalem church, believers gather in the temple (2.46; 5.12, 42). Acts 2.46 indicates that while members of the Jerusalem believing community meet in groups in various homes, the temple is where they gather 'together', ὁμοθυμαδόν. By this word Luke does not simply mean that they continue to take part in temple worship (which 3.1 indicates) but that they assemble as a unified group within temple space.[117] Solomon's Portico becomes the regular place of meeting in the temple complex for the believing community at large (5.12). The summary statement of 5.42 emphasizes that the apostles teach and preach in the temple on a daily basis.[118] The gathering of believers in the temple apparently continues until persecution forces members of the Jerusalem church out of the city (8.1). The σχολή of Tyrannus in Ephesus serves as teaching centre for believers ('the disciples') as well as outsiders (19.9). Precisely what Luke means by σχολή has been perennially debated. Abraham Malherbe argues that Luke intends for his readers to understand the σχολή as a collegial building,[119] which is possible. More likely, a building or room used formally for teaching is meant.[120] Loveday Alexander takes the σχολή to be 'an auditorium used for lectures by visiting philosophers or rhetors, perhaps for regular classes'.[121] An auditorium could be part of an elite house, but the fact that Luke uses neither οἶκος nor οἰκία in 19.9-10 suggests that he is not thinking of a room in a house. It is worth bearing in mind that classrooms could be located in and above shops (see Chapter 6). The Western text specifies Paul's teaching hours, 'from the fifth to the tenth hour'. The period

117   Barrett 1994: 170.
118   According to Klauck (1981: 50), Acts 5.42 follows a chiastic pattern that links preaching with the temple and teaching with what takes place in the house. Gehring (2004: 74), in line with this understanding of the verse, translates it as: 'Day by day, they never stopped proclaiming Jesus as the Christ in the temple and teaching in the individual houses'. But that Luke means to link only preaching and not teaching with the temple completely flies in the face of the immediate context: the section to which 5.41-42 forms a conclusion is about the apostles teaching in the temple and the Sanhedrin's attempt to stop them doing so (5.21, 25, 28). In Luke's Gospel and in Acts, teaching is frequently a public activity. Luke's point in 5.42 is that the apostles continued their habitual practice of *both* teaching and preaching in *both* temple and houses.
119   Malherbe 1977: 89–90.
120   The word σχολή is used synonymously with διδασκαλεῖον ('classroom') in Plutarch, *De Recta Rat.* 42A (as noted in Barrett 1998: 905).
121   Alexander 2002: 235

specified is presumably to be understood as a part of the day during which the lecture-hall or classroom was not normally in use.[122] In his speech to the Ephesian elders at Miletus (20.18-38), Paul speaks retrospectively, in 20.20, about having taught the believers in Ephesus both 'publicly', δημοσίᾳ, and at home. It is usually thought that by δημοσίᾳ, Paul is referring to the σχολή of Tyrannus,[123] but as Jerome Neyrey has shown, the σχολή is likely to have been classified as 'private' rather than 'public' space.[124] In 16.37, δημοσία refers to the marketplace or agora,[125] and this is probably what is in view in 20.20. Luke has already shown Paul disputing in the agora at Athens (17.17). The agora was a natural site for teaching (see Chapter 8). A reference to urban open space fits with the fact that Paul's asseveration in 20.20 is structurally parallel to the statements of 2.46 and 5.42, in which meeting/teaching at home is complemented by meeting/teaching in the public setting of the temple.[126] Paul's speech to the Ephesian elders, the only formal speech addressed to believers in Acts, seems to take place at the harbour at Miletus (20.18-38).[127] At the end of his week's stay in Tyre, Paul prays with the local believers, including women and children, 'on the beach' (21.5) before boarding a ship for Jerusalem. Watersides, schoolrooms and urban open space, as we will see, are credible non-house meeting places of the early Christians.

122 Barrett 1994: 905.
123 E.g. Alexander 2002: 236; Stowers 1984: 61.
124 Neyrey 2003: 91. Neyrey himself thinks that δημοσία 'refers to the residences of governors and kings and city centers' (102). He interprets the statement of 20.20 as a statement about Paul's general activity across the narrative of Acts. However, Paul is talking specifically here about his modus operandi in *Ephesus* (ὑμῖν...ὑμᾶς).
125 Paul's statement in 16.37, 'they have beaten us in public' (δείραντες ἡμᾶς δημοσίᾳ), refers back to the public flogging in the Philippian agora narrated in 16.19-23.
126 It is not a problem that there is no mention of teaching in the agora in the foregoing account of Paul's mission in Ephesus in 19.1–20.1. There is no mention of his teaching in believers' homes in this passage either. Luke's recapitulations of Paul's conversion (22.3-21; 26.9-18) famously give details not narrated in the original account (9.1-19). We are perhaps meant to infer that Paul taught in the marketplace after his two-year tenure of the school came to an end (according to 20.31, he spent three years at Ephesus).
127 So Kistemaker 1990: 39. A harbour setting is suggested by the fact that he boards ship immediately after concluding the speech (20.38).

3. *Conclusion*

The Synoptic house settings of Jesus' teaching and social dining do not constitute direct evidence of the use of houses as early Christian meeting places since the Gospels are accounts of the ministry of Jesus and not descriptions of early church life. It is not injudicious to hypothesize a connection between the Gospel settings of Jesus' ministry and the settings in which early Christians gather, but the range of spaces in which Jesus teaches and has fellowship with others (especially his disciples) needs to be taken into account. The varied settings of Jesus' ministry in the (four) Gospels cohere with a broadened understanding of early Christian meeting places.

The book of Acts bears strong textual witness to houses as church-meeting locales, but that testimony is not nearly as extensive as has often been claimed. While a number of passages in Acts unequivocally depict house meetings and houses as meeting places, other passages taken as illustrative of the house as meeting places are more ambiguous, and in yet others, the claimed reference to a 'house church' is no more than a speculative inference. Moreover, other gathering places are also indicated. The evidence in Acts, therefore, does not comport with the consensus view that the earliest Christian meetings were 'almost exclusively' in houses.

Chapter 3

LITERARY EVIDENCE FROM 100 TO 313 CE

Having investigated the evidence for the house as the church's meeting place in the New Testament, we turn now to look at literary evidence outside and beyond it. We cover written (including papyrological) sources relating, more or less, to the period 100 to 313 CE, from around the beginning of the second century to the institution of the 'Peace' under Constantine.[1] Given the wider chronological parameters and larger database, we cannot examine all this material in the same detail as we treated some of the key New Testament passages.

On the common reconstruction of Christian assembly venues in the pre-Constantinian era, Christians met first in unmodified houses, until around 200 CE, then in partially or wholly adapted houses and finally in hall-type buildings. Our interest in the present study lies in the first stage, the so-called house church phase of assembly, but it is necessary to consider what evidence there is for domestic *domus ecclesiae* in the literature relating to the third and early fourth centuries, since extensive evidence for adapted houses as church buildings would count as strong support for a previous pattern of gathering 'almost exclusively' in houses. The chapter is thus divided into discussion of written evidence for (unmodified) houses as Christian meeting places, and discussion of literary evidence for modified and renovated houses as church buildings, following a broadly chronological path. Many of the relevant data have been collated by White.[2]

1   The date, 100 CE, to be clear, is a symbolic one. A second-century date is posited by many scholars for some New Testament documents (e.g. 2 Peter), and *1 Clement* is traditionally dated c. 96 CE.

2   White 1997: 36–120, 160–71. Traditions and legends linking Rome's titular churches with pre-Constantinian 'house churches' (on which see Lanzoni 1925) are not considered in this review. These traditions, found in sources such as the *Liber Pontificalis*, church council records and Roman martyrdom accounts, stem from the fifth and sixth centuries CE and cannot be used as *ante-pacem* evidence for the use of houses as places of worship (see further the next chapter). Also disregarded is the

1. *Evidence for Houses as Meeting Places*

Evidence for the use of believers' houses as Christian meeting places has been detected in a number of literary sources relating to the second and early third centuries CE, especially the Apocryphal Acts. We first look at evidence dating to the (very) late first and early second centuries, i.e., data in the 'apostolic fathers', and then consider evidence from the later second and early third centuries. It is convenient to take the Apocryphal Acts together and discuss the relevant data in them in a discrete section.

1.1. *The Late First and Early Second Centuries*
In his treatment of the ministry in the Christian communities represented by the Shepherd of Hermas, *1 Clement*, and the letters of Ignatius, Harry Maier maintains that 'the church meeting in households provides the social setting of the development of leadership structures in these early churches'.[3] He maintains that the typical leaders of these communities were '*patresfamilias* with houses large enough to accommodate meetings in their homes'.[4] Maier's account of emerging ecclesial leadership patterns is presented as a trajectory that begins with Paul and extends to Rome (Hermas), Corinth (*1 Clement*) and the communities in Asia Minor addressed by Ignatius.[5] The 'house-church' setting, which Maier sees reflected in the Pauline epistles, is understood to be 'a relatively firm setting from which to approach the later documents'.[6]

Maier presupposes a 'house-church' context for Hermas but finds the assumption corroborated in references to hospitality in the document.[7] In *Man.* 8.10, the list of virtuous duties commended includes 'being hospitable' (φιλόξενος), motivated by the knowledge that 'the practice of hospitality (φιλοξενία) results in doing good'. According to Maier, this exhortation 'would have had its most pertinent reference to wealthy

---

hagiographical narrative of the Abitinian martyrs, which tells of their worship, during Diocletian's persecution, in the homes of Octavius Felix and Emeritus (for the relevant passage from the *Passio Saturnini*, see White 1997: 87–9). As Dearn (2004) has shown, the text was composed more than a century after the events it purports to describe and cannot be accepted as a reliable record of them.

3   Maier 1991: 4.
4   Maier 1991: 4.
5   Maier (1991: 55–8) dates Hermas unusually early at 100 CE. Most have dated it to the middle of the second century CE (cf. Campbell 1994: 223). Osiek (1999: 20) dates it to an expanded period from the end of the first century to the middle of the second century.
6   Maier 1991: 10.
7   So also Lampe 2003: 374 n. 4.

persons, who had an important role in providing meeting places for the worshipping community'.[8] However, the words φιλόξενος and φιλοξενία have to do with welcoming strangers and visitors, not hosting meetings of fellow believers in one's house (members of one's own community could hardly be regarded as strangers).[9] There is nothing in the passage or its wider context to indicate that anything other than 'hospitality' in its accepted sense is in mind. In *Sim.* 8.10.3, the pastor refers to those who 'gladly welcomed God's servants into their houses' (καὶ εἰς τοὺς οἴκους αὐτῶν ἡδέως ὑπεδέξαντο τοὺς δούλους τοῦ θεοῦ).[10] In *Sim.* 9.27.2, he similarly speaks of 'bishops and hospitable people who were always glad to welcome God's servants into their homes' (ἡδέως εἰς τοὺς οἴκους ἑαυτῶν πάντοτε ὑπεδέξαντο τοὺς δούλους τοῦ θεοῦ). Maier thinks that patrons of 'house churches' are in view,[11] but in both places, the reference is more obviously to those who receive 'travelling believers, especially itinerant preachers and missionaries'.[12] Maier contends that a 'house-church' setting provides a plausible background to the community divisions indicated in Hermas,[13] especially the divisions between leaders (*Vis.* 3.9.9-10; *Sim.* 9.31.6).[14] The schisms documented in Hermas certainly fit well against a background of multiple congregations in Rome (as indicated in Rom. 16) but the text does not require us to presume that all these groups are meeting in believers' houses.

Maier also focuses on mentions of hospitality when attempting to find specific evidence of 'house churches' at Corinth in *1 Clement*. According to Maier, Clement's references to hospitality (*1 Clem.* 1.2; 10.7; 11.1; 12.1; cf. 35.5) have little do with the entertainment of visitors, a topic that otherwise receives no development in the letter; rather they reflect the 'the general setting of the church gathered in wealthier persons' homes'.[15] However, the fact that Clement cites as exemplars of hospitality Old Testament figures renowned for entertaining strangers (Abraham, 10.7; Lot, 11.1; Rahab, 12.1) makes it quite clear that the kindly reception of guests and visitors (travelling Christians) is precisely what

---

8   Maier 1991: 61.

9   BDAG 1058; *TNDT* 5.1–36.

10   Maier (1991: 61) points out that the pastor can use the phrase 'slaves of God' for the wider community (*Sim.* 1.1.1), but here and in *Sim.* 9.27.2, a reference to dedicated Christian workers or missionaries seems more likely.

11   Maier 1961: 63.

12   Osiek 1999: 209–10.

13   Maier 1991: 93.

14   Maier 1991: 63–4.

15   Maier 1991: 93.

he has in view. Maier interprets the conflict at Corinth that Clement addresses as a conflict between 'house churches'.[16] It need not be denied that conflict between Christian groups at Corinth had something to do with the dispute that Clement tries to resolve, but we are not compelled to suppose that the Corinthian groups necessarily all met in houses.

The correspondence of Ignatius, according to Maier, indicates that the churches in Asia Minor with which Ignatius was in contact were suffering from division.[17] A context of meeting in houses, in his view, provides the backdrop to these divisions. He speculates that at each location there were a number of household meetings usually led by presbyters ('house-church' hosts) alongside the common assembly,[18] which most likely took place in the home of the 'leading presbyter-bishop', the ἐπίσκοπος.[19] Ignatius attempts to increase the control of the ἐπίσκοπος and delegitimize meetings other than the common assembly.[20] Maier is by no means alone in seeing 'house churches' reflected in Ignatius's writings.[21] However, as Maier freely concedes, 'There is no direct mention in Ignatius' letters of household meetings'.[22] In *Eph.* 6.1, Ignatius depicts God as the master of the house, with the ἐπίσκοπος as his steward.[23] But, as stressed in Chapter 1, the application of household language to the ordering of the church is not contingent upon an actual habit of meeting in houses and so need not reflect it.[24] The epistles bear witness to the existence of believing households (*Smyrn.* 13.1; cf. *Eph.* 16.1). Two are named in greetings ('the household of Gavia [or Tavia]' in *Smyrn.* 13.2; 'the widow of Epitropus together with the whole household belonging to her and the

16   Maier 1991: 87–94.
17   Passages describing or presupposing ecclesial division include: *Eph.* 5.2-3; *Mag.* 4.1; *Trall.* 2.2; 7.2; *Smyrn.* 7.1; 8.1-2; *Phld* 3.3; cf. Maier 1991: 148. No division is indicated for Rome.
18   Maier 1991: 153. A common assembly is certainly attested for Ephesus (*Eph.* 5.3: 'Therefore whoever does not meet with the congregation thereby demonstrates his arrogance and has separated himself'; cf. 20.2) and is probably indicated for Magnesia (*Mag.* 7.2: 'run together as to one temple of God, as to one altar'). Cf. Trebilco 2004: 650.
19   Maier 1991: 181.
20   Maier 1991: 153–5, 177–81.
21   So also Corwin 1960: 65; Schoedel 1985: 240; Trebilco 2004: 650.
22   Maier 1991: 148.
23   Schoedel (1985: 56 n. 15) identifies two elements at work in this verse: the householder who sends his servants to his vineyard (Mt. 21.33-41); the idea of receiving Christ's representative as Christ himself (Mt. 10.40; Gal. 4.14).
24   The term 'householder' (οἰκοδεσπότης) occurs only here in Ignatius, and the word οἰκονομία elsewhere is used for the divine plan (*Eph.* 18.2; 20.1). Cf. Schoedel 1985: 56 n. 15.

children' in *Pol.* 8.2).[25] However, we should not automatically assume that believing households were 'churches at the home' (in the Pauline sense); neither the formulation ἡ κατ' οἶκον ἐκκλησία nor a variant of it appears in Ignatius' writings.[26] The existence of multiple gatherings in the Asian locations addressed by Ignatius fits with the community divisions reflected, but again we do not have to conclude that all these gatherings were based in houses. If, in some places, the separate groups all came together to worship, it might be easier to imagine the whole-church gathering happening in some place other than the home of an individual.

I want to be clear that I am not denying the existence of house-based congregations in the localities covered by these early Christians writings. The point I am making is that claimed exegetical evidence for 'house churches' in these works does not hold up under scrutiny. The documents do not overtly attest to the use of houses as congregational meeting places.

1.2. *The Later Second and Early Third Centuries*

The *Martyrdom of Justin* describes the trial, sentencing and execution of Justin and his companions, c. 164/165. The record is generally regarded as reliable. The trial is presided over by Q. Junius Rusticus, who was urban prefect from 162 to 168. An exchange between the prefect and Justin in *M. Just.* 3 runs as follows:

> Rusticus the prefect said, 'Where do you (Christians) assemble?'
> 'Wherever is chosen and it is possible for each one', said Justin, 'for do you think it possible for all of us to gather in the same place (of assembly)?'
> Rusticus the prefect said, 'Tell me, where do you assemble, that is, in what place?'
> Justin said, 'I have been staying above the baths of Myrtinus for the entire period I have resided in Rome for this the second time. And I know no other meeting place except the one there. If anyone wishes to come to me there, I am accustomed to share with him the words of truth.'[27]

The text is corrupt at the point at which Justin names the baths. The *Martydrom of Justin* comes down to us in three recensions. Recension B

25 Schoedel (1985: 281 n. 14) wonders whether Gavia/Tavia and the wife of Epitropus are one and the same.

26 The epistle *To Hero* 9 has the more explicit 'house church' greeting, 'Salute thou also Mary my daughter, distinguished both for gravity and erudition, as also "the Church which is in her house"'. However, the letter is spurious. The 'house church' greeting is taken from Col. 4.15.

27 Following White's (1997: 43) translation.

gives his residence as 'above the bath of a certain Martinos son of Timiotinus', while Recension C lacks any reference to a specific location. Recension A, reproduced above, is generally considered to be the most original. However, there is no known bathhouse in the city of Rome associated with someone called Myrtinos. Indeed, the name itself is unattested in the epigraphic record. In a recent article, Harlow Snyder argues for the identification of Justin's bathhouse with a bathhouse known to have existed in Rome at the time: the bath of Mamertinus (possibly Marcus Petronius Mamertinus, who served as praetorian prefect in Rome, 139–143 CE), located on southeast side of the city, within Region I.[28] A scribal misstep, he thinks, would explain the corruption of Mamertinus to Myrtinos, which in turn could have given rise to Martinos (changing an unusual name to a more recognizable one).[29]

Despite the uncertainty surrounding the name and location of the bathhouse, the information that Justin was living 'above' a bathing complex is generally taken as trustworthy. That one could reside above a bathing establishment is clear from Seneca, who also at one time stayed in such circumstances and gives a vivid account of his experience (*Ep.* 56).[30] Such a residential arrangement is archaeologically demonstrated by the Sarno Baths at Pompeii (see further in Chapter 7).

It is persistently assumed that Justin's living quarters 'above the baths' were also the meeting place of his group, and thus the passage is taken as proof of the existence of 'house churches' in Rome in the second half of the second century. However, the Greek wording could be understood to mean that Justin and his fellow worshippers, i.e., his students,[31] met within the bathhouse itself rather than in his abode on top of it.[32] A bathing establishment was an environment in which a philosopher like

28   H.G. Snyder 2007: 350. H.G. Snyder (2007: 355) thinks that the bathhouse can be located more precisely at 'the point where the Via Latina branches off the Via Appia'.

29   H.G. Snyder (2007: 357 n. 77) thinks that Rusticus would have known the establishment; hence he does not question him further about it.

30   Seneca complains about the range of noises he had to endure residing in such an environment, but as H.G. Snyder notes (2007: 349), living over or around a bathhouse 'would have offered several distinct advantages to a teacher such as Justin' (cf. 346–8).

31   The named individuals arrested and tried alongside Justin are Euelpistus, Chariton, Hierax, Paion, Liberianus and Charito. Lampe (2003: 277) believes that these individuals constituted the whole membership of Justin's school at the time.

32   Ἐγὼ ἐπάνω μένω τοῦ Μυρτίνου βαλανείου παρὰ πάντα τὸν χρόνον ὃν ἐπεδήμησα τὸ δεύτερον τῇ Ῥωμαίων πόλει· οὐ γινώσκω δὲ ἄλλην τινὰ συνέλευσιν εἰ μὴ τὴν ἐκεῖ.

Justin might well operate. It is highly likely that pedagogical activity took place in grand *thermae* and also in some large neighbourhood bath-houses, or *balnea* (see Chapter 7). The Baths of Sura, a large neighbour-hood *balneum* in Rome, are called a γυμνάσιον by Dio Cassius (68.15.3), suggesting that they had educational facilities (see Chapter 7).[33] The Baths of Mamertinus, which Snyder thinks were Justin's baths, were probably comparable to the Baths of Sura.[34] Whether or not Snyder is correct in his identification of Justin's bathhouse, a scenario in which he taught in rented space *inside* the bathing complex above which he was staying is an entirely possible one.[35]

An intriguing feature of this passage, and one that is constantly over-looked, is Justin's claim, in response to Rusiticus's questioning, that the Christians gather, 'wherever is chosen and it is possible for each one'.[36] The answer implies that Roman Christians at the time utilized *whatever* space (not just *domestic* space) they could for meeting purposes.

In his *True Word*, dating to around 177–180 CE,[37] extant only in citations from Origen's *Contra Celsum*, Celsus complains about the recruitment strategy of the Christians:

> In private houses we see wool-workers, cobblers, laundry makers, and the most illiterate and bucolic yokels, who would not dare to say anything at all in front of their elders and more intelligent masters. But whenever they get hold of children in private and some stupid women with them, they let out some astounding statements as, for example, that they must not pay attention to their father and school-teachers, but must obey them; they say that these talk nonsense and have no understanding, and that in reality they neither know nor are able to do anything good, but are taken up with mere empty chatter. But they alone, they say, know the right way to live, and if the children would believe them, they would become happy

33   The Baths of Sura were commissioned in the early second century by L. Licinius Sura, a confidant of Trajan. The bathhouse has not survived but its basic layout is known from the Marble Plan (see Yegül 1992: 66), in which it is labeled 'Bal Surae' (short for *Balnea Surae*). The plan shows a bathing area with a row of interconnected rooms and a colonnaded palaestra fronted by *tabernae*.

34   H.G. Snyder 2007: 356–7.

35   As Lampe emphasizes, in Justin's school not only did instruction take place but apparently also worship and Eucharistic celebration (cf. *Apol.* 1.67). Lampe (2003: 279) suggests that Justin's school took the form of a philosophical/religious association, in which were cultivated 'common meals and discussions'. Justin may also have conducted baptism (*Apol.* 1.61, 64). If so, the baptismal act could have been conveniently performed in the *frigadiarum* of the bathhouse.

36   Ἔνθα ἑκάστῳ προαίρεσις καὶ δύναμίς ἐστιν.

37   Chadwick 1953: xxviii.

and make their home happy as well. And if just as they are speaking they see one of the school-teachers coming, or some intelligent person, or even the father himself, the more cautious of them flee in all directions; but the more reckless urge the children on to rebel. They whisper to them that in the presence of their father and their schoolmasters they do not feel able to explain anything to the children.… But if they like, they should leave father and their school-masters, and go along with the women and little children who are their playfellows to the wooldresser's shop, or to the cobbler's or the washerwoman's shop [i.e. the fuller's shop], that they may learn perfection. And by saying this they persuade them (*C. Cels.* 3.55).[38]

According to Michael Green, Celsus reflects here the Christians' use of houses for evangelistic purposes: 'it was in private houses that the wool workers and cobblers, the laundry workers and the yokels whom he so profoundly despised did their proselytizing'.[39] However, a closer look at the passage indicates that while initial contact was made 'in private houses', it was in shops and workshops that Christian instruction took place.[40] Celsus thus bears important witness to the use of commercial and industrial premises as sites of Christian activity and meeting (see further in Chapter 6).

In his *Apology*, Tertullian, written around 200 CE, argues that churches should have their place among the tolerated associations, since they are not like the troublesome *factiones* dreaded by the state. In the course of his argument, he describes a Christian communal meal:

> Yet about the modest supper-room of the Christians alone a great ado is made. Our feast explains itself by its name. The Greeks call it *agapè*, i.e., affection… The participants, before reclining, taste first of prayer to God. As much is eaten as satisfies the cravings of hunger; as much is drunk as befits the chaste. They say it is enough, as those who remember that even during the night they have to worship God; they talk as those who know that the Lord is one of their auditors. After manual ablution, and the bringing in of lights, each is asked to stand forth and sing, as he can, a hymn to God, either one from the holy Scriptures or one of his own composing, – a proof of the measure of our drinking. As the feast commenced with prayer, so with prayer it is closed (*Apol.* 39).

---

38   Taken from Chadwick 1953: 165–6.
39   Green 1970: 208.
40   Osiek and MacDonald (2006: 222) suggest that the movement from house to shop could have been from 'one section of a house to another', but Celsus firmly distinguishes 'private houses' from shops, implying that the latter were architecturally and spatially separate from the former.

From the reference to the 'supper-room (*triclinium*) of the Christians', Alan Doig thinks that 'a private domestic setting'[41] is presupposed. However, the formulation could also apply to rented dining rooms (see Chapter 7). Comments made by Tertullian in other writings could be interpreted as indicating the existence of more formal Christian edifices in Carthage in his time (see below). If that interpretation is correct, the 'supper-room of the Christians' would presumably be a room within a dedicated church building (though not necessarily a domestic *domus ecclesiae*).

The *Apostolic Tradition* is a manual of church order and practice conventionally attributed to Hippolytus of Rome and so dated to the early third century. Recent scholarship on the document, though, has distanced itself from the attribution to Hippolytus. Thus Paul Bradshaw, Maxwell Johnson and L. Edward Phillips, in their 2002 commentary on the *Apostolic Tradition*, view the work as an aggregate of material drawn from different sources, diverse regions and different periods 'perhaps as early as the mid-second century to as late as the mid-fourth century'.[42] A striking feature of the work is the clear distinction drawn between fellowship meals called 'Lord's Suppers' (*Ap. Trad.* 27–29) and celebrations of the Eucharist.[43] Lord's Suppers were evidently hosted by local Christians. Invitations by these patrons are directly referred to in 27.2:

> But through the whole offering let him who offers be mindful of him who invited him, because for that reason he [the host] entreated that he [the guest] should enter under his roof (*sub tecto eius*).[44]

It is legitimate to conclude, as Bradshaw, Johnson and Phillips do, that the patrons hosted these fellowship meals in their homes,[45] but a patron could also host a meal in a hired dining room. Such space would still count as *sub tecto eius* understood more loosely. Church assembly proper in the *Apostolic Tradition* is quite formalized (e.g. men and women stand apart, *Ap. Trad.* 18). The material context of assembly seems to be some kind of hall,[46] whether a small hall within a renovated house (as in Dura Europos) or a larger hall building.

---

41 Doig 2008: 3.

42 Bradshaw, Johnson and Phillips 2002: 14.

43 The separation of the Eucharist from the communal meal may also be reflected in Clement of Alexandria, *Paed.* 2.1.

44 Translation from Bradshaw, Johnson and Phillips 2002: 144. For the Latin, see Bobertz 1993: 172.

45 Bradshaw, Johnson and Phillips 2002: 145, following Bobertz 1993. So also Lampe 2003: 375.

46 So White 1990: 120.

1.3. *The Apocryphal Acts*

Houses figure prominently as settings in which believers gather and missionary proclamation takes place in the Apocryphal Acts (including the Pseudo-Clementines).[47] In the *Acts of Paul*, the apostle preaches in the house of Onesiphorus in Iconium.[48] When he arrives at the house, he breaks bread with those present and expatiates on sexual abstinence and the resurrection (*Acts of Paul* 3.5).[49] While Paul is speaking 'in the midst of the church in the house', Thecla sits at the window of the house next door. She listens to him 'day and night' as he preaches, and she absorbs his teaching about virginal celibacy (3.7).[50] Paul also speaks to companies of believers in the house of Aquila and Priscilla in Ephesus,[51] the house of Epiphanius at Corinth (*Acts of Paul* 9), and the house of Claudius in Italy (*Acts of Paul* 10).

In the *Acts of Peter*, when the apostle reaches Rome, he lodges with Narcissus and preaches in his house (13). Narcissus is one of the few believers in the city not to have been swayed by Simon Magus. Peter learns that Marcellus the Senator, a former benefactor of the Christian community in Rome, has fallen under Simon's spell and allowed the heretic into his house. Peter goes to the house to confront Simon, but Simon refuses to come out. Marcellus, though, repents. He subsequently ejects Simon and cleanses the house of all traces of him. He then invites Peter to his home where widows and old people have gathered to hear

---

47   The five chief Acts were probably written in the second and third centuries. The order in which these Acts were written cannot be determined with certainty. J.K. Elliott (2009: 229) thinks that the compositional sequence could be: *Acts of Paul*; *Acts of Peter*; *Acts of John*; *Acts of Andrew*; *Acts of Thomas*. Klauck (2008: 18), following an earlier line of scholarship, dates the *Acts of John* first (ca. 150–160). For convenience rather than out of conviction, I follow Elliott's relative sequence. I also cite from Elliott's translation (which is a revision of that of M.R. James). The *Homilies* and *Recognitions* of Clement are two versions of the same work. The original text or *Grundschrift* from which they derive has not survived. The *Homilies*, written in Greek, dates to the early fourth century (300–320 CE). The *Recognitions*, penned in Latin, is later and may date to around the mid-fourth century. The underlying text on which these two were based, however, probably belongs to the first half of the third century, and some material in it could be even earlier (Klauck 2008: 200).

48   In contrast to the canonical book of Acts, in the *Acts of Paul*, the communities that Paul visits are not founded by him, but already exist (Klauck 2008: 73).

49   *Acts of Paul* 3 = the *Acts of Paul and Thecla*.

50   Later in the narrative (3.41), Thecla herself speaks to a gathered company in a house.

51   Following the Coptic papyrus of the Ephesian episode; see Schneemelcher 1992: 263–5.

the apostle speak. Peter enters the dining room of the house and sees the gospel being read (20). After rolling up the book, he proceeds to expound the passage (apparently the transfiguration). Miraculous healings follow Peter's sermon, and Marcellus offers his house as a dwelling for 'the virgins of the Lord' (22).

The houses of Lycomedes and Andronicus are John's preaching bases in Ephesus in the *Acts of John*. The apostle first preaches in the house of Lycomedes, whom he has raised from the dead and converted. As John teaches, Lycomedes has an artist secretly paint his portrait (27). Later in the narrative, John conducts a service in the home of Andronicus, another convert (46). He preaches, prays, celebrates the Eucharist and lays hands on each person assembled. When John returns to Ephesus after ministering elsewhere, he stays with Andronicus. As soon as the Ephesian Christians hear of John's return, they run to the house to meet him (62). John's final assembly with the brethren at Ephesus takes place in a house (106-110; cf. 111), presumably that of Andronicus.

In the *Acts of Andrew*, the apostle gives evangelistic preaching in the houses of Demetrius in Amasea and Lesbius at Patras.[52] Demetrius, hearing of the apostle's miraculous powers, beseeches him to restore to life his slave who has just died. Andrew comes to Demetrius' house, preaches a sermon and raises the boy. All believe and are baptized (*Epitome of the Acts of Andrew* 3). Lesbius the proconsul, who has been seeking to kill Andrew, gets beaten up by two Ethiopians. As he lies close to death on his bed, he sends for Andrew. The apostle comes to his house, preaches the word, heals the proconsul, and he and all those present believe and are confirmed in the faith (*Epitome of the Acts of Andrew* 22). When Andrew returns to Patras, he heals and converts Maximilla, the wife of the new proconsul Aegeates. Maximilla brings the apostle and all the brethren into her bedroom, where Andrew preaches (*Acts of Andrew* 6-10). The believers gather together night and day at the praetorium. One Sunday, the brethren are assembled in Maximilla's bedroom listening to Andrew preach when Aegeates returns, but the apostles and the other believers are able to leave the house unnoticed (13).

The house of Siphor, a captain in the army of the Indian King Misdaeus converted by Thomas, serves as a preaching place for the apostle in the *Acts of Thomas*. The apostle is frequently shown sitting and teaching in Siphor's house (105, 131-33). In the last of these scenes, the king bursts into the house, seizes the chair on which Thomas is seated and hits him on the head with it. The apostle is taken away to

52   We also read of household conversions: *Epitome of the Acts of Andrew* 4.5, 29.

judgment. The king's son, Vazan, secretly brings him from prison to his house, where he, his wife and the king's wife are baptized and receive the Eucharist (155-58).

In the Pseudo-Clementines, in Tripolis, the house of Maro is Peter's preaching centre in Tripolis for the duration of his three-month stay (*Rec.* 4.2, 6-7; 6.15). It is important to note, however, that Peter actually preaches in the *garden* attached to the house rather than within the house itself. This garden is also the regular location of Peter's private teaching to his companions during the sojourn in Tripolis.[53] The mission in Tripolis results in the establishment of a church. Peter appoints Maro as bishop, along with twelve presbyters and deacons (*Rec.* 6.15). In Laodicea (in Syria), a chief man of the city offers Peter the use of his house for teaching (*Rec.* 8.36). When Peter and his colleagues come to the house, they are welcomed by the master of the house and taken to 'a certain apartment, arranged after the manner of a theatre, and beautifully built'. There Peter preaches to a large crowd already assembled (8.38). Finally, in Antioch, Theophilus, a prominent figure in Antioch,

> consecrated the great palace (*ingentem basilicam*) of his house under the name of a church, and a chair was placed in it for the Apostle Peter by all the people; and the whole multitude assembling daily to hear the word, believed in the healthful doctrine which was avouched by the efficacy of cures.[54] (*Rec.* 10.71)

In the Apocryphal Acts, then, houses are recurring preaching places and meeting locales. However, they are by no means the only settings of missionary speech.[55] Nor are they the only places where believers gather for teaching, the Eucharist prayer, etc. Other places of meeting explicitly mentioned include barns, inns, bathhouses, gardens, watersides, and tombs. We will pick up the references to these other meeting sites in Part II of the book. The Apocryphal Acts are works of pious fiction, but

53   A group of twelve, with Clement making up a thirteenth member of the entourage (*Rec.* 3.68). Cf. Klauck 2008: 218.

54   Although this passage has sometimes been taken as indicating a domestic *domus ecclesiae*, as Sessa (2009: 98) observes, the text is 'almost certainly not suggesting a physically renovated house church, since the only change described was the introduction of a single piece of furniture, Peter's *cathedra*'.

55   Some of the more spectacular locations include the forum in Rome, where, after winning the contest with Simon Magus, Peter urges the spectators to repent (*Acts of Peter* 28-29); the theatre at Ephesus, where John preaches to the 'whole city' there gathered and conducts a mass healing (*Acts of John* 31-36); the temple of Artemis at Ephesus, where John ascends a platform and addresses a crowd gathered to celebrate the birthday of the goddess (*Acts of John* 37-45; the temple crumbles at John's prayer, and many convert).

they must have had a certain degree of 'verisimilitude' precisely 'in order to have gained and held a wide readership'.[56] It is generally accepted that the scenes of meetings in houses – even though the houses depicted are often improbably grand – reflect a historical reality of assembling in houses in the second century and into the third. But other places of meeting referred to must also have resonated with Christian readers. In Part II, I will try to show that barns, inns, bathhouses, etc., are locations in which early Christians could plausibly have met.

Taken together, the Apocryphal Acts give us the clearest and best literary evidence for houses as early meeting places, but they also provide important literary evidence for early Christian use of other kinds of spaces for meeting besides houses.

2. *Evidence for Adapted Houses as Church Buildings*

Around the beginning of the third century, we begin to get literary signals of dedicated church buildings. Some of the early signals are debatable, but others seem to be more definite. On the standard view, the earliest church buildings, those of the first half of the third century, were adapted houses. But to what extent is this borne out by the literary data?

Large church buildings are clearly documented for the later third and early fourth centuries. Eusebius bears witness to a period of numerical growth before the onset of the Great Persecution, necessitating architectural expansion:

> And how could one fully describe those assemblies thronged with count-less men, and the multitudes that gathered together in every city, and the famed concourses in the places of prayer; by reason of which they were no longer satisfied with the buildings of olden time, and would erect from the foundations churches of spacious dimensions throughout all the cities? (*H.E.* 8.1.5)[57]

White categorizes these large church buildings as *aula ecclesiae*. In his view, these new hall structures (which were still mainly adaptive structures) did not displace *domus ecclesiae* but overlapped with them. To what extent, then, do domestic *domus ecclesiae* show up in the literary record for the second half of the third century and into fourth? We begin with written evidence relating to the period from 200 to around 250 CE.

---

56   Green 1970: 199.

57   Lactantius (*De mort. pers.* 12) gives an account of the destruction of the church building at Nicomedia on 23 February 303, at the beginning of the persecution, calling the structure a 'very lofty edifice'.

2.1. *The First Half of the Third Century*

Clement of Alexandria is the earliest writer to speak of 'going to church', using the Greek word ἐκκλησία. In *Paedagogus* 3.11 (c. 200 CE), he writes:

> Woman and man are to go to church (τὴν ἐκκλησίαν) decently attired, with natural step, embracing silence, possessing unfeigned love, pure in body, pure in heart, fit to pray to God. Let the woman observe this, further. Let her be entirely covered, unless she happen to be at home (πλὴν εἰ μὴ οἴκοι τύχοι). For that style of dress is grave, and protects from being gazed at. And she will never fall, who puts before her eyes modesty, and her shawl; nor will she invite another to fall into sin by uncovering her face. For this is the wish of the Word, since it is becoming for her to pray veiled....
>
>   Such ought those who are consecrated to Christ appear, and frame themselves in their whole life, as they fashion themselves in the church for the sake of gravity; and to be, not to seem such – so meek, so pious, so loving. But now I know not how people change their fashions and manners with the place. As they say that polypi, assimilated to the rocks to which they adhere, are in colour such as they; so, laying aside the inspiration of the assembly (συναγωγῆς), after their departure from it, they become like others with whom they associate. Nay, in laying aside the artificial mask of solemnity, they are proved to be what they secretly were. After having paid reverence to the discourse about God, they leave within [the church] what they have heard. And outside they foolishly amuse themselves with impious playing, and amatory quavering, occupied with flute-playing, and dancing, and intoxication, and all kinds of trash.

White thinks that by ἐκκλησία, the place of assembly, i.e., the building, is meant.[58] Valeriy Alikin, on the other hand, sees no reason to presume that the word means anything other than 'assembly'.[59] Going to the ἐκκλησία is clearly contrasted with being 'at home'. It is reasonable to deduce, therefore, that the meeting place, whether or not the term ἐκκλησία refers to it, is not the ordinary home of a believer.[60] Since the passage lacks any description of the meeting venue, it cannot be used as evidence of domestic *domus ecclesiae*.

---

58   White 1997: 53 n. 9.

59   Alikin 2010: 55. Note that in *Strom.* 7.5, Clement states, 'it is not now the place, but the assemblage of the elect, that I call the Church'.

60   Origen, in *De Orat.* 31.4-5 (White 1997: 67–8), also presumes a clear distinction between the 'place of prayer', which is the 'the spot where believers come together in one place', and the ordinary homes in which believers live. For Origen, the fact that marital sex takes place in the home renders it unsuitable for truly effectual prayer (Bowes 2008a: 53–54).

In *De Pud.* 3.4-5, Tertullian speaks of repentance standing before the church's 'doors' (*pro foribus eius*),[61] and then in 4.5, he states that adultery and fornication should be driven 'not only from the threshold, but from all shelter of the Church' (*omni ecclesiae tecto*).[62] In *De Idol.* 7.1, Tertullian bewails 'that a Christian should come from idols into the Church (*ecclesia*); should come from an adversary workshop into the house of God'. These remarks seem to suggest that the *ecclesia* is a building. White takes the view that such comments by Tertullian 'suggest a move toward a domus ecclesiae type of structure'.[63] However, in these passages Tertullian could simply be referring to the 'assembly', metaphorically representing it as a building. Even if he is speaking of a church building, he gives no clue as to its architectural form. The expression 'house of God', *domus Dei*, used in *De Idol.* 7.1, is a symbolic descriptor (probably connoting the temple); it does not indicate the domestic character of the building. We have already seen that in *Apol.* 38–39, Tertullian speaks of the '*triclinium* of the Christians'. This would fit, of course, with a renovated house as the formal church meeting place, but it would also be consistent with the church building being a remodelled restaurant building (see below). Indeed, almost any kind of private structure would have provided space that could be adapted for dining. In sum, while Tertullian *might* reflect a shift toward dedicated church buildings in Carthage at the turn of the third century, he offers no clear evidence that such buildings were adapted houses.

The apologetic dialogue *Octavius* by Minucius Felix seems to exhibit a literary relationship with Tertullian's *Apology*, though it is a matter of ongoing debate whether Tertullian made use of the *Octavius* or the *Octavius* was dependent on Tertullian. In *Oct.* 9.1, Caecilius, the pagan critic, speaks of 'those abominable shrines (*sacraria*) of an impious assembly', which are appearing throughout the world.[64] This is the first instance of the use of the word *sacrarium* in a Christian cultic connection. Lampe speculates that domestic rooms set apart for Christian

61   The antecedent of *eius* is *ecclesia* in the previous sentence.

62   White (1997: 61) translates *omni ecclesiae tecto* as 'the entire church building'.

63   White 1990: 195 n. 81. All the relevant passages in Tertullian are collected in White 1997: 54–62.

64   This reference to Christian *sacaria* stands at odds with the perception of Christians represented in *Oct.* 8.4; 32.1: that they have no altars, no sanctuaries and never meet openly. According to Lampe (2003: 369), the difference between these passages and *Oct.* 9.1 reflects the difference between the second and third centuries. Presumably, then, Lampe thinks that the *Octavius* was composed over a lengthy period.

worship are in view.[65] This is of course possible, but the text does not make this specification.

A clear-cut and securely dated reference to a dedicated church building is found in the Syriac *Edessene Chronicle* for the year 201 CE, which mentions the king's palace and 'the temple of the church of the Christians' among the buildings damaged or destroyed in a flood that engulfed the city that year.[66] White warns against taking this passage at face value as pointing to a monumental church building; such structures are not otherwise attested until later in the third century. He takes the edifice to be 'a renovated domus ecclesiae', finding support for this interpretation from the *Edessene Chronicle* for 313 CE, which records the building of the 'church' at Edessa, begun under Bishop Kune (c. 282–313) and completed under Bishop Sa'ad (313–324).[67] The later 'church' referred to, in White's view, must have been a monumental structure erected as a replacement for an earlier more primitive building.[68] However, for Peter Richardson, the fact that the earlier church building is mentioned in the chronicle for 201 CE alongside 'the great and magnificent palace' of the king indicates that the Christian building was 'a large visible structure'.[69] He thinks that the 'temple of the church' was probably a purpose-built church building. I am inclined to agree with Richardson here; monumental church architecture may have emerged in the kingdom of Edessa much earlier than it did elsewhere in the empire. Yet, the possibility that the church building was an adaptive structure, perhaps even a large renovated house, cannot be ruled out. All we can glean from *Edessene Chronicle* for the year 201 CE is the existence of a large dedicated church building in Edessa; the precise archaeological form it took is basically guesswork.

The *Historia Augusta* (*S.H.A. Sev. Alex.* 49.6) reports a clash between *popinarii* (restaurateurs) and Christians over a piece of property during the reign of Alexander Severus (222–235 CE). The dispute somehow came to the attention of the emperor, who decided in favour of the Christians:

> And when the Christians took possession of a certain place, which had previously been public property, and the keepers of an eating-house (*popinarii*) maintained that it belonged to then, Alexander rendered the

---

65 Lampe 2003: 369. The word *sacrarium* is normally used for 'a sanctuary or shrine in which sacred objects are kept': OLD 1675.
66 White 1997: 102–3.
67 White 1990: 118.
68 White 1990: 118.
69 P. Richardson 2004a: 145.

> decision that it was better for some sort of a god to be worshipped there
> than for the place to be handed to the keepers of an eating-house
> (*popinarii*).

The report seems to testify to Christian takeover of a pre-existing building for the purpose of worship. The structure was evidently some kind of public place rather than a private house, and it may have been a rental property. That *popinarii* were interested in it suggests it was a restaurant building rather than a house. The building must have been relatively sizeable for the emperor to get involved in the wrangle.

Cyprian makes passing mention in his letters of the physical space in which gathering takes place. The spatial references seem to imply a setting of assembly in Carthage around 250 CE in which there was a separate area for the clergy and a raised platform.[70] According to White, 'While the general plan of Cyprian's church building cannot be ascertained, it suggests something of a larger rectangular hall'.[71]

In sum, then, from possible and more definite literary signals of early, dedicated church buildings, there is no explicit indication that they were adapted houses. This is not, of course, to deny that adapted houses were ever used as Christian cultic spaces in the first half of the third century. It is simply to point out that they do not overtly appear in the literary record.

2.2. *The Later Third and Early Fourth Centuries*
Porphyry, the Neoplatonist philosopher, refers to church buildings in his book *Against the Christians* (fr. 76), written around 268–270 CE:

> But the Christians, imitating the construction of temples, erect great
> buildings (μεγίστους οἴκους) in which they meet to pray, though there is
> nothing to prevent them from doing this in their own homes (ἐν ταῖς
> οἰκίας) since, of course, their Lord hears them everywhere.[72]

---

70   White 1990: 124. There is a distinct area (*congestum*) for clergy (*Ep.* 59.18.1), and an elevated pulpit (*Ep.* 38.2). For texts and translations, see White 1997: 68–9, 75–6.

71   White 2000: 718. The late third-century Syrian work, *Didascalia Apostolorum*, envisages segregated assembly space, with distinct areas for bishops and presbyters, laymen, married women, young women, aged women, and widows (*Didascal.* 12.44b-46b; for text and translation, see White 1997: 78–83). The importance of sitting in one's correct place is emphasized: 'let the deacon see that each one of them on entering goes to his place, that no one may sit out of his place'. Again, a large hall seems to be suggested.

72   For text and translation, see White 1997: 104.

He calls these structures literally 'great houses', μεγίστους οἴκους. He is not, though, suggesting thereby that they were modified domestic houses. The word οἶκος is being use in the general sense of 'building'. These ecclesiastical constructions were evidently large public buildings, comparable, at least in scale if not in style, to some 'pagan' temples.

Eusebius gives us the first attested instances of the expression οἶκος τῆς ἐκκλησίας, the Greek equivalent to the Latin expression *domus ecclesiae*.[73] However, as Kristina Sessa has shown, he does not mean by the expression a domestic building specially adapted for ecclesial purposes. Rather, he employs it 'to denote the physical church building in its most generic sense, with no hint that the church bore any special architectural relationship to a house'.[74] Sessa's conclusion also applies to Eusebius' use of οἶκος on its own to denote a church building.[75]

One passage in Eusebius, though, has been taken as indicating 'the renovation of *oikoi* to serve as churches'.[76] In *Martyrs of Palestine* 13.1, Eusebius refers to a lull in persecution when Palestinian Christians were able οἴκους εἰς ἐκκλησίας δείμασθαι. But Eusebius is not talking here about the conversion of domestic houses into church buildings; as Sessa notes, the wording conveys 'the act of building cult spaces for the Christian communities of Palestine, with the former articulated as

73   The expression occurs in *H.E.* 8.13.13; 9.9a11; *VC* 3.43.3, 58.3. See Sessa 2009: 101–4. In *H.E.* 7.30.19, it is applied to the church building that Paul of Samosata refused to relinquish when he was ejected from his charge as bishop of Antioch (260–270). In *H.E.* 8.13.13, Eusebius commends Constantius I for not destroying the church buildings (when dealing with Diocletian's edicts against Christians). In *H.E.* 9.9a11, he states with regard to Maximinus's letter about the Christians (in response to the Edict of Milan) that 'it gave no orders about holding meetings or erecting church-buildings'. In *VC* 3.43.3, the expression is used of a church building commissioned by Helena on the Mount of Olives, and in *VC* 3.58.3, it denotes a church building commissioned by Constantine in Heliopolis.

74   Sessa 2009: 103. The church building occupied by Paul of Samosata (*H.E.* 7.30.19) was plainly a significant public building and not a revamped house. The synodal letter, cited by Eusebius (*H.E.* 7.30.9-11), tells how Paul had embellished it, adding a bema and a *secretum*, or private audience chamber, which, as White (1990: 195 n. 84) points out, were elements of civic architecture. The church buildings commissioned by Helena on the Mount of Olives (*VC* 3.43.3) and by Constantine in Heliopolis (*VC* 3.58.3) were probably basilicas.

75   This is clear from Eusebius' application of the word οἶκος to the new church building at Tyre, dedicated in 317. From the description of the building in Eusebius's own panegyric delivered at the festival of dedication and recorded in *H.E.* 10.4, it is clearly a monumental construction, at least 'an elaborated aula ecclesiae' (so White 1990: 136) if not a basilica.

76   Thomas 1987: 11.

"houses" (οἴκους) and the latter as "assemblies" (ἐκκλησίας)'.[77] Eusebius' point is that believers in Palestine were able to build (δέμω) houses, i.e., sacred buildings, to serve the assemblies/churches.

An official report details the search of a church meeting place in Cirta in Numidia on 19 May 303, during the Great Persecution, gives us our best literary evidence for a pre-Constantinian domestic *domus ecclesiae*.[78] The search was carried out by an official named Munatius Felix, and its purpose was to find and confiscate scripture. The meeting place is described as the 'house in which the Christians would assemble' (*domus in qua Christiani conveniebant*). It had a library with cupboards and barrels and also a dining room (*triclinium*) in which was found four large jars and six barrels. It seems clear that the church building was an actual house. The other places searched that day were actual houses (the homes of seven readers). The building appears to have been a domestic habitation largely given over to ecclesial use. The inventory includes many items of clothing (82 women's tunics, 16 men's tunics, 13 pairs of men's shoes, 47 pairs of women's shoes, etc.), which clearly did not form a personal wardrobe. They may have been liturgical vestments, or clothes for charity.[79] There is little in the passage, though, to suggest that the house had undergone much physical adaptation (unlike the Christian building at Dura Europos).[80] There is no mention, for example, of cultic fixtures or decorations. White thinks that as well as serving as a Christian meeting place, it may have also functioned as the bishop's residence.[81]

A street survey from Panopolis (*P. Gen. Inv.* 108), Egypt, dated between c. 298 and 341, mentions 'the house which is also the ---- of the church'.[82] The text is extant in fragmentary papyrus remains, and there is a lacuna precisely at the point of interest. The 'house' was evidently located in a domestic quarter: all the other structures indicated for this region were domiciles.[83] The house could thus have been a domestic *domus ecclesiae*.[84] But it is also possible that the house in question was a

77   Sessa 2009: 103. Thus Lawlor and Oulton (1927: 396) translate the phrase as 'to build houses for church assemblies'.
78   *Acta Munati Felicis* preserved in the *Gesta apud Zenophilum*. For text and translation, see White 1997: 105–10.
79   Luijendijk 2008: 350 n. 25.
80   White 1990: 122.
81   So White 1990: 126.
82   White 1997: 160–2.
83   White 1997: 160.
84   White (1997: 161 n. 60) observes that the formula used, οἰκία ἤτοι, is employed at other points in the text by the same recorder to designate a domestic building that was used for some other purpose.

dependency of the church building, with the latter located elsewhere (since it is not otherwise mentioned in the census). The damaged state of the text makes it impossible to know the exact relationship of the οἰκία to the ἐκκλησία. As White concludes, whether the οἰκία 'was the actual church building, a renovated domus ecclesiae, or some other dependency, cannot be determined with more certainty'.[85]

Two other papyrological texts from around the same time are similarly ambiguous. A papyrus from Oxyrhynchus (*P. Oxy.* 43), dating to around 295, contains a list of street wardens and the streets for which they are responsible.[86] Of interest are two streets identified as 'North-Church Street' and 'South-Church Street'. Most of the streets in this document are named after a prominent house or building they contain. We can deduce, therefore, that buildings known as ἐκκλησίαι were sufficiently prominent that they served to identify the streets on which they stand. What we cannot deduce, however, is the architectural forms of these church buildings: they could have been adapted houses or other adaptive structures, but they could also have been, as Richardson thinks,[87] purpose-built church buildings. A papyrus document (*P. Oxy.* 2673) records a declaration made on 5 February 304 by a lector of the church in Chysis, Egypt, of the church's property in compliance with Diocletian's decree.[88] The church building, designated ἐκκλησία, had apparently been seized earlier. The document bears similarity with the record of the search at Cirta, Numidia. On this basis, White surmises that a *domus ecclesiae* is indicated.[89] However, once again, it is not possible to determine whether this church building was a renovated house or some other kind of structure.[90]

The edict of toleration issued by the Emperor Galerius on 30 April 311, as recorded by Eusebius, permitted Christians to exist and to have 'the houses in which they used to assemble' (τοὺς οἴκους ἐν οἷς συνή-γοντο, Eusebius, *H.E.* 8.17.9).[91] The word οἶκοι here is being used with the sense of 'sacred buildings' and is not calling attention to the domestic nature of Christian meeting places. Maximinus's ordinance of 313, as

85   White 1990: 123.
86   For text and translation, see White 1997: 164–6.
87   P. Richardson 2004a: 144.
88   White 1997: 166–70.
89   White 1990: 123.
90   That the only valuables recorded as having been recovered in it were some bronze vessels might suggest that the congregation was poor. However, the congregation might have tried to conceal its possessions (as suggested by Luijendijk 2008: 352).
91   White 1997: 110–11.

reproduced by Eusebius (*H.E.* 9.10.10-11), allowed Christians to construct their 'Lord's houses' (τὰ κυριακὰ τὰ οἰκεῖα). Again the expression does not point to domestic architecture but is a generic term for Christian buildings.

All in all, the report of the search of the 'house in which the Christians would assemble' at Cirta in 303 is the only overt evidence of a domestic *domus ecclesiae* in the period from 250 to 313 CE. From the information given, there is little sign of the domestic edifice having undergone much physical alteration. This is not to claim that domestic *domus ecclesiae* were rare or virtually non-existent during this period. What I wish to emphasize is how rarely they explicitly show up in the literary record.

3. *Conclusion*

Explicit evidence for (unaltered) houses as Christian meeting places in literature relative to the second and early third centuries is more or less confined to the Apocryphal Acts. These writings undoubtedly testify to the use of houses as meeting places, but they provide good evidence for Christian gatherings in various other places as well. Other texts of the period (*Martyrdom of Justin*, Celsus's *True Word*) similarly indicate that meeting places were more varied than just houses.

Explicit literary evidence for adapted houses as church buildings in the third and early fourth centuries is extremely thin. It is pretty much limited to the record of the search of the house in which Christians assembled in Cirta in 303 (and the house does not appear to have experienced significant architectural adaptation). A widespread *ante-pacem* practice of transforming houses into cultic spaces, which would tend to imply a prior widespread pattern of gathering in unaltered houses, is thus not documented in the literature. Unquestionably, modified houses were among the earliest dedicated church buildings (see the next chapter). But it is likely that Christians also adapted other structures as well. *S.H.A. Sev. Alex. 49.6* seems to bear witness to a Christian adoption of some kind of restaurant building for ritual use. The literary evidence appears to indicate that larger halls of various sorts were the 'normative' form of Christian architecture by the beginning of the fourth century.

In sum, written evidence for the period 100–313 CE does not substantiate the view Christians during the first two centuries met 'almost exclusively' in houses.

Chapter 4

ARCHAEOLOGICAL EVIDENCE

From the literary evidence, we switch now to the archaeological evidence. Ordinary, unaltered homes that served as Christian meeting places, if any has survived, are virtually impossible to detect archaeologically, since by definition they are indistinguishable from other surviving domestic structures. Consequently, attention must focus on domestic *domus ecclesiae*. We have seen that houses physically modified for Christian use hardly show up in literary sources relating to the third and early fourth centuries. We now consider the question: To what extent have they left their mark on the archaeological record?

There is one building that we can confidently identify as a pre-Constantinian house-turned-church building: the Christian building at Dura Europos. We thus begin with an account of this edifice. We next discuss the Megiddo 'prayer hall', discovered in 2005. We then turn to possible domestic sites of assembly underlying Rome's titular churches. Finally, we look at other possible cases of domestic *domus ecclesiae* relating to the pre-Constantinian era.

1. *The Christian Building at Dura Europos*

The Christian building at Dura Europos, in modern Syria, was discovered in 1931, and excavated from 1932 to 1933.[1] The final excavation report was written by Carl Kraeling and published posthumously in 1967.[2] The structure remains the most important discovery of pre-Constantinian ecclesiastical architecture.

Dura was a Roman garrison city, with a population of 6000 to 8000.[3] It was captured from the Parthians in the 160s CE and made a Roman

---

1. White 1997: 123.
2. Kraeling 1967; summarized in G.F. Snyder 2003: 128–34; White 1997: 123–31.
3. MacMullen 2009: 1; on the history of Dura, see Mell 2010: 69–78.

colony in 211.[4] The city came under increasing Sassanian attack in the 250s, finally falling to Sassanids in 256. It was abandoned and never re-inhabited. Dura was eventually covered by blown sands and hidden from sight until its chance rediscovery by soldiers in the aftermath of World War I.[5]

The Christian building lay on the edge of the town on the street adjacent to the western wall (opposite Tower 17). It was constructed on an irregularly shaped (trapezoidal) plot of land.[6] The house was partially demolished and filled in when the wall was strengthened as a defensive manoeuvre just prior to the final collapse of the city.[7] The same defensive fill preserved the nearby synagogue building and other houses on the street. The back (west side) of the Christian structure was almost completely preserved, while the front (east side) was almost entirely levelled.[8]

The Christian building stood on the corner of a block designated M8, which was mainly residential in character.[9] Externally, its form was that of a typical private house in Dura.[10] Internally, though, it had undergone significant adaptation to turn it into a building for Christian assembly.

Before its renovation for Christian usage, the house consisted of eight rooms, including an inner court (see Fig. 1).[11] The house was bigger than the majority of houses in Dura; only a few residences were larger.[12] Entrance into the house was by means of an ordinary doorway, which opened into a vestibule (Room 8), leading, via an archway, into the central courtyard (Room 1), from which the main chambers were accessed.[13] Upon entering the house through the main doorway, one had to turn right to proceed through the archway into the inner court. The relative positioning of the outer and inner openings functioned as a screening device, which ensured that no one could see directly into the courtyard from the street.[14] This provided some privacy when the house was converted into a church building.

4. Mell 2010: 72.
5. MacMullen 2009: 2.
6. Kraeling 1967: 9.
7. Kraeling 1967: 6.
8. Kraeling 1967: 5; G.F. Snyder 2003: 129.
9. Kraeling 1967: 3.
10. Kraeling 1967: 3.
11. Following Kraeling 1967: 7–32.
12. Kraeling 1967: 10.
13. Kraeling 1967: 3.
14. Kraeling 1967: 4; cf. G.F. Snyder 2003: 131.

The courtyard was fairly typical of Dura architecture. Its surface was beaten red earth with sprinklings of dry plaster.[15] In the northwest corner, just in front of the entrance to Room 6, was a latrine, the cesspool of which went down 3 m below the level of the courtyard.[16] To the east, on the left side of the courtyard, was a long portico (Room 2), which would have provided space for cooking and storage.[17] On the south side of the courtyard, opposite the entrance, was a suite of three rooms, comprising a dining room, Room 4A, with two linked chambers, Room 4B and Room 3, at either end.[18] Room 4A was the largest room in the house, measuring 8 m × 5.15 m.[19] Benches made of rubble and plaster ran around all four sides of the chamber, and a Bacchic frieze decorated all four walls.[20] Room 3, which was accessed only through Room 4A, may have served as the storage area for the dining room. Room 4B seems also to have had a storage function. This is suggested by the rows of peg-holes on the west and south walls, which are typical features of a store room linked with a dining room in this kind of house.[21] The floor level in Room 4B was 0.15 m lower than that of Room 4A.

To the right, or west, of the courtyard were two rooms, Rooms 5 and 6.[22] Room 5 was the second largest room in the house, connecting with Rooms 4B and 6 through doorways at either end. Rooms 5 and 6, Kraeling conjectures, could have served as the women's quarters.[23] Room 6, which could also be accessed from the courtyard, was poorly lit and ventilated and was located near the latrine and cesspool. One stepped down into the room (its floor level was lower than any other room of the house). The chamber, Kraeling thinks, may have functioned simultaneously as a storage room for housekeeping items and the bedroom of a female slave.[24] A stairwell and alcove (under the stairs) comprised Rooms 7A and B.[25] The stairway led to the roof, which would have been used during the summer as a spot for sleeping and relaxation.[26]

15. Kraeling 1967: 11.
16. Kraeling 1967: 11.
17. Kraeling 1967: 13.
18. Kraeling 1967: 14–20.
19. Kraeling 1967: 15.
20. Kraeling 1967: 15.
21. Kraeling 1967: 16.
22. Kraeling 1967: 20–8.
23. White 1997: 129.
24. Kraeling 1967: 22.
25. Kraeling 1967: 28–9.
26. Kraeling 1967: 29.

A graffito in Room 4B, calling for Dorotheos to be remembered, inscribed on wet plaster and subsequently recoated, gives the date 232/233.[27] Dorotheos was probably the craftsman who originally plastered the walls. The date given is thus most likely the date of the erection of the house.[28]

The alterations that turned the private house into a Christian edifice (see Fig. 2) all took place in a single phase of remodelling rather than in successive stages.[29] The courtyard was tiled (raising the court level in the process), and two L-shaped (plastered rubble) benches were added, one at the southwest corner of the court and the other at the northwest corner.[30] The latrine was removed and the cesspool covered over. The decommissioning of the latrine, according to Kraeling, 'necessarily put an end to the use of the building for domestic and residential purposes'.[31]

The wall between Rooms 4A and 4B was removed to make a single large chamber (Room 4), 12.9 m long and 5.15 m wide, which functioned as the assembly hall of the Christian congregation.[32] The floor level was raised to a level above the benches in what had been Room 4A.[33] This served to reduce dampness, but it also increased the seating capacity of the hall.[34] The new floor had a slight gradient, being 0.07 m higher at the west than at the east.[35] What was left of the Bacchic frieze was (surprisingly) not removed but covered over with a thin layer of plaster.[36] Two low windows were added to the wall facing the courtyard, giving added light.[37] Against the eastern wall of the room was set a plaster and rubble dais or platform.[38] To the right of this installation is a lump of plaster with a hole at the top, which White thinks may have served as a socket for a torch or lampstand.[39] To the left of the platform a door opened into Room 3, which probably operated as a storage facility for ecclesiastical items. A graffito on the north wall of Room 4 restored by White

27. Kraeling 1967: 17.
28. Kraeling 1967: 34–9; White 1997: 124, 132 n. 6.
29. White 1997: 124.
30. Kraeling 1967: 11.
31. Kraeling 1967: 12. But not many homes had a latrine!
32. Kraeling 1967: 14, 19.
33. Kraeling 1967: 18.
34. Kraeling 1967: 19.
35. Kraeling 1967: 18.
36. Kraeling 1967: 19.
37. Kraeling 1967: 19.
38. Kraeling 1967: 19.
39. White 1997: 129.

as, 'Remember Paul and -----, son of Paul, the bishop and (people)',[40] appears to make some sort of reference to the congregation and its leadership.[41]

Two main changes were made to Room 5: a low-level window was installed in the court-facing wall, and an unusually elaborate trim was applied to the door leading from Room 5 to Room 6.[42] The function of Room 5 within the Christian complex is unclear. Kraeling doubts that it was the setting of the agape or Eucharistic meal since the room lacks typical dining installations.[43] He thinks that the chamber may have served as an *exorcisterium* or *pistikon*, an antechamber entered as a preliminary to baptism.[44] Ramsay MacMullen interprets the room as a *katechumenion*, where those who wished to become full members of the Christian community underwent their initiatory instruction.[45]

Room 6 was the most extensively adapted room in the building: it was turned into what appears to have been a baptistery.[46] Having held the least importance in the former house, it now became the most sacred room in the building.[47] Originally the room had the same height as the other main chambers of the house (around 5.22 m).[48] In the reconstruction, the ceiling was lowered to a height of 3.2 m above floor level,[49] and a small upper room was created, which was accessed from a landing of the staircase in Room 7. The upper room is too small, in Kraeling's view, to have served as the living quarters of a member of the clergy, though it could have been used for sleeping purposes by a night watchman in cold weather.[50] A new plaster floor was laid in Room 6, raising the level of the floor 0.04 m above the former level.[51] Into the west side of the room was introduced what appears to have been a baptismal font, consisting of a

40. White 1997: 134.
41. White 1997: 134 n. 12.
42. Kraeling 1967: 21–2.
43. Kraeling 1967: 153. He does not consider the possibility that portable couches could have been used for meals.
44. Kraeling 1967: 153.
45. MacMullen 2009: 3–4. Kraeling (1967: 153) thinks it possible that the room could have served this function in addition to its primary use as a chamber for the first part of the baptismal ritual.
46.   In personal conversation with me, Professor Samuel Lieu cast considerable doubt on the identification of Room 6 as a bapistery.
47. Kraeling 1967: 24.
48. White 1997: 129.
49. Kraeling 1967: 27.
50. Kraeling 1967: 155.
51. Kraeling 1967: 27.

basin and canopy. The basin was made of brick and mortar.[52] The canopy over the basin rested on two rubble pilasters at the back and two columns made of rubble and plaster at the front.[53] The canopy itself was made of stone, rubble and plaster, and took the form of a barrel vault, running east and west with arches at the sides.[54] A niche in the south wall between the two doorways, which was originally rectangular, was shaped into an arch in line with the shape of the canopy. Below the niche, projecting from the wall, was a table or ledge (a feature retained from the original construction).[55]

The room was richly decorated. The ceiling was painted dark blue with white stars and dots to emulate the night sky.[56] The columns supporting the canopy were painted to imitate marble, while the facing sides of the pilasters were each painted with grape and leaf designs set within a rectangular field.[57] The vault of the canopy was painted in the same style as the ceiling. On the front of the canopy were fruit designs.[58] The walls of the room were adorned with frescos.[59] The west wall, where the canopy and basin were installed, was embellished with a painting of the good shepherd and his sheep. To the bottom left of the picture, another artist subsequently added a scene of Adam, Eve, the serpent and the tree. On the upper register of the south wall was a garden scene, perhaps a representation of the heavenly paradise.[60] On the lower register of the south wall was a picture of the woman at the well and further along was a composition of David and Goliath. The upper portion of the north wall was decorated with scenes of the healing of the paralyzed man and the walking on the water. A resurrection sequence with women approaching the empty tomb ran along the lower register of the east and north walls.

The final changes were to the exterior of the house.[61] First, a rubble flange was set against the west wall, running its entire length. Second, a bench made of rubble was added to the north wall of the edifice.

52. Kraeling 1967: 26.
53. Kraeling 1967: 26.
54. Kraeling 1967: 26.
55. Kraeling 1967: 24.
56. Kraeling 1967: 43.
57. Kraeling 1967: 44.
58. Kraeling 1967: 44.
59. Kraeling 1967: 50–88.
60. So Kraeling 1967: 67.
61. Kraeling 1967: 29–30.

The renovation took place sometime between 232/233, when the house was built, and 256, when the city was destroyed. Kraeling put the renovation in the forties 'approximately half way between' these two dates.[62] White thinks it occurred c. 240/241.[63] The building evidently operated as a Christian meeting place until the final days of the city. Even though the structure looked like a private house from the outside, its identity as a Christian place of worship was evidently no secret.[64] The renovation programme itself would have attracted considerable public attention.

According to Kraeling, the assembly hall of the renovated building could have accommodated 65 to 75 persons on 'mats spread over the floor'.[65] MacMullen believes that wooden chairs and benches would have been used at least for the older and more well respected members of the congregation, including the clergy.[66] MacMullen also thinks that men and women would have been seated separately (with men to the right in eastern fashion).[67] If Kraeling and others are correct in doubting that Room 5 could have been used for dining, the Dura building would reflect a situation in which the Eucharist was celebrated independently of a communal meal.[68]

The Christian building at Dura Europos is a clear-cut case of a private house renovated and turned into a dedicated Christian meeting place. However, two cautionary points must be made. First, the remodelling campaign that turned the dwelling house into a church building was a single operation. This building does not, therefore, provide archaeological confirmation of the alleged process by which the home of an individual believer was gradually turned into a formal church building. Second, as White fully acknowledges, there is no evidence to indicate that the unrenovated house at Dura served as a Christian meeting place.[69] Nor is there any evidence to indicate that the house was owned by a Christian prior to its change of usage. When the structure became a Christian building it ceased to be a dwelling house, and no connection between the building and the Christian community can be established archaeologically before its Christianizing transformation.

62. Kraeling 1967: 38.
63. White 1997: 124.
64. Kraeling 1967: 110; White 1990: 121–2.
65. Kraeling 1967: 19.
66. MacMullen 2009: 3.
67. MacMullen 2009: 5. In *Didascal.* 12, women are consigned to the back of the room.
68. White 1990: 120.
69. White 1997: 123.

2. *The Christian Prayer Hall at Megiddo*

Excavations at the Megiddo Prison in northern Israel in 2005 brought to light the remains of an early Christian place of worship, which has been hailed as the oldest surviving Christian building. The meeting hall was part of what was apparently a domestic building and so is of particular relevance to this inquiry.

The building lay on the outskirts of the ancient Jewish village of Kefar 'Othnay.[70] To the east of the village, a Roman army camp was established where the Sixth Legion Ferrata and other legions were stationed, giving rise to the name Legio by which the site was commonly known in Rome times (conserved in its Arabic name, El Lajjun, used until the mid-twentieth century). The building was uncovered in an area designated Area Q.[71] Only foundations, floors and parts of walls survive. The edifice, located on the north side of an alley, measured at least 20 × 30 m. It had a long entrance corridor leading to four wings with twelve main rooms, a number of smaller rooms and an inner and outer courtyard. In the latter, the larger of the two courtyards, a couple of clay ovens were found. Finds in the northern wing (jugs, cooking pots and jars) indicate the domestic nature of the building. The western wing, at the end of the long corridor, consisted of an antechamber that led into a small service room and then into a rectangular room, measuring 5 × 10 m, lying (more or less) north to south, which was paved with a mosaic floor. This was the room that served as the Christian meeting hall.

The complex as a whole, according to the excavator, Yotam Tepper, seems to have been a residential building connected with the Roman army.[72] Military artefacts, including two Roman bread stamps, were found in the building. The bread stamps were inscribed with the names and military statuses of the bakers. Tepper concludes that the building served as a residence for Roman army officers who did not live in the army camp nearby, probably because they had families.[73] Part of the building seems to have been used for the production of bread for the army. Tepper doubts that the building was privately owned; he thinks that it was the property of either the army or the state.

70. On the site, see Tepper and Di Segni 2006: 8–16.
71. On the building, see Tepper and Di Segni 2006: 22–4. For an image of Area Q, see http://www.hadashot-esi.org.il/images//4411-2.jpg.
72. Tepper and Di Segni 2006: 29–31.
73. Tepper and Di Segni 2006: 50–1.

The floor of the Christian meeting room has been well preserved.[74] It was covered by a layer of debris containing sherds of pottery and fragments of fresco, which served to protect it. The fresco remnants indicate that the walls of the room were colourfully painted. Monolithic pilasters projected from the western and eastern walls. These pilasters may have supported an arch. In the centre of the floor stand two raised stones, which probably served as the base for the podium of the Eucharistic table referred to in one of the inscriptions. The mosaic is made up of limestone tesserae of ten different colours.[75] It comprises four panels on each of the four sides of the central podium. The panel to the north is the most ornate. It contains a dedicatory inscription and a rectangle with geometric designs enclosing an octagon with a central disc featuring two fish. The panel to the south bears two Greek inscriptions opposite each other. The panels on the west and east sides have no inscriptions, consisting only of rhomboid patterns.

The dedicatory inscription in the north panel identifies the donor of the paved floor as 'Gaianus, also called Porphyrius, centurion'. He was a Roman army officer and was evidently a member of the congregation ('our brother'[76]). He was not, though, the owner of the building (he would hardly have recorded an act of generosity toward himself!).[77] The epigraph in the western side of the southern mosaic panel records the donation of a table (τραπέζα) by a woman called Akeptous. The table referred to was almost certainly a table that served for the celebration of the Eucharist.[78] Tepper and Di Segni think that communal meals 'could have taken place around this table on special occasions'.[79] The inscription in the eastern side of the southern mosaic panel petitions the remembrance of four named women (Primilla, Cyriaca, Dorothea, and Chreste). Noting that the female names appear on the one side of the room, while the male names (Gaiaus, who paid for the mosaic floor, and Brutius, the

74. Tepper and Di Segni 2006: 24–5. For view of the mosaic floor, see http://www.hadashot-esi.org.il/images//4411-4.jpg.
75. On the mosaic, see Tepper and Di Segni 2006: 31–4.
76. The language of brotherhood, as we have already observed (p.24), was not exclusive to Christians in the Graeco-Roman world, so this in itself does not indicate that he belonged to a Christian congregation. However, it carries this significance when taken in conjunction with the overtly Christian nature of the Akeptous inscription.
77. Tepper and Di Segni 2006: 35.
78. The fish symbol is found in connection with early Christian fellowship meals and the Eucharist; see G.F. Snyder 2003: 30–5.
79. Tepper and Di Segni 2006: 40.

artist who laid it) appear at the other, Di Segni wonders whether a pattern of gender separation was in force when the congregation celebrated the Eucharist.[80]

Numismatic and ceramic evidence leads Tepper to conclude that the building, including the Christian meeting room, was erected about 230 CE, in an alleged brief period of peace for the church broken by the death of Severus Alexander and the accession of Maximinus in 235 CE.[81] Such a date of construction would indeed make it the earliest surviving dedicated Christian meeting place, predating the Christianizing renovation at Dura Europos by a few years (on White's dating of the latter). Tepper's dating of the meeting room, therefore, has met with a cautious response. Vassilios Tzaferis argues for a date in the second half of the third century, during a period of peace that continued until the Great Persecution of Diocletian (which began in 303).[82] During this time, he points out, there was an increase in the number of Christians serving in the Roman army. However, others have wondered whether the Christian meeting room can be pre-Constantinian at all. Reacting to the initial announcement, Joe Zias, a former curator for the Israel Antiquities Authority, doubted whether the mosaic could be pre-Constantinian.[83] He thinks it unlikely that a Roman army officer of the third century would have put his name on it.[84] In Zias' view, the building is probably a Roman building adapted for Christian use at a later date. The presence of a Christian cult-room within state- or army-owned property allegedly

80. Tepper and Di Segni 2006: 42.

81. Tepper and Di Segni 2006: 50.

82. Tzaferis 2007.

83. http://www.nytimes.com/2005/11/07/international/middleeast/07mideast. html?_r=0.

84. One must not imagine that Christians in the Roman army were continually persecuted throughout the *ante-pacem* era. Many Christians served in the Roman army before the early fourth century and apparently met little trouble, except during the Great Persecution (see Helgeland 1979; Helgeland, Daly and Patout Burns 1985). Yet, 'the Christian in the army was caught in a net of exceedingly fine mesh' (Helgeland, Daly and Patout Burns 1985: 51). Roman military religion was so pervasive, it would have been impossible for Christian soldiers to avoid it completely. Most seem to have got along by performing their army religious obligations (whenever such duties could not be eluded) while keeping their Christian faith a private matter, so as to prevent an outright clash between the two (Helgeland 1979: 819). By making a public declaration of his allegiance to Christ on army or state property (as Tepper has it), Gaianus would be inviting the kind of religious conflict that others took care to avoid. Cf. Eusebius' account of the martyrdom of the army official, Marinus (Eusebius, *H.E.* 7.15-16).

dating to the pre-Constantian era is certainly anomalous and awaits a convincing explanation. Tepper is clear that his conclusions are based on a preliminary analysis of the finds and that more extensive excavation is required.

On Tepper's analysis, the building at Kefar 'Othnay was a 'dwelling house',[85] though not a private house but one owned by the military or the state, and the Christian meeting room was a 'domestic chapel'.[86] Yet he resists calling the edifice a *domus ecclesiae* because it was not legally owned by the congregation. Moreover, the building was not adapted for Christian use: the Christian room was purpose-built at the same time as the rest of the building. Tepper calls the Christian meeting room a 'Christian prayer hall'. Whatever the nomenclature, what we would have at Megiddo, on Tepper's reconstruction, is a formal Christian meeting room or chapel in a functioning residential building (where workshop activity was also carried out). However, until further research is carried out on the site and the building is dated more conclusively, it cannot be taken as certain archaeological evidence of Christian cultic space in an *ante-pacem* dwelling house.

3. *The Titular Churches of Rome*

Domestic buildings have been discovered under a number of Rome's ancient titular churches. For example, one of the constructions underlying the Church of S. Clemente (*Titulus Clementis*) was a large *domus* dating to the late first or early second century.[87] The Church of S. Caecilia is built on the site of a Roman domestic structure dating from the first century BCE and was in use until the fourth century CE.[88] As noted in Chapter 1, underneath the Church of S. Prisca is a large *domus* in which, in the third century, a mithraeum was installed. In older scholarship, it was assumed that such domiciles were the original meeting places of the *tituli*.[89] However, the literary evidence used in support of that assumption is no earlier than the late fifth century.[90] It is now generally accepted that

---

85. Tepper and Di Segni 2006: 50.
86. Tepper and Di Segni 2006: 53.
87. The house was arranged around a central cortile colonnaded on all sides (White 1997: 224–5). In the first half of the third century, the cortile was transformed into a mithraeum.
88. White 1997: 438.
89. E.g. Kirsch 1918.
90. As noted on p.68 n.2, above.

the *tituli* were a post-Constantinian phenomenon.[91] Moreover, it is now more widely acknowledged that the presence of earlier buildings on the sites of the *tituli* does not imply that the earlier structures were used as church meeting places.[92]

One site, however, has been thought to provide archaeological evidence of both a *domus ecclesiae* and (later) an *aula ecclesia* dating to the pre-Constantinian era within a tenement block: the basilica of SS. Giovanni e Paolo (*Titulus Byzantis*), situated on the Caelian Hill (see Fig. 3). According to Graydon Snyder, SS. Giovanni e Paolo ranks with the Christian building at Dura Europos as 'one of the two most important extant complexes of pre-Constantinian church architecture'.[93] He continues: 'the reconstructed architectural development of this complex gives us more insight into the growth of congregational life and worship than any other architectural site'. The building history to which Synder refers is that of Krautheimer,[94] a summary of which now follows.

Four structures, dating from the middle of the second century to the early third, originally occupied the area subsequently taken up by the basilica.[95] Two were domestic buildings that remained in private use until the construction of the basilica. These two houses are situated one under the apse and the other under the front part of the basilica.[96] Of the other two structures, one was 'a private residence with a thermal establishment on the lower floor, or a thermal establishment with apartments on the upper storeys'.[97] In the last quarter of the second century, this building

91. Bowes 2008a: 65. According to Bowes (66), fourth- and early fifth-century sources for the *tituli* offer little or no evidence for their pre-Nicene origins, but in the later fifth and sixth centuries, there is an increasing concern to legitimate the *tituli* 'through reference to a mythic pre-Nicene past'.

92. G.F. Snyder 2003: 142. The western part of the house with mithraeum underneath the Church of S.Prisca is thought to have been a Christian meeting place (White 1997: 438). But the hypothesis is largely based on tradition associating the site with Prisca (Vermaseren and Van Essen 1965: 116) and not on clear-cut archaeological evidence. At the beginning of the fifth century, Christians constructed the Church of S. Prisca on the site, re-using the *domus* in the process (Vermaseren and Van Essen 1965: 242). The mithraeum was filled in with debris, which included some Christian objects (marbles and lamps with Christian symbols). But this material seems to have come from a cemetery, which probably lay nearby (Vermaseren and Van Essen 1965: 242), rather than from elsewhere in the house.

93. G.F. Snyder 2003: 144.

94. *CBCR* 1.267–303; summarized in Krautheimer 1939: 129–32; G.F. Snyder 2003: 144–9; White 1997: 219–8.

95. Krautheimer 1939: 129.

96. Krautheimer 1939: 129.

97. *CBCR* 1.278.

underwent some remodelling. The reconstructive work included the setting up of a nymphaeum-courtyard at the west end of the house.[98] The remaining structure was an apartment block with a row of four or five shops, or *tabernae*, on the ground floor.[99] Each of the first three *tabernae* to the west consisted of a front shop/workshop area and a back room, connected by a doorway. Beam holes and the remnants of a staircase in the first *taberna* indicate the existence of a mezzanine floor (in all probability in all the ground-floor *tabernae*), at a height of 2.4 m from the ground floor.[100] The *tabernae* opened onto the *Clivus Scauri* but at a distance of ca. 6 m from the street. The space between was either an open plaza or a portico.[101] Around the middle of the third century, the *balineum*-residence was joined to the apartment block by a vaulted corridor, or *cryptoporticus*, spanning the lane between the two structures. This created an upper terrace that made possible communication between these buildings on the upper floors, while they remained separated at ground level. Krautheimer supposes that the owners of the *balineum*-residence bought the apartment block in order to merge the two. The merger created a new complex of considerable size.[102]

Slightly later in the third century, further enlargement and adaptation took place. In the front of the complex, and the apartment block in particular, a façade was built along the *Clivus Scauri*, replacing the plaza or portico that had apparently previously filled the space between the *tabernae* and the street (see Fig. 4). The new front opened in six arches into a portico that ran along the *tabernae* (though the six arches did not spatially correspond to the five shops).[103] The façade generated more space on the upper floors of the building, but it darkened the interior of the *tabernae* units.[104] The façade displays an unusual pattern of fenestration on the first and second floors (US second and third floors), which is still visible in the church's south wall. On each floor, there are five windows to the left, one in the centre and seven to the right (see Fig. 5). The five windows on the west side fall into two groups of two and three, suggesting two rooms. Krautheimer conjectures that 'two apartments consisting of several rooms each occupied the two upper floors on the left side'.[105] The distances between the windows on the right side,

98. *CBCR* 1.279.
99. *CBCR* 1.279.
100. *CBCR* 1.280.
101. *CBCR* 1.280.
102. *CBCR* 1.293.
103. *CBCR* 1.282, 293.
104. *CBCR* 1.282.
105. *CBCR* 1.293.

however, are too small to allow for separate rooms. The arrangement points, in Krautheimer's view, to a single large hall, which apparently rose through both the first and second floors.[106] A strong supporting wall was built between the fourth and fifth shops, evidently to support the floor of the hall and to carry a row of piers to bear its high ceiling. Such a large hall, claims Krautheimer, would have served no purpose in an apartment block; it could only have been used as a large meeting area.[107] Krautheimer concludes that the hall was built in order to accommodate a Christian assembly.

While it cannot be proved that the building was used by a Christian community at the time of this remodelling, it had become Christianized, according to Krautheimer, by the beginning of the fourth century, when the back room of the third *taberna* (see Fig. 4) was decorated with Christian frescoes. Krautheimer acknowledges that 'the Christian element [in the wall decorations] is rather slight', but takes the image of an *orans* as 'certainly Christian'.[108] Some time later, a large staircase was built in the cryptoporticus. The stairs apparently led directly from ground level to the first floor and thus to the hall. The stairway was then altered in a subsequent building operation to include a mezzanine landing. In the rear of the landing, the upper section of a *confessio* (a repository for relics) was built.[109] The *confessio* belongs to the last third of the fourth century.[110] Krautheimer believes that the top of the *confessio* projected into the floor of the hall and that an altar was placed near it.[111]

Around 410 CE the construction of the basilica began, a venture that was executed in two distinct projects: the first project apparently aimed at extending the upper hall and was quickly abandoned; the second envisaged a properly basilical structure.[112] The construction was completed by the middle of the fifth century.

White, following Krautheimer's reconstruction, sees in this complex 'a continuum of Christian adaptation' beginning with worship in a shop.[113] Snyder sums up the reconstructed pre-Constantinian history as follows:

106. Krautheimer 1939: 131.
107. Krauhteimer 1939: 131.
108. *CBCR* 1.283. This is disputed by Brenk (1995), who takes the *orans* to be a representation of *pietas*. See further p. 103 n.116, below.
109. *CBCR* 1.286.
110. Krautheimer 1986: 30.
111. *CBCR* 1.296.
112. *CBCR* 1.297–301.
113. White 1990: 114.

> In this remarkable complex building we can see the use of a third century shop as a Christian meeting place. The shop Christians eventually gained control of the entire insula so that about the time of Constantine they could create an *aula ecclesiae* above the row of shops and residences.[114]

What is notable here is the idea that the initial meeting place was a ground-floor shop rather than a house. This fits well with the thesis being developed in the present book. Unfortunately, the suggestion cannot be confirmed archaeologically, since the Christian decoration of the back room of the third *taberna* unit dates from the early fourth century, after the introduction of the alleged *aula ecclesiae*.[115] The use of a *taberna* for a meeting place thus can only be hypothetically maintained for SS. Giovanni e Paolo.[116]

It should be noted that it is not only *domus* and apartment blocks with ground-floor *tabernae* that underlie titular churches. The earliest structure underneath the Church of S. Clemente is a first-century *horreum* or warehouse (see Chapter 6). The main structure underneath the Church of S. Martino ai Monti is a large hall (17.2 × 14.2 m) with six cross vaults creating six bays, which was probably a market hall or commercial building.[117] The Church of S. Pudenziana (*Titulus Pudentis*) partially rests upon a second-century bathhouse (see Chapter 7). One of the structures underneath the Church of San Sebastiano was a quadrangular roofed hall that apparently served for funerary *refrigeria* (see Chapter 8). The Church of S. Sinfosa similarly was built over a funerary chapel.[118] It must be emphasized that there is no archaeological evidence that any of these earlier, non-house buildings was used as an early Christian meeting place. Nevertheless, if, as White suggests, the kind of structures Christians took over and adapted were the kind of places where they were already accustomed to gather,[119] the range of edifices utilized in the

114. G.F. Snyder 2003: 149.

115. *CBCR* 1.295.

116. Not all scholars accept Krautheimer's chronology and building history; see, e.g., Apollonj-Getti 1978: 493–502; Brenk 1995. According to Brenk, the main building beneath the basilica was a huge private dwelling, which was never in the possession of a Christian community. The earliest evidence of Christian presence in the building is the reliquary/shrine installed on the mezzanine landing of the staircase towards the end of the fourth century. The frescoes in the back room of the third shop, Brenk (1995: 188) argues, are not distinctively Christian; they rather indicate an interest in religious, philosophical and bucolic themes by the owner of the house at the time.

117. *CBCR* 3.87–124; G.F. Snyder 2003: 149–50; White 1997: 228–33.

118. White 1997: 438.

119. Cf. White 1990: 114.

construction of early church buildings in Rome would suggest that Christians, at least in this city, did not meet 'almost exclusively' in houses.

4. *Other Claimed Pre-Constantinian Domestic*
Domus Ecclesiae

Other sites have been thought to provide evidence of a domestic *domus ecclesiae*, which if not dating to the pre-Constantinian era at least illustrates the kind of constructed meeting space that was typical during the *domus ecclesiae* phase of early Christian assembly.

In Qirqbize, northern Syria, a small basilical church was discovered next to a large villa. The church building in its final form dates to the sixth century, but, according to Georges Tchalenko, who investigated the site in the 1950s,[120] it was originally constructed as a modest ecclesiastical edifice in the first third of the fourth century. J.G. Davies describes the church building as 'a house adapted for use as a [Christian] community building',[121] but the structure was erected from the outset as a church building and was originally physically distinct from the villa beside it.[122] It was not, therefore, a domestic *domus ecclesiae*.

Excavations conducted by H.C. Butler at Umm-el-Jimal in the Southern Haurân in 1904–1905, uncovered a small basilica set within a complex of six courtyard houses.[123] On the basis of an inscription, Butler identified the basilica as the 'Julianos Church' and dated it to 344 CE. However, the inscription has since been shown to be a gravestone epitaph reused in the construction of the basilica.[124] Renewed investigations in 1956 by Spencer Corbett determined that the basilica was built within the framework of one of the houses, House C, incorporating the remains of a monumental structure with a triple gate that stood in the courtyard of that house.[125] Corbett cautiously indentified the 'Triple Gate' building

---

120.   Tchalenko 1953: 319–42, summarized in White 1997: 135–40.

121.   J.G. Davies 1968: 8.

122.   A small alleyway separated the two buildings: White 1997: 136. The church was apparently built as a dependency of the owners of the villa for themselves and other local Christians (White 1997: 136–7).

123.   On the building history of the 'Julianos Church', see Corbett 1957; White 1997: 141–51. See also the summary in Blue 1994: 146–50.

124.   White 1997: 141. It nevertheless offers, as White notes, a *terminus a quo* for the completion of the basilica.

125.   Corbett 1957.

as an old Nabatean temple, which the builders of House C for some reason decided to integrate wholesale into the courtyard. Corbett thought that the triportal building might have been used as a Christian place of worship. When the Christians that met there outgrew the building, they enlarged it, constructing a basilica that also utilized the north portion of the house.[126] Corbett dated the basilical construction to the late fourth or early fifth century (around c. 400).[127] White thinks it more likely that the Triple Gate building was installed in the courtyard of House C sometime after the domicile was constructed (he dates the house to the late third or early fourth century).[128] White finds Corbett's suggestion that the Triple Gate building served as a Christian meeting place 'intriguing', but he points out that there are other cultic possibilities.[129] White favours the idea that the building was a synagogue, since a triportal entrance was a feature of some synagogues in northern Palestine in the fourth century and later. To be clear, the building which Corbett proposes as the meeting place of a Christian community was not a house but a cultic structure situated in the courtyard of a house. Thus, it is misleading to raise the possibility, as Blue does, that it was a 'house church'.[130] Moreover, Christian use of the building prior to the erection of the basilica is simply hypothesized by Corbett; it cannot be substantiated from the archaeology. It offers no evidence, therefore, of a pre-Constantinian domestic *domus ecclesiae*.

One of the most well known, and most controversial, alleged domestic *domus ecclesiae* of the *ante-pacem* period is the so-called House of St Peter in Capernaum.[131] The excavations that uncovered the house were carried out in 1968 under the direction of Virgilio Corbo. The dig focused on the remains of an octagonal building close to the excavated synagogue. The octagonal structure was identified as a fifth-century church consisting of two concentric octagons and a portico on five sides (the other three sides were taken up with an apse and two sacristies on either

126. Corbett 1957: 65.
127. White 1997: 150; Corbett 1957: 65.
128. White 1997: 148. For White, this explanation fits better with the 'diminutive courtyard'.
129. White 1997: 150.
130. Blue 1994: 146. Blue, in fact, concludes that the 'Julianos Church', prior to the construction of the basilica, is actually an example of an *aula ecclesiae*. He states (150), 'The question of a former *domus ecclesiae* or house church must be left unanswered'.
131. Corbo 1969; G.F. Snyder 2003: 134–6; Strange and Shanks 1982; Taylor 1993: 268–94; White 1997: 152–9.

side of it).[132] Octagonal churches were typically memorial churches, suggesting that the octagonal church at Capernaum marked a site of special significance.[133] Excavations beneath the octagonal church revealed a set of buildings within a quadrilateral enclosure (see Fig. 6). The largest room in the complex was clearly venerated: its plastered walls were marked by Christian graffiti. Further investigation indicated that the 'venerated hall' originally belonged to a house within a complex of humble habitations dating to the first century. Corbo identified the house, on the basis of tradition, as the house of Peter. The house, according to Corbo, was transformed into 'one of the most ancient house churches (perhaps the most ancient) which is known'.[134] The architectural development is summed up as follows:

1. A complex of poor habitations existed in the area in the first century.
2. Within this complex, one hall was venerated from the first century onwards by the local community of Jewish Christians, who continued to live in the other rooms next to the revered one.
3. About the fourth century, the 'primitive house church' was enlarged by the addition of an atrium on the east and dependencies on the north; the site was then enclosed within a 'sacred precinct'.
4. The belief in the sanctity of the place, which tradition indicates was the house of Peter, found expression in graffiti on the walls of the venerated hall.
5. An octagonal church was constructed over the venerated site.[135]

Corbo's architectural reconstruction, however, has failed to gain general approval.[136] As White points out, Corbo's report, which the author acknowledges is of a preliminary kind, is technically deficient. The proposed architectural development is not backed up by a thorough analysis of the layers of architectural remains.[137] A serious problem with Corbo's claims, for White, is the fact that there is no evidence of Christian presence at the site until the creation of the quadrilateral complex – what

132.   Corbo 1969: 71.
133.   Strange and Shanks 1982: 6.
134.   Corbo 1969: 53–4.
135.   Corbo 1969: 71.
136.   However, recently Runesson (2007: 240–2) has registered his support of Corbo's reconstruction.
137.   White 1997: 154. So also P. Richardson 2004a: 106.

Corbo calls the 'sacred precinct' – in the fourth century.[138] All the graffiti examined point to a fourth-century date (and none can be linked with the earlier house).[139] It seems that around this time the site was considered to have been Peter's house and was revered accordingly.[140] The construction of the quadrilateral complex would appear to belong to the period of Constantine's sponsorship of the development of sacred sites in the holy land. In White's view, the quadrilateral structure should be understood as 'a sanctuary, *memoria*, or holy place associated with the tradition of St. Peter and the Gospels'.[141] White insists that it is illegitimate to use the terms 'house church' and *domus ecclesiae* in connection with it, since, there is no evidence (from the information provided by Corbo) that any of the houses, either in unaltered or renovated form, was ever used as a place of Christian assembly.[142]

The Eufrasian Basilica in Poreč, Croatia, is a sixth-century complex, named after the bishop (Euphrasius, c. 550–559 CE) who commissioned its construction.[143] The basilica has retained many of its original features. Excavations conducted in the late nineteenth century showed that the existing basilica was built over an earlier fifth-century basilica, which was in turn erected on the site of an earlier hall church, dating to the fourth century. The hall church (configured as two adjoining rectilinear halls, one of which served as the main hall of the church) was found to include elements of a third-century Roman structure. Ante Sonje argued that the third-century edifice was a large Roman villa transformed into a *domus ecclesiae* in the late third or early fourth century. However, subsequent research has called into question these claims. The domestic nature of the structure preceding the hall church is not archaeologically demonstrable. Moreover, whatever the structure was, there is no evidence of Christian use of it. The first indications of Christian usage relate to the hall church.

Restoration work on the eleventh-century Cathedral of Aquileia brought to light an earlier pre-basilical church building dating to the

138. White 1997: 159.

139. White 1997: 157 n. 56, referring to research by E. Testa. See also Taylor's analysis of the graffiti.

140. Cf. Taylor (1993: 294) who concludes that 'Veneration of the place known as the House of Peter appears to have begun in the fourth century'.

141. White 1997: 159. Taylor (1993: 288–90) identifies the construction as the work of Joseph of Tiberius as attested by Epiphanius, *Pan.* 30.11.10.

142. White 1997: 159.

143. On the Eufrasiana complex, see White 1997: 186–99, on which the summary above is based.

fourth century.[144] This building consists of two large rectangular halls set in parallel to each other, a third hall that allowed communication between the parallel halls, and other smaller rooms arranged around the connecting hall. Some of the smaller rooms may have formed an episcopal residence. An inscription in the mosaic floor of the south hall identifies the complex as the Church of Bishop Theodore, who was known to have attended the synod of Arles in 314, and whose period of office as bishop ran from 308 to 319/20. It is reasonable to assume that the construction of the church at least commenced during his episcopate.[145] Various proposals have been advanced regarding an earlier domestic *domus ecclesiae* on the site. According to one theory, the north hall was built over a large *domus*, which had served as the meeting place of the Christian community.[146] More recent research has shown that the hall church was immediately preceded by a large complex that included a row of shops.[147] Although it is possible that some part of that building was owned by a believer and used as a Christian meeting place, no evidence has been discovered that would support such a scenario.[148] As with the Eufrasian complex, the earliest demonstrable links with Christianity stem from the hall-church phase of construction.

A small room (measuring 3 × 2.7 m) in an upper storey apartment of the House of the Bicentenary at Herculaneum (V.16-17) contains a cross marking on its rear wall.[149] The house belonged to a certain Gaius Petronius Stephanus and was one of the largest in Herculaneum.[150] The upper floor contained two apartments, which were probably rented out. The room with the cruciform mark apparently belonged to the smaller of the two flats. The cross impression was made on a stucco surface. What appear to be nail markings can be seen in and around the cross imprint.[151] Under the stucco a small wooden cabinet, which was possibly a *lararium*, was found.[152] Amedeo Maiuri, who discovered and excavated the building

144.   See G.F. Snyder 2003: 137–40; White 1997: 199–209. The review in the main text summarizes White.

145.   Sometime in the later fourth century, the north hall was enlarged to nearly double its original size, swallowing up a number of the rooms between the two main halls and part of the transverse hall in the process (White 1997: 203). This new enlarged hall would serve as the basis for the medieval cathedral.

146.   For details, see White 1997: 205.

147.   White 1997: 206.

148.   White 1997: 206.

149.   Barnard 1984; Green 1970: 214–16.

150.   Green 1970: 214.

151.   Barnard 1984: 16.

152.   Green 1970: 215.

in 1938, proposed that the imprint on the wall was made by a Christian cross.[153] On this basis, it has been proposed that the room was Christian cultic space. Thus, Michael Green writes:

> The conclusion suggests itself that here we have a Christian chapel, and the cross on the wall was snatched away as a prized possession when the Christian occupant fled before the rising mud and lava which engulfed the stricken town on August 24th, A.D. 79.[154]

However, most scholarship has not followed Maiuri's interpretation of the cross marking. Representing the consensus view, Graydon Snyder states: 'this so-called cross could have been anything attached to the wall by two cross pieces'.[155] It is generally thought unlikely that the cross was an object of Christian veneration at this time.[156] Unfortunately, there is nothing else to indicate this was a place where Christians lived and/or worshipped.

The *Domus dei Pesci* (IV.3) at Ostia is a rich house built in the first half of the third century CE. On the floor of the vestibule is a white mosaic with a central coloured panel in which there is a chalice with one fish inside and two outside (on either side of the stem of the chalice).[157] In the central courtyard, there is a large semicircular basin in the marble floor on which a dolphin was pictured. It has been suggested that the *domus* was a Christian place of worship and that the semicircular basin was a baptistery. That we have here a domestic *domus ecclesiae* is a tantalizing possibility, but without more specific Christian identification it is no more than that.[158]

---

153. Maiuri 1939.
154. Green 1970: 215.
155. G.F. Snyder 2003: 61.
156. But see Barnard (1984: 19–20), who points out that in early biblical manuscripts, the *tau-rho* Christogram is used to represent the word σταυρός. The *tau-rho* Christogram is a visual representation of a figure on a cross (cf. Hurtado 2006: 152) and points to the existence of Christian cross symbolism by at least the final decades of the second century (Hurtado 2006: 142). Note also Barn. 9.7-9.
157. G.F. Snyder 2003: 206–7; White 1997: 436; http://www.ostia-antica.org/regio4/3/3-3.htm.
158. White 1997: 436. Another Ostian house was renovated extensively in the fourth century. One room was turned into a (collegial) hall. The decorations of the room include a representation of Christ. It has been argued that the *domus* served a Christian function, whilst also remaining a house. White (1997: 436) treats the claim with caution, but, in any case, it does not appear to be a pre-Constantinian renovation.

The Roman villa at Lullingstone, Kent (England) can confidently be described as a domestic *domus ecclesiae*.[159] The structure was a large country villa, built around 90 CE, which underwent several renovations and continued in use until it was destroyed by fire and abandoned in the early fifth century CE. Around the middle of the fourth century CE, a Christian chapel was installed in the north wing of the house, in a room directly above the 'Deep Room', which lay about 2.4 m below the ground floor level of the house (see Fig. 7). The Deep Room, which was probably originally a storeroom,[160] had been functioning as a pagan cult room (originally a nymphaeum), and it retained this function even after the chapel above was created.[161] A room adjoining the chapel room was converted into a vestibule with a door that opened to the outside (see Fig. 8). That the chapel had its own entrance on the north side of the house suggests that it served not only those living in the house but also others from the wider local community.[162] There may also have been a door leading into the chapel from the living quarters of the house. The chapel collapsed into the Deep Room when the house burned down, but some of its décor can be determined from debris that fell into the lower room. On the west wall was a painting of six figures, including a man, a woman, a young man and a child, all in an orans posture.[163] The figures may represent the owner of the house and his family. On the south wall was a *chi-rho* fresco.[164] The rest of the wall contained some kind of landscape painting. The east wall, which had two windows, seems to have been decorated with geometric patterns, and perhaps also a *chi-rho*. This *chi-rho* fresco, of which there are only traces, may have stood in an arched niche, of which there are also remnants.[165] Alternatively, the arch may have framed the putative doorway connecting the chapel to the rest of the house. The house gradually fell into a state of neglect, but the chapel wing continued in use until the villa was destroyed at the beginning of the fifth century.[166]

159.   White 1997: 243–57. Cf. de la Bédoyere 2001: 130–1; Fulford 2003; Meates 1979–87. The description in the main text is based on White.
160.   White 1997: 246.
161.   White 1997: 254.
162.   White 1997: 255.
163.   White 1997: 256.
164.   White 1997: 256.
165.   A third *chi-rho* monogram was also found on the wall of another room in the wing: White 1997: 256.
166.   White 1997: 257.

The Lullingstone Villa is the most secure example of a house partially renovated for Christian use during the first four centuries of the Christian era, and White appeals to it to illustrate the *domus ecclesiae* phase of Christian assembly. Blue goes as far as to cite it as an example of what was possible in Paul's day.[167] However, the fact remains that it is not a pre-Constantinian *domus ecclesiae*. What it primarily reflects are the realities and possibilities of the time to which it belongs.[168]

5. *Conclusion*

The only certain archaeological example of a house adapted into a church building, dating to the Pre-Constantinian era, is the Christian building at Dura Europos. The house at Dura was changed into a Christian edifice in one campaign of renovation. It does not, therefore, exemplify the progressive transformation of a house into a dedicated church building. Moreover, it cannot be shown that the house was previously owned by a believer. It may have been a structure with which the Christian community at Dura had no previous connection.[169] Thus, it does not provide archaeological evidence for the use of a church member's dwelling as a Christian meeting place. The 'prayer hall' at Megiddo may be a Christian chapel within a functioning (army) residential complex, dating to the third century, but the site needs further investigation for the excavator's interpretation and dating to be established securely.

The domestic buildings underneath Rome's titular churches offer little or no direct evidence of pre-Constantinian Christian usage as sites of assembly. The structure that offers the best evidence (such as it is) of such usage is the large apartment block underneath the Church of SS. Giovanni e Paolo. However, the scenario it suggests is one in which the initial meeting place was a ground-floor shop. Other claimed examples, beyond the city of Rome, of Pre-Constantinian, domestic *domus ecclesiae*

167.   Blue (1994: 162) writes: 'The Lullingtsone example must be precisely the sort of arrangement Paul is referring to when he writes that Gaius is host to the whole church'.

168.   Bowes (2008a: 130–5) treats the Lullingstone villa as part of the phenomena of intra-villa churches, in the fourth and fifth centuries, of which there are other examples.

169.   According to Bowes (2008b: 581), 'Dura Europos is emerging not as the tip of a *domus ecclesiae* iceberg, but as an unicum'. It could in fact be understood not as reflecting a normative pattern, but as 'a radical break from Christian practice in other cities, produced by particular local exigencies'.

do not survive scrutiny. Only the Roman villa at Lullingstone offers clear evidence of a domestic *domus ecclesiae*, but the Christian chapel is post-Constantinian.

In sum, the *ante-pacem* archaeological evidence hardly bears witness to an extensive Christian practice of renovating houses for worship, and thus to a prior phase of gathering 'almost exclusively' in unaltered houses. Indeed, if the variety of buildings underneath Rome's titular churches allow us to hypothesize at all about the places in which early Christians originally met, they support a scenario in which Christians did not limit themselves to houses as gathering sites.

Chapter 5

COMPARATIVE EVIDENCE

Scholars have identified certain parallels in the Graeco-Roman world
to the early Christian use of houses as worship and meeting places: the
domestic cult; the use of houses as teaching centres; the utilization of
houses and renovated houses by associations as meeting places; 'house
synagogues'. These seemingly parallel phenomena relate to the four
'models from the environment' with which the early churches have often
been compared: households, schools, associations, and local (Diaspora)
Jewish communities.[1] The analogous use of houses by similar groups
forms a line of comparative evidence for the view that early Christians
met almost always in houses. It is also seen as providing a kind of
rationale for the Christian practice: in employing houses as venues for
worship, teaching and meeting, the early Christians were simply following a widespread pattern in their social environment.

The parallels are without doubt impressive, but they are delineated
precisely on the assumption that the early Christians characteristically
and consistently met in houses. A properly broadened understanding of
the contemporary parallel phenomena supports a broader view of early
Christian meeting places.

1. *The Domestic Cult*

The domestic or household cult, i.e., the variety of religious practices
conducted within the household, was an important aspect of religion in
Graeco-Roman antiquity. Greek households typically honoured Zeus as
Zeus Ktesios (Zeus of Possessions) and *Zeus Herkios* (Zeus of the
Courtyard).[2] Of the other deities worshipped, the most significant was
Hestia, the goddess of the hearth.[3] The hearth also featured in Roman

1   See esp. Meeks 1983: 75–84.
2   Boedeker 2008: 230–4.
3   Boedeker 2008: 234.

domestic religion. There, sacrifices were made to Vesta, the Roman
equivalent to Hestia.[4] According to Cato (*De re Rustica* 143.2), garlands
were hung on the hearth on holy days.

As well as Vesta, Roman households venerated the *Penates* and the
Lares. The *Penates* were originally the guardian deities who defended
the storeroom and protected the food supply, ensuring the household's
subsistence.[5] Eventually, they came to be viewed more broadly as 'the
gods who have a concern for all things in the *potestas* of the masters of
the house'.[6] While some scholars think that the *Lares* were originally
gods of the fields, more likely they were deified spirits of ancestors.[7]
Their role was a tutelary one, watching over all the living members of a
household. In shrines, the *Lares* are usually depicted as dancing youths.
The *Lares* were worshipped in close alliance with the *genius* of the
family, especially of the *paterfamilias*. The *genius* was regarded as 'the
living spirit of the *paterfamilias*'. It represented fertility and 'the watch-
ful power to continue the family *nomen* and *gens* from one generation to
another'.[8] The *genius* was honoured especially on the birthday of the
paterfamilias and at his wedding.[9]

In a Roman house, worship normally took place at the household
shrine. Domestic shrines, conventionally called *lararia*, were located
in kitchens, dining rooms and others rooms, and also in peristyles and
gardens.[10] Many *lararia* have been discovered in Pompeii, Herculaneum,
Ostia and other places. These take standard forms.[11] The simplest type is
a niche, especially in a wall, with a painted representation of the god or
gods worshipped. The niche would also have contained a statuette or
statuettes of the deity or deities. Another kind of *lararium* is an *aedicula*,
which is a miniature temple resting on a podium. A variant of this type is
a pseudo-*aedicula*, which is a combination of wall-niche and podium
(the niche is usually framed with an aedicular façade). A wall painting
with an altar is yet another type. The rarest but most impressive form of
shrine is a *sacellum* or cult-room. All these shrine-types have in common
a depiction of the deity/deities and a provision for sacrifice.

---

4   Orr 1978: 1561.
5   Orr 1978: 1563.
6   Harmon 1978: 1593.
7   Orr 1978: 1564.
8   Orr 1978: 1570.
9   Orr 1978: 1571.
10   Bodel 2008: 255–6.
11   Orr 1978: 1576–8.

From Roman literary sources and *lararia* paintings, we learn that domestic worship mainly consisted of prayer and the offering of sacrifices.[12] Sacrificial offerings tended to be fairly small: incense, wine and small items of food. Animal sacrifices, especially pigs, could sometimes be offered.[13] Worship was offered on special family occasions: births and birthdays; a boy's adoption of the *toga virilis* (or *libera*); a girl's marriage; the death of a family member and its annual commemoration.[14] Pious families, though, probably prayed and made some small offering to the household gods every day.[15]

The domestic cult is an obvious parallel to and precedent for early Christian use of house space as ritual space. Since religion as expressed in the household cult was part of the Greek and Roman household long before the arrival of Christianity, it would seem natural that Christians should use their homes for worship.

However, it was not case that 'pagan' domestic-cultic activity consistently occurred, as Branick claims, 'within the confines and privacy of the home'.[16] The most important festival in honour of the *Lares*, the Compitalia, which happened once a year, was celebrated at crossroads. The feast was normally convened a few days after the Saturnalia, and like the Saturnalia slaves participated in it.[17] At the crossroads would be suspended wooden dolls, one for each free man, woman and child in the family, and wooden balls, one for each slave in the family.[18] Dinners marking birthdays, marriages and a son's coming of age might be held in rentable dining rooms in temples and other places rather than at home (see further Chapter 7).[19] Moreover, funerary meals normally took place at the site of burial (see further Chapter 8).

12 See esp. Plautus' *Aulularia*, prologue (spoken by the household god of Euclio).
13 Jashemski 1979: 120.
14 Harmon 1978; Bakker 1994: 9.
15 Jashemski 1979: 118.
16 Branick 1989: 43.
17 Harmon 1978: 1594.
18 Harmon 1978: 1595.
19 That family events such as weddings and birthdays were occasions for banquets to which guests were formally invited is clear from papyrus dinner invitations, written variously between the first and fourth centuries CE, recovered in Egypt (mainly Oxyrhynchus). See Alston 1997: 35–6; Kim 1975. Alston (1997: 36) notes that of 31 invitations from Oxyrhynchus, 16 are to temples (nine specifically to the Serapeum).

Recent research has established that the domestic cult, during the period of interest to us in this study, belonged to a larger phenomenon categorized from a legal perspective as *sacra privata* or 'private religion'. Bowes writes:

> Much of the literature on 'private cult' tends to focus only on the cult of the Lares or household gods, the result of a modern tendency to define private religion as familial. Yet the household cults were but the tip of a vast private iceberg: any rituals, structures, or groups which were not funded through the public treasury AND not directed towards the well-being of a politically constituted unit, were, by default, private.[20]

Bowes points out that in the city of Rome alone private religion 'embraced a huge range of rituals and spaces'.[21] In his inventory of *lararia* in Pompeii published in 1939, George Boyce had already shown that 'household cult' was not limited to houses.[22] He documented shrines in shops, workshops, hotels and inns and other private buildings. Jan Bakker, in his 1994 study of private religion in ancient Ostia, similarly demonstrates the array of urban locales in which cultic activity was expressed.[23] Bakker's important work is known and referred to by New Testament scholars,[24] but what seems to have gone wholly unnoticed is its potential significance for an understanding of early Christian meeting places: it decentres the house as the locus of private religious activity and shows that other types of urban spaces could be transformed into private ritual spaces.

2. *Houses as 'Schools' and Places of Teaching*

In a widely cited article published in 1984, Stanley Stowers discusses the circumstances of Paul's preaching.[25] While Paul preached in the synagogue many times, the most important place for his preaching activity,

---

20   Bowes 2008a: 21. The legal distinction between private and public in Roman religion is articulated by Festus, as follows: 'Public rites are those which are performed at public expense on behalf of the [whole] people, and also those which are performed for the hills, villages, clans, and chapels, in contrast to private rites which are performed on behalf of individual persons, households, or family lineages'. Cited from Bowes 2008a: 20.
21   Bowes 2008a: 21.
22   Boyce 1937.
23   Bakker 1994.
24   E.g. Osiek and Balch 1997: 21, 203, 228 n. 32, 229 n. 30, etc.
25   Stowers 1984.

according to Stowers, was the private house.[26] Stowers seeks to demon-
strate that a private house would have been considered an entirely
appropriate locale for speaking to an audience. The private house, he
maintains, 'was a center of intellectual activity and the customary place
for many types of speakers and teachers to do their work'.[27] Occasional
lectures and recitations often occurred in houses. These were usually
private events with invited audiences.[28] Invitations might be delivered
orally in the manner reported by Epictetus—'come around to-day and
hear me deliver a discourse in the house of Quadratus' (*Diss.* 3.23.23)—
or, they might be issued more formally in writing. The wealthy liked
having philosophers frequenting their houses,[29] and philosophers benefited from the social approbation that association with wealthy home-
owners provided. As well as occasional teaching, houses, Stowers points
out, also accommodated schools of higher education. Seneca (*Ep.* 76.4)
speaks of walking to the house of the philosopher Metronax to attend his
lectures. Plutarch turned his house in Chaeronea into a philosophical
school.[30] Aulus Gellius in the mid-second century studied philosophy in
Athens under the Platonist philosopher Taurus who taught in his house
(*Attic Nights* 7.13.1-4). Marcus Aurelius, we are told, was such a dedicated student of the Stoic philosopher Apollonius of Chalcedon that
even after he became a member of the imperial family he still went to
Apollonius' house for instruction.[31] In the light of contemporary practice,
then, Paul's use of the house for preaching and teaching was not irregular
but 'an accepted and recognized way of doing such things'.[32]

Yet, as Stowers recognizes, and to an extent shows in this article,
houses were far from the only places where teaching was carried out.[33]
At elementary level, common was open-air teaching in streets, street
corners, porticos and arcades.[34] More permanent locales included shops
or mezzanines above shops (called *pergulae*; see further the next
chapter). Teachers of higher education too might operate in or above

26   Stowers 1984: 65, 81.
27   Stowers 1984: 65.
28   Stowers 1984: 65–66.
29   E.g. Dio Chrysostom, *Or.* 77.1-78.34. For further references, see Stowers
1984: 66 n. 37.
30   Stowers 1984: 67. Stowers (1984: 67 n.47) draws attention to *De sollertia
animalium*, which is set in Plutarch's school.
31   *S.H.A., Marcus Aurelius* 3.1.
32   Stowers 1984: 70.
33   Though Stowers (1984: 66) maintains that the private house was apparently
'the most popular place for philosophers and sophists to hold their classes'. In
support, he cites Lynch 1972: 174.
34   Yegül 1992: 178.

shops.[35] More typically, higher education was associated 'with imperial
fora and temple precincts, architectural complexes with open spaces,
courtyards, colonnades, and exedrae'.[36] Emulating the Greek gymnasia, it
is likely that the larger Roman bathing complexes provided spaces for
teachers and philosophers to meet with their students.[37] Stowers does not
regard these other conventional teaching locales as relevant, having
already determined that the private house was Paul's favoured teaching
site. Also, he thinks that such places would either have been inaccessible
to Paul or would have been deemed by him as unsuitable. On the one
hand, public speaking in the public centres of higher education required
status and recognition, which Paul did not have;[38] on the other, urban
outdoor spaces such as streets, street corners and marketplaces were
typically the haunts of Cynics, who harangued and forced themselves on
strangers in a manner that Paul is unlikely to have replicated.[39] However,
as we have already seen, nowhere in the Pauline epistles do we read of
Paul preaching or giving instruction in a house. While Luke in Acts does
present the apostle as preaching and teaching in houses (Acts 16.40;
20.7-12, 20; 28.23, 30), as has been observed, Paul is also shown speaking in various other locations too. The literary evidence does not force
us, therefore, to concentrate narrowly on houses when considering the
comparative data. One may readily agree that prestigious public teaching
venues such as forum colonnades and temple precincts would not have
been available to Paul and other Christian teachers. However, other
recognized teaching sites such as shops and workshops were certainly
accessible, and Stowers concedes that Paul, like some Cynics, may have
taught in a workshop while he worked.[40] It may also be acknowledged
that it was not Paul's style to thrust himself on people as some Cynics
did, but that does not mean that he would have avoided places in which
Cynics were known to operate, especially if these places were free public spaces also used in a more respectable fashion by humble school-
teachers. Luke in Acts 17.17 explicitly presents Paul as dialoguing with
(not accosting) strangers in the agora at the Athens, and in 20.20, Luke
depicts him as having taught believers 'publicly' in Ephesus, which may
mean, as we have seen, that he taught them in the agora.[41]

35   Cf. Libanius, *Or.* 1.102; see the next chapter.
36   Yegül 2010: 124.
37   Yegül 1992: 178.
38   Stowers 1984: 74–5.
39   See, e.g., Dio Chrysostom, *Or.* 32.9. Stowers 1984: 75–6.
40   Stowers 1984: 80–1.
41   Stowers (1984: 60–62) doubts the historicity of Luke's depiction of Paul
engaging in evangelistic conversation in Acts 17.17. It seems to me entirely possible

The point I wish to emphasize here is that 'teaching was carried on in a wide variety of locations, both indoors and out'.[42] Christian teachers and leaders were not bound by some pedagogical convention to give instruction in houses only.

3. *Houses as Collegial Meeting Places*

There has been growing acceptance over recent years that Graeco-Roman 'associations' offer an appropriate and useful typology for understanding early Christian groups.[43] Associations are attested in literary and epigraphic sources under a wide variety of names: θίασοι and numerous other terms in Greek; *collegia* and various other descriptors in Latin. Associations were organized clubs or guilds formed around a household, a common cult, an ethnic group, a neighbourhood, or a common trade or profession (these networks often overlapped).[44] Their purposes were varied, but in functional terms they provided social interchange and group identity for their members. An important service they offered was participation in and contribution to funerals of their members.[45] Associations met regularly; many, it seems, met on at least a monthly basis. Inscriptions refer to business meetings and especially meal meetings. As Smith states, 'The banquet was often the central activity of clubs'.[46]

Many *collegia* would, of course, have met in the houses of their patrons.[47] The use of private houses as meeting places is attested in literature (e.g. Tacitus, *Ann.* 1.73) and inscriptions.[48] A well-known

that Paul dialogued with passers-by in the agora at Athens just as he did in other cities (following Goodrich 2012: 115).

   42   Alexander 2002: 74.
   43   See esp. Kloppenborg 1993a, 1993b, 1996a, 1996b; Ascough 2003; Harland 2003. That Christian groups could be perceived, at least sometimes, as associations is clear from Pliny the Younger, *Ep.* 10.33-34; Tertullian, *Apol.* 38–39; Origen, *C. Cels.* 1.1; 8.7. See further Wilken 1984: 31–47; cf. Wilken 1970: 452–6.
   44   Harland 2003: 29; Kloppenborg and Ascough 2011: 1.
   45   Kloppenborg and Ascough 2011: 8.
   46   Smith 2003: 124.
   47   Smith 2003: 105.
   48   The words οἶκος and οἰκία appear in numerous Greek inscriptions relating to associations, but one needs to pay careful attention to how the terminology is being used in each instance. While a private house as the site of the association is sometimes indicated, this is not always the case. A decree of the *oregeones* of Bendis, dating to 330–324/3 BCE (for text, translation and commentary, see Kloppenborg and

series of inscriptions refers to 'an association in the house of Sergia Paullina' (*collegium quod est in domo Sergiae Paulinae*).[49] According to Branick, meetings and ceremonies of associations formed around households 'took place in private houses'.[50] Yet, like non-collegial households, it is reasonable to assume that some so-called domestic *collegia*[51] would at least occasionally dine in hired dining facilities. Also, associations initially located in private homes would often outgrow their original meeting places.[52]

Many associations had their own formal buildings or clubhouses, which served as their meeting places. Remnants of various collegial buildings have survived.[53] According to White, collegial halls 'typically resembled domestic architecture'.[54] The meeting place of the association of merchants and shippers from Berytus in Delos, White points out, was known as the 'House of the Poseidonists from Berytus'.[55] Architecturally it is like a house with a peristyle and a large assembly room, but instead of residential quarters, it had a room with altars to and statues of the gods. At Ostia, where some of the best-preserved remains of association buildings are to be found, a number 'came from the realm of domestic architecture'.[56] Thus the headquarters of the *Fabri Navales* or ship-builders (III.3.1-2), situated on the main street of Ostia, the Decumanus

Ascough 2011: 33–9) refers to an οἰκία, but the 'house' is distinct from the sanctuary (ἱερον), and it is the latter that is the meeting place of the association ('The supervisors and the sacrifice makers shall arrange as assembly and convocation in the sanctuary...'). The house, which was evidently next to or close to the ἱερον, was evidently the property of the association and was rented out by it for an income. Sometimes the word οἶκος is used to denote the clubhouse or cultic centre of the association, as in the decree of the Athenian *thiasotai* of the Mother of the Gods, dating to 265/4 BCE (for text, translation and commentary, see Kloppenborg and Ascough 2011: 100–104), which refers to the construction of the 'house', i.e., the sanctuary. In some inscriptions, οἶκος designates the association itself (see Robert 1969).

49   CIL 6.9148, 9149, 10260-4 (referred to already above, p.18 n.8).
50   Branick 1989: 47.
51   Ascough (2003: 24 n. 41) questions the validity of this category. He argues that even associations based in households had as their main focus the worship of a particular deity and so should be categorized as religious associations.
52   Ascough 2003: 39.
53   Ascough, Harland and Kloppenborg 2012: 221–40; Bollman 1998; Hermansen 1981: 61–87.
54   White 2000: 696.
55   White 2000: 696.
56   White 2000: 697.

Maximus, was, White claims, built in a lot previously occupied by a peristyle house.[57] Directly across the street from it was the *Schola Traiana* (IV.5.15), which was the guildhall of *Naviculariei*, or ship owners. It was similarly formed out of a large peristyle house.[58]

Donald Binder has disputed White's interpretation of the House of the Poseidoniasts in Delos.[59] Binder points out that this building is not a 'house' in the sense of a 'domestic residence' but a 'guild house' or 'cultic house'. Architecturally, its size classifies it as a hall. The House of the Poseidonists, he insists, never served as a domestic building; rather, 'the structure was erected as a public, monumental building that served as a commercial and cultic center'.[60] While some Ostian collegial buildings were adapted from domestic structures, others were not. Recent excavations have confirmed that the structure preceding the guildhall of the *Fabri Navales* was actually a fullonica.[61] The collegial hall of the *stupparores*, or caulk makers (I.10.4), was partially built over a bathing establishment.[62] The meeting place of the guild of *lennucularii*, or ferry-men (I.2.3), was originally a basilica-like building (though probably not an actual basilica).[63] The previous state of Ostia's guildhalls, however, is less important than their architectural re-styling for collegial purposes. Temple architecture, it is clear, was the dominant influence on Ostian guildhalls.[64] Several edifices, including the guildhall of the *Fabri Navales* and that of the *stupparores*, were monumental courtyard temples. Another group, which includes the ship owners' guildhall, adopted the same pattern but had a tablinium-type sanctuary instead of a temple proper. Others had full temples but the surroundings were not laid out artistically.[65] As Katherine Dunbabin states, 'There is no single architectural form' for collegial buildings; 'various building types could be adapted to the needs of the group'.[66]

57 White 2000: 697.
58 White 2000: 697.
59 Binder 1999: 312–14.
60 Binder 1999: 314.
61 http://www.ostia-antica.org/regio3/2/2-1.htm This does not exclude the possibility that the structure was originally a peristyle house, since some Pompeian fulleries were converted *domus*; see the next chapter.
62 Hermansen 1981: 119.
63 Hermansen 1981: 65, 115–19.
64 Hermansen 1981: 74.
65 The collegial building of the *lennucularii*, though, was unique in Ostia: Hermansen 1981: 74.
66 Dunbabin 2003: 94.

One of the most important collegial buildings to have been excavated is the meeting hall of the *Iobakchoi* (the devotees of Dionysus Bacchus) at Athens, dating to the mid-second century CE (see Fig. 9).[67] The structure, known as the Baccheion, is located in an area west of the acropolis, between the Pnyx and the Areopagus. The Baccheion measures 18.8 × 11.25 m and comprises a large hall with two rows of columns dividing the internal space into a central nave and two aisles.[68] At the eastern end, there is a rectangular apse, within which was found an altar with Dionysiac decorations. Although the entrance has not survived, the layout would suggest that it was in the west wall opposite the apse. The building is thus like a basilica in form.[69] The building is identified as the meeting site of the *Iobakchoi* by a stele found next to the altar. The text on the column is one of the longest inscriptions relating to an association from the Roman era, giving comparatively detailed information about the club.[70] The regulations indicate two main types of meeting: business meetings and banquets. Meal meetings were evidently monthly (line 42), but there were a number of additional feasting occasions, including a yearly festival (probably the Dionysaic *Anthesteria* festival), which featured a special libation and a discourse or sermon (lines 113-15). Another festival involved a dramatic presentation (lines 123-24). The excavated hall was suitable for business meetings, speeches, religious rites and even dramatic performances, but, as Smith observes, it did not have a conventional dining area, which is odd since the text makes explicit mention of a 'banquet hall' (ἑστιατορειον, line 141). Meal meetings, especially the yearly festival, are called στιβάδα (lines 48-49, 52, 63, 70, 112, 152). The term στιβάς refers to the leaves or foliage on which participants at a picnic or outdoor banquet reclined, whether strewn on the ground or stuffed into mattresses or cushions.[71] Reclining on mats of leaves was the preferred style of dining for Dionysian feasts.[72] According to Philostratus, Herodes Atticus supplied wine for both citizens and strangers 'as they lay...on couches of ivy leaves' (κατα-κειμένους ἐπὶ στιβάδων κιττοῦ) during the feast of Dionysius.[73] Smith

67   Described briefly in Harland 2003: 81–3; Smith 2003: 123.
68   Smith 2003: 123.
69   Smith 2003: 123.
70   For text, translation and commentary, see Kloppenborg and Ascough 2011: 241–57. See also Smith 2003: 111–23, 129–31.
71   Dunbabin 1991: 134. E.g. Plato, *Rep.* 3.372b. The related Latin term *stibadium* came to refer to a semi-circular couch first used for outdoor dining and subsequently introduced into Roman dining rooms.
72   Smith 2003: 114.
73   Philostratus, *Vit. Soph.* 2.3.

thus suggests that in times of banquets, rather than lay out couches, the *Iobakchoi* of Athens 'utilized the more rustic dining arrangement in which straw mats were spread on the floor'.[74] The meeting hall could then easily be turned into to a 'banquet hall'.

The Baccheion at Athens illustrates how internal space in collegial buildings was 'multipurpose'.[75] Where there were no formal dining rooms, the main hall, the courtyard or porticos could be changed into dining space using moveable equipment.[76]

The meeting places of associations were not just private houses and specially designated clubhouses.[77] Many associations met in dining rooms attaching to public temples. The Egyptian guild of Zeus Hypsistos, whose regulations survive in a papyrus dating from 69 to 58 BCE,[78] held its banquets in a 'common room', ἀνδρῶνι κοινῷ, in the temple, which was a civic temple.[79] The word κοινός in this context more precisely means 'belonging to the association', which probably indicates that the guild hired it.[80] Egyptian associations, it seems, commonly dined in temple dining rooms. Roman *collegia* too often met in public temples.[81] The society of Diana and Antinous in Lanuvium, Italy, for example, held its banquets in the temple of Antinous.[82] The worshippers of Hercules met in the temple of Herclues, and the *convictores concordiae* dined in the temple of Concord.[83] Many associations, especially those with no fixed place of their own, evidently met regularly in hospitality establishments, such as inns and restaurants. According to Cassius Dio (60.6-7), when Claudius 'disbanded the clubs' he 'abolished the taverns where they were wont to gather and drink, and commanded that no boiled meat or hot water should be sold'. The emperor's action implies that inns and *popinae* were well-known gathering places of *collegia*. Material evidence for inns as association meeting places has been found in Pompeii (see Chapter 7). Associations could dine in gardens and other outdoor settings (see Chapter 8). Athletic clubs were sometimes based in bathhouses. A set of inscriptions indicates that an association of athletes

74   Smith 2003: 114.
75   Dunbabin 2003: 94.
76   Dunbabin 2003: 94.
77   As Dunbabin (2003: 99) notes, many *collegia* were small and humble bodies. They 'will have had to use whatever space was available for their feasts'.
78   Roberts, Skeat and Nock 1936.
79   Roberts, Skeat and Nock 1936: 48.
80   Roberts, Skeat and Nock 1936: 48.
81   Smith 2003: 102.
82   Smith 2003: 102.
83   Smith 2003: 102.

belonging to the cult of Hercules had its guild seat somewhere in the Thermae of Trajan.[84] Funerary activities of an association took place at the burial site, which was sometimes the property of the group.[85] An appreciation of the diversity of settings in which associations could meet fits well with a broader view of early Christian meeting places.

4. *House Synagogues*

The process that White sees at work in early Christianity, whereby a congregation first meets in the home of a patron and then adapts or wholly transforms a domestic residence for religious use, he also finds in Jewish communities of the Diaspora in the pre-Constantinian period. The apparent use of houses and adapted houses as gathering places by Diaspora Jews appears to give powerful comparative support to the AEH perspective.

In his chapter on 'Synagogues in the Graeco-Roman Diaspora' in the first volume of *The Social Origins of Christian Architecture*, White discusses six Diaspora synagogues;[86] each is given a fuller treatment in the second volume. All six, he points out, are adaptive structures. One synagogue was adapted from a civic bath-gymnasium complex acquired by the Jews of Sardis. The renovation took place, according to White (following the archaeological reports) in two main stages, the first dating to the late third century, and the second, involving the construction of a colonnaded forecourt and mosaic floors, to the fourth or fifth century.[87] All the others, White claims, were adapted from domestic architecture.

The oldest is the alleged synagogue at Delos. The building, designated GD 80, was excavated in 1912/13 by Andre Plassart and identified by him as a synagogue.[88] Although the identification has been questioned because the building lacks overt Jewish symbolism or architectural features, strong circumstantial evidence, in White's view, makes the identification sound.[89] Located at the seaside, it was, according to White, previously a private house. The renovation took place in two phases, the first in the late second century BCE and the second in the mid-first

---

84   Yegül 2010: 122.
85   Harland 2003: 85.
86   White 1990: 62–77; cf. 2000: 702.
87   White 1997: 310–21. Magness (2005) has challenged the dating of the mosaic floors, arguing that they date to the sixth century.
88   White 1997: 332.
89   White 1997: 338.

century CE.[90] In the first phase, the largest room in the house, which at some point during its domestic existence was partitioned, was turned into an undivided assembly hall; the second phase involved reconstruction of the front wall and improvement of the portico.[91] The synagogue in Priene was built as an overhaul of a Hellenistic domicile typical of contemporary Priene houses.[92] The renovation occurred in the second century CE and involved extensive transformation of the interior but comparatively little change to the outside of the house. The synagogue at Ostia (discovered in 1961), located near what was once the shoreline, was thought by the original excavator, Maria Florian Squarciapino, to have been a purpose-built synagogue, first built in the first century CE and remodelled on subsequent occasions, its present structure stemming from the fourth century CE.[93] According to White in his *Social Origins*, it was a house or, more likely, an *insula* complex, dating to the late first or early second century, converted to a synagogue in at least three stages (see Fig. 10).[94] First, in the late second or early third century, the interior was modified to create an assembly hall with a bema at the end and benches along the wall. Second, in the early to mid-fourth century, significant structural alterations were made to create a 'monumental' synagogue. The changes included the raising of the top level of the assembly hall through the second storey and the introduction of columns to support the new ceiling. Also, an elaborate Torah shrine was installed. Third, from the middle of the fourth century and until the abandonment of the building, various smaller embellishments, such as floor decoration, took place. The original synagogue at Stobi, dating to the second or third century CE, was located on the lower level of a large *domus* owned by Claudius Tiberius Polycharmos who, as an inscription informs us, donated that part of his house to the Jewish community while retaining control of the upper rooms.[95] The house was apparently damaged or destroyed by fire, and the synagogue was rebuilt next door some time around the early fourth century. In the fifth century the site was taken up by a Christian basilica. Finally, the synagogue at Dura Europos was, like

90 White 1990: 64.

91 White 1997: 336–8.

92 White 1990: 67–9; 1997: 325–32. The synagogue was originally, and wrongly, identified by the excavators as a *Hauskirche*, and is taken as such by Filson (1939: 108–9).

93 See White 1997: 387–8.

94 White 1997: 390–1; cf. 1990: 70–1.

95 White 1990: 71; 1997: 343–52. For text and translation of the inscription, see White 1997: 352–6.

its Christian counterpart, a regular Durene house.[96] It was renovated in two distinct phases. The earlier phase, dating to c. 150–200 CE, brought change to the internal space, with the introduction of a small assembly hall. The subsequent renovation, dating to 244/245, was a more thorough-going reconstruction. The house was virtually rebuilt as a synagogue with a large hall of assembly. The construction also took over the house next door.

White thus sees a general pattern in Diaspora Judaism. In the earliest diffusion, 'local congregations probably met in the homes of individuals'.[97] Over time, private quarters 'were gradually adapted more to the peculiar needs of religious use in accordance with the social circumstances of the community'.[98]

Binder, in his study of synagogues in the Second Temple period, has challenged White's overall thesis regarding the domestic origins of synagogue buildings.[99] Binder makes the point that White overlooks important inscriptional evidence from Egypt that clearly points to the existence of monumental synagogue architecture from the second century BCE.[100] Reference to architectural features, such as pylons, exedras and precincts, suggest structures consisting of 'a walled outer precinct with a monumental gate and a cultic hall in the midst of the sacred area'.[101] References in Philo and Josephus also seem to indicate that some Diaspora synagogues were 'consecrated buildings, not houses that remained in private use'.[102] Binder does not engage with White's interpretation of the synagogue buildings at Priene, Stobi and Dura, which are beyond the parameters of his own study (the Second Temple period), but he disputes White's understanding of the structures at Delos and Ostia.[103]

In Binder's view, the dimensions of the assembly room (16.9 × 14.4 m) of building GD 80 at Delos make it unlikely to have been originally a room in a private house. Such dimensions, he points out, are unparalleled in Delian domestic architecture.[104] The chamber must have been erected

---

96   White 1990: 74–7; 1997: 272–87.
97   White 1990: 64
98   White 1990: 101.
99   Binder 1999.
100   Binder 1999: 229. P. Richardson (2004a: 143) similarly believes that such references indicate the presence of purpose-built synagogues or 'houses of prayer' in Egypt in the second century BCE.
101   Binder 1999: 484.
102   Binder 1999: 229. See the references given there.
103   Binder 1999: 297–317, 322–6.
104   Binder 1999: 307.

not as a room in a private house but as a hall within a public edifice. Moreover, the length of the stylobate forming the edge of the portico (18 m) 'dwarfs those found inside the courtyards of private homes, which all run less than 10 m in length'.[105] The columns of the portico are also much taller than columns of Delian houses and are more like those found in public buildings on the island. The structure as a whole, he points out, is quite similar to the House of the Poseidoniasts, which White takes to be a renovated house but which Binder argues was constructed as a monumental building. Binder thinks that GD 80 was either 'originally constructed as a cultic hall by a pagan association' and was subsequently transformed into a synagogue building, or was from the outset built as a synagogue and subsequently modified with a partition wall being erected in the hall of assembly.[106] Binder similarly stresses the disparity between the synagogue building and local domestic architecture in his discussion of the Ostia synagogue. It is very different, he insists, from both Ostian peristyle houses and *insula* buildings.[107] He finds little in White's reappraisal to overturn Squarciapino's original analysis. He thus takes the Ostia synagogue in its first phase to be a first-century construction exhibiting 'most of the features commonly associated with Second Temple synagogues' (large hall with benches on three sides, well and basin for purifications, banquet area).[108]

After a review of all the relevant literary, epigraphic and archaeological data, Binder rejects White's theory that Diaspora synagogues arose out of gatherings in houses. He thinks rather that they emerged from meetings in urban open places such as the forum or agora, and especially from gatherings by bodies of water, finding it significant that Diaspora synagogues were often built close to bodies of water.[109] Binder's larger work also takes in Palestinian synagogues.[110] In contrast to White, who claims in his *Social Origins* that there is no archaeological evidence for dedicated synagogue buildings in the homeland dating to the first century,[111] Binder identifies four constructions 'that we can confidently state are the remains of synagogues built in Palestine during the period of the Second Temple'.[112] These are the buildings at Gamla (in the southern

105   Binder 1999: 308.
106   Binder 1999: 314.
107   Binder 1999: 331–2.
108   Binder 1999: 334.
109   Binder 1999: 339.
110   Binder 1999: 155–226.
111   White 1990: 61. It must be remembered that White was writing before the archaeological discoveries of recent years.
112   Binder 1999: 199.

Golan), Masada, Herodium and Capernaum. Binder argues that the antecedents of Palestinian synagogues were meetings at city gates.[113] He believes that pre-70 synagogues, both in Palestine and the Diaspora, were strongly linked to the Jerusalem temple. In the Diaspora, synagogues provided a way of being connected to the central sanctuary while remaining physically distant from it.[114]

White's interpretation of building GD 80 as a house-turned-synagogue has also been challenged by Monika Trümper in an article published in 2004.[115] In Trümper's opinion, 'The building was certainly never conceived and used as a domestic dwelling'.[116] Like Binder, she observes that the architectural form differs sharply from the many excavated private houses on the island. She also dismisses one of the two possibilities mooted by Binder: that it was built as the cultic hall of a pagan association. Features integral to the original design of the building, such as a large hall, a water reservoir and orientation toward the east, strongly suggest to her that the building was planned from the beginning as a synagogue.[117] Trümper is undecided on the date of the initial construction: it could be the second century BCE, but 'a date in the third century B.C. or at the very beginning of the first century B.C. cannot be excluded'.[118]

Lidia Matassa, in an article appearing in 2007, re-expresses earlier doubts about the identification of building GD 80 as a synagogue. She argues that the circumstantial evidence on which the identification largely depends (literary and epigraphic evidence) is insufficient to support it.[119] Taken on its own, while there is nothing that excludes building GD 80 from being a synagogue, 'there is not one piece of evidence that would suggest that it actually *was* a synagogue'.[120] The internal layout, she argues, is similar to two of the Sarapeia on the island.[121] Most large buildings on Delos, she points out, had their own cisterns.[122] She also maintains that the building is not oriented eastwards.[123]

113   Binder 1999: 226, following Levine 1996.
114   Binder 1999: 341.
115   Trümper 2004.
116   Trümper 2004: 592.
117   Trümper 2004: 592.
118   Trümper 2004: 593.
119   Matassa 2007: 84–94.
120   Matassa 2007: 111.
121   Matassa 2007: 97.
122   Matassa 2007: 98.
123   Matassa 2007: 98–9.

Anders Runesson, in an article published in 1999 as part of an exchange with White on the Ostia synagogue, argued that the edifice 'was constructed de novo as a synagogue'.[124] Although some features were unique, the 'temple-like' design of the original building was most likely inspired by the architecture of Ostian guildhalls.[125] Runesson dated the synagogue to the second half of the first century CE. In his response to Runesson, White defended his interpretation while modifying it slightly to include the possibility that the original *insula* could have contained a collegial hall.[126] Runesson has written further on the Ostia synagogue,[127] but the exchange between him and White, and all previous discussion of the synagogue since Squarciapino, has been completely overtaken by a thorough reexcavation of the site by the Department of Classics at the University of Texas at Austin under White's directorship. A goal of the project is to provide a definitive plan and architectural history of the synagogue. At a presentation of the annual meeting of the Society of Biblical Literature in 2011, White proposed a provisional new phasing of the synagogue complex in the light of excavations so far. What he cautiously calls the 'Early Synagogue' is dated to the early Severan period, late second to early third century CE.

Synagogal origins is a hotly contested topic, with an array of sub-debates about particular structures and also particular texts. The field is also a very fast-moving one. Since Binder's study, other ancient Palestinian 'synagogues' have been discovered (at Jericho, Mod'in, Khirbet Qana, and Migdal).[128] It is with due caution, therefore, that I make the following points.

First, the archaeological picture relating to early synagogue buildings is more varied than White allows. The synagogues at Priene, Stobi and Dura Europos are (at least so far) uncontested examples of 'house synagogues', private domestic buildings renovated for synagogal use. The earliest synagogue at Stobi is a particularly interesting example because the upper quarters of the building apparently remained in domestic use after the lower level became the Jewish community's meeting place.[129]

124   Runesson 1999: 432.
125   Runesson 1999: 432.
126   White 1999. The debate between Runesson and White is neatly summarized in Catto 2007: 55–8.
127   Runesson 2001a, 2001b, 2002, Runesson, Binder, and Olsson 2008: 223–30.
128   For a more up-to-date review of the archaeological evidence, see Catto 2007: 82–104. On the structure discovered at Migdal, provisionally identified as a synagogue dating to 50–100 CE, see online: http://www.antiquities.org.il/article_Item_eng.asp?sec_id=25&subj_id=240&id=1601&module_id=#as.
129   White 1990: 71.

Some synagogues, though, were apparently adapted from other structures. The synagogue at Herodium was originally the *triclinium* of the palace fortress.[130] The structure at Masada identified as a synagogue may have originally been built as stables.[131] The claimed first-century synagogue at Modi'in was apparently originally a Hellenic hall.[132] Moreover, the synagogue in Gamla was almost certainly a purpose-built synagogue.[133] The building was excavated in 1976 by Shmaryahu Gutman, who identified it as a synagogue. It consists of a main hall measuring 19.6 × 15.1 m and other smaller chambers, the whole complex occupying space of 25.5 × 17 m.[134] Stone benches (two to four rows) run along all four walls of the main room, interrupted only by the main entrance. The hall was colonnaded, with four rows of four columns. A small niche in the western corner of the building may have been used for the storage of Torah scrolls. A lintel with carvings was found near the main entrance. An exedra fronts the main entrance into the hall. About 10 m to the southwest of the building lies a *mikveh* (4 × 4.5 m). While it has been maintained that the building was simply a private house used for prayer gatherings,[135] such a claim cannot be sustained. The structure is nothing like surrounding domestic architecture and shows no evidence of having been adapted from a house.[136] Features including a large hall with benches around the walls, a water supply, the orientation toward Jerusalem, the carved lintel and the overall quality of the stonework[137] all point to the classification of the building as a synagogue. Coin and artefactual deposits indicate a date of construction around the beginning of the first century CE.[138]

One must, of course, be careful about generalizing from a very limited number of archaeological examples, most of which are subject to conflicting interpretations, but the evidence seems to indicate that pre-Constantinian synagogues were architecturally varied and not all renovated houses.

130	Binder 1999: 182.
131	A suggestion proposed by Ehud Netzer and cautiously accepted by Binder: see Binder 1999: 176–7.
132	Catto 2007: 98.
133	Binder 1999: 162–72; Catto 2007: 93–6.
134	Catto 2007: 93. Further details in the main text are taken from Catto's description.
135	E.g. Kee 1990: 8–9.
136	Binder 1999: 167.
137	Catto 2007: 96.
138	Catto 2007: 95.

Second, there is relatively little evidence for synagogue gatherings in unaltered private houses. White deduces a practice of gathering as congregations in private homes from the use of renovated houses as synagogue buildings. Yet, as Binder points out, 'in no case…has White demonstrated that Jews used a private house as a synagogue prior to its architectural transformation into a public building'.[139] Literary evidence for the use of ordinary houses as synagogue venues is also lacking.[140] To be clear, then, Jewish use of unaltered houses as congregational meeting places is to a large extent *hypothesized*. Recognizing the hypothesized nature of the alleged phenomenon significantly reduces its value as comparative evidence for 'house churches'.[141] As Catto emphasizes, it is likely that domestic space of some sort would often have been used for Sabbath gatherings,[142] but it would be precarious to assume that the use of ordinary houses as synagogues was standard practice in Diaspora and Palestinian Judaism.

Third, literary sources witness to Jewish meetings in open urban space[143] and especially at watersides. In *Mos.* 2.41-42, Philo describes an annual Alexandrian festival celebrating the production of the Septuagint. He tells how Jews cross over to the island of Pharos, both to honour the place were the task of translation was carried out and to thank God for the achievement. He continues:

> after the prayers and thanksgivings, some fixing tents on the seaside and others reclining on the sandy beach in the open air feast with their relations and friends, counting that shore for the time a more magnificent lodging than the fine mansions in the royal precincts.

139   Binder 1999: 229 n. 2. This applies even to the early synagogue at Stobi. The Polycharmos inscription does not explicitly indicate that Polycharmos' house had been functioning as a meeting place for the Jewish community before the renovation to his house for use of part of it as a synagogue. It would not, though, be unreasonable to deduce such prior usage.

140   Binder (1999: 147) points out that while the terms οἶκος and οἴκημα appear occasionally with reference to a synagogue, 'their usage is in the general sense of "building" or "chamber" rather than "domestic residence"'.

141   Indeed, Jewish use of plain houses as synagogue buildings is hypothesized on the basis of early Christian use of houses as meeting places. Cf. Oster 1993: 193.

142   Catto 2007: 104. Rabbinic traditions (e.g. *m. Saab.* 1.4) indicate that Jewish leaders and heads of schools often met in the upper chambers of houses. See further Safrai 1976: II, 731. The home was also the setting of various family religious rituals in Diaspora Judaism, especially during the major festivals (Barclay 1997: 70–72).

143   Cicero, *Flac.* 28.66; *Taan.* 2.1 (as noted in Catto 2004: 161).

In another passage (*Flacc.* 122), Philo states that, when they learned of
Flaccus' arrest, the Jews of Alexandria poured out through the gates of
the city at dawn and 'made their way to the parts of the beach near at
hand, since their meeting-houses had been taken from them'. There, in
space Philo regards as 'most pure' (καθαρωτάτος), they engaged in
worship and celebration. Binder thinks that the use of the beach as a
worship site on this occasion probably reflects the practices of Alexandrian Jews prior to the construction of synagogues: when their synagogues were confiscated, they reverted to an earlier mode of gathering.[144]
In *Ant.* 14.257-58, Josephus cites a decree from the city of Halicarnassus,
dating to the mid-first century CE. The ruling permits the Jews of the city
to observe the Sabbath and perform their sacred rites according to their
law, and also τὰς προσευχὰς ποιεῖσθαι πρὸς τῇ θαλάττῃ. This clause is
often understood as meaning that the Jews were allowed to build 'places
of prayer by the sea',[145] taking προσευχὰς as referring to synagogue
buildings. However, Catto has argued convincingly that the clause
should be rendered 'to offer prayers beside the sea'.[146] That watersides
were quite commonly used as meeting places by Jews in the absence of
formal synagogue buildings is suggested by Acts 16.13: 'we went
outside the gate by the river, where we supposed (ἐνομίζομεν) there was a
place of prayer'. As Catto notes, 'the use of νομίζω…shows that Luke
supposes that there were frequently such places for meeting near
water'.[147] According to Binder,

> the beach or the riverside would have served as a natural meeting site for
> Jews, since either provided the means for the ritual washings that appear
> to have been customary before worship or the explication of scripture…
> A spot outside or near the edge of town appears to have been preferred in
> many cases…perhaps as a way to avoid interference from gawking
> Gentiles.[148]

Whether or not formal synagogues emerged from gatherings by water,
watersides were evidently established places of meeting for Diaspora
Jews in the period under consideration.

144   Binder 1999: 339.
145   As in the Loeb translation.
146   Catto 2004.
147   Catto 2007: 190. According to Tertullian, on fast days, Jews pray in the
open air at the shore (*De Ieiunio* 16).
148   Binder 1999: 339–40.

5. *Conclusion*

The domestic cult, the use of houses as teaching centres, the adoption of houses and renovated houses as collegial buildings, and 'house synagogues' seem to offer comparative support for the view that early Christians met almost always in houses. The claimed analogies, however, are predetermined and circumscribed by this view. Domestic religion was part of the larger phenomenon of private religion, the settings of which were multiple. Teaching was exercised in a wide assortment of spaces. Associations met in a variety of locations and by no means only in houses or renovated houses. The extent to which houses served as synagogues, either informally or formally (through architectural adaptation), is fiercely debated. That (unrenovated) private houses were often used for Sabbath gatherings in the absence of formal synagogue buildings does seem likely, though firm evidence for this is very slim. But Jewish gatherings could also take place in the open air, especially at watersides, and there is good evidence that a waterside locale was often the preferred meeting place. A broader appreciation of the spaces in which private religion occurred and in which analogous groups met thus supports a broader view of early Christian meeting places.

Part II

EVIDENCE AND POSSIBILITIES
FOR NON-HOUSE MEETING PLACES

Chapter 6

RETAIL, INDUSTRIAL AND STORAGE SPACES

In the first part of the book it was shown that while there is good evidence for houses as early Christian meeting places, it is not as abundant as is usually thought. Moreover, it was noted, mainly in passing, that other places of meeting are indicated or suggested by the data. The evidence, therefore, does not justify the conviction that Christians in the first two centuries met 'almost exclusively' in houses. These next three chapters identify on the basis of evidence a number of alternative types of venues that could well have served, at least sometimes in some localities, as settings for early Christian meetings.

The space-types discussed in these chapters are grouped for convenience into three categories: retail, industrial and storage spaces; commercial hospitality and leisure spaces; outdoor spaces and burial places. The present chapter deals with retail and industrial locations and storage facilities, and treats shops and workshops, barns and warehouses. As explained in the Introduction, in discussing each space-type, in most cases, a three-step approach is followed. First, literary and/or archaeological evidence for the space-type as a Christian meeting place is noted. Next, the space-type is described and illustrated with archaeological examples. Then, using the criteria of availability, analogous usage, adequacy and advantageousness (not consistently all four in every case), attempt is made to establish the plausibility of the space-type as a setting for Christian assembly. We begin, then, with shops and workshops.

1. *Shops and Workshops*

1.1. *Evidence for Shops and Workshops as Christian Meeting Places*
As argued in Chapter 1, the κατ' οἶκον ἐκκλησία of Prisca and Aquila, both in Ephesus and in Rome, was probably located in a workshop dwelling. Clear literary evidence for shops and workshops as centres

of Christian activity is provided by Celsus, as reported by Origen (*C. Cels.* 3.55). The passage was cited in full in Chapter 3.[1] Celsus identifies the wooldresser's shop,[2] the cobbler's workshop and the fuller's workshop as settings in which Christian instruction typically takes place. As we saw in Chapter 4, the use of a third-century shop as a Christian meeting place is suggested, though not proven, by the archaeology of SS. Giovanni e Paolo. A Pompeian bakery (VI.6.17-21) was identified as 'Panificio dei Cristiani', or the Bakery of the Christians, on the basis of the discovery of a cross-shaped stucco relief, which has since disappeared, on the eastern wall of the main shop area (VI. 6.20-21; see Fig. 11; the bakery is indicated in the plan of the *Insula Arriana Polliana* in Fig. 12).[3] However, the interpretation of the relief as a Christian cross is now regarded as doubtful.[4] From a later period, the Byzantine shops with Christian symbols excavated in Sardis provide definite evidence of Christian occupation of *tabernae*.[5] Peter Richardson wonders whether these *tabernae* were used as small meeting places as well as shops and workplaces.[6]

1.2. *Roman Shops and Workshops*

A 'shop' is normally defined as a place in which goods or services are sold, whereas a 'workshop' is a place in which goods are prepared, manufactured or repaired. But it is difficult to maintain a hard distinction between shops and workshops in the Roman world since many small businesses involved both manufacturing and sales, with both going on in the same premises, which was usually the modest *taberna*.

According to Ardle MacMahon, 'the *taberna* was the most ubiquitous and dominant urban architectural form in Rome and throughout the

---

1   See pp.74–5, above.

2   For γυναικωντῖτις as having in this sense in this passage, see den Boer 1950; cf. Sande 1999: 12.

3   See Steffani 2005. On the western wall of the shop room, there was a sacred painting (*lararium*) with the image of a serpent. In a recess above the oven in the main bakery area (VI.6.17) was a red-coloured plaque with a representation of a phallus and the inscription, *hic habitat felicitas* ('Here dwells happiness'). The plaque is now kept in the Museo Archaeologico di Napoli. According to Stefani (2005: 139), the phallic image was not an erotic (or obscene) one; rather it served an apotropaic function, warding off evil and protecting the activity that took place in the workroom.

4   For the same reason that the cross in the House of the Bicentenary at Herculaneum is generally doubted to be a Christian cross. See pp.109–9, above.

5   On the Byzantine shops at Sardis, see Crawford 1990, 1999.

6   P. Richardson 2004b: 62.

Roman world'.[7] The form 'was common throughout the cities of the empire, both in east and west'.[8] Rows of *tabernae*, often behind colonnades, lined streets or surrounded forums and markets. The Marble Plan (203–211 CE) shows rows of *tabernae* along main streets, side streets and alleys of the city of Rome.[9] Ruins of *tabernae* have been found at almost every major Roman archaeological site.[10] In Pompeii, 577 structures identified as *tabernae* have been counted; the number of *tabernae* found in Ostia has been put at 806.[11]

The characteristic architectural feature of a *taberna* structure is its wide front leading into a rectangular room.[12] In Pompeii, *taberna* fronts tend to be 2 to 3 m wide, and in Ostia, the average width is about 3 m.[13] *Taberna* thresholds in Pompeii and Ostia often have a long groove in them in which vertical wooden shutters, used to close the building at night, could be placed.[14] At the side of the groove (usually to the right of it), there is a depression into which the shutters would have been inserted and slid into position. When the shutters were in place, a 'night door' would then have been slotted into the depression.[15] A pivot hole in the threshold allowed the door to swing inwards. The night door allowed access to the *taberna* outside of business hours. Some *tabernae* had fixed counters, across which business was conducted.[16] These were usually placed at or near the entrance. Surviving *taberna* counters from Pompeii, Herculaneum and Ostia are solid structures made of cement, brick or rubble, sometimes decorated with a marble veneer.[17] Many *tabernae* would have a makeshift or portable counter, and many types of *tabernae*, especially those functioning as workshops, would not have needed a

7   MacMahon 2003: 9. Martial (*Ep.* 7.61) complained that shopkeepers had taken over the entire city of Rome, and that until Domitian stepped in to curb their expansion, the whole city was 'a big shop'.

8   Murphy-O'Connor 2002: 194.

9   MacMahon 2003: 9.

10   One of the most impressive and imposing arrangements of *tabernae* in Rome, still visible today, is Trajan's Market, which had shops on five different levels: Stambaugh 1988: 153.

11   Bakker 1994: 80.

12   Though according to MacMahon (2003: 91), 'a wide doorway, although very common, was not always necessary in a *taberna*. A great number must have had quite ordinary doorways…'

13   MacMahon 2003: 91–2.

14   On *taberna* doorways, see MacMahon 2003: 91–9.

15   MacMahon 2003: 92.

16   On *taberna* counters, see MacMahon 2003: 80–90.

17   MacMahon 2003: 80.

counter.[18] Frequently, shop wares would spill out on to the street, and laws were introduced requiring vendors to keep their goods within their shops.[19]

A *taberna* might simply consist of the open-fronted room, but often there would be at least one back or side room. Some Pompeian *tabernae* even had a small back garden.[20] Many *tabernae* had a mezzanine, known as a *pergula*.[21] This is a floor above the shop (but not a proper upper storey), accessible via an internal stair, which was often simply a wooden ladder resting on a podium.[22] A window above the shop entrance would illuminate the *pergula.* Rear rooms and especially *pergulae* would have been used as living quarters. Latrines, bed-niches and the remnants of wall decoration in back or side rooms provide material evidence of the habitation of *tabernae.*[23] For shops with living quarters attached Axel Boëthius coined the term 'shop-houses' or '*tabernae*-houses'.[24] However, as MacMahon emphasizes, *tabernae* 'were not really domiciles in the modern sense, but were at their most basic level an extension to a retailer's place of business'.[25] Nevertheless, *tabernae* contributed significantly to Roman urban housing. They account for more than 40 per cent of housing units at Pompeii, and in Herculaneum they constitute over 30 per cent.[26] A notice from the *Insula Arriana Polliana* (VI.6, see Fig. 12) in Pompeii advertises '*tabernae* with their *pergulae*' for rent.[27]

Tabernae were often integrated into larger buildings, both public complexes, such as *thermae*, and domestic buildings. Shops/workshops could take up the front of a *domus*, as in the aforementioned *Insula Arriana Polliana* in Pompeii (Fig. 12).[28] The main structure is an atrium-peristyle house, known as the House of Pansa. A row of *tabernae*, with trademark wide openings, flanks the main entrance to the house. One *taberna* (VI.6.22) communicates with the main house and was probably operated by a slave of this household. Four *tabernae* (VI.6.2, 3, 4, 23), however, have no access into the house and are likely to have been

18   MacMahon 2003: 81.
19   Martial, *Ep.* 7.61; *Dig.* 43.10.1.4; cf. Stambaugh 1988: 152–3.
20   Jashemski 1979: 167–81.
21   Pirson 2007: 468.
22   Bakker 1994: 80.
23   Pirson 2007: 469.
24   Boëthius 1934: 168.
25   MacMahon 2003: 57.
26   Pirson 2007: 468.
27   CIL 4.138. For the text of the inscription and its translation, see Pirson 1997: 168.
28   Pirson 1997; 2007: 470.

rented units, probably the '*tabernae* with their *pergulae*' referred to in the advertisement.[29] *Tabernae* could also occupy the ground floor of a multi-storey apartment block. In Rome, the *tabernae* forming the lowest level of the *Insula Aracoeli* illustrate this arrangement (see Fig. 13),[30] as do the ground-floor *tabernae* subsumed under SS. Giovanni e Paolo.

While small-scale industrial activity took place in *tabernae,* larger businesses required larger structures. In Pompeii, the three biggest fullonicae were formed out of *domus*.[31] The fullonica of Stephanus, on Pompeii's Via dell'Abbondanza, was an adapted atrium-peristyle house (see Fig. 14).[32] The main industrial area was at the back of the building, where the fulling stalls and washing basins were to be found for the first phase of the fulling operation. The peristyle was probably used for drying.[33] In the atrium, the *impluvium* was built up with masonry to form a large vat (see Fig. 15). Near the entrance of the building stood a fulling press for the final stages of the fulling process. The fullonica was thus laid out with 'a degree of industrial rationalization' with the cloth moving forward from the rear to the front of the building.[34] The presence of a kitchen and latrine at the southeast corner of the building indicates that at least some of the staff lived on the premises, probably in the upper floor.[35] The fullonica of Lucius Veranius Hypsaeus (VI.8.20-21, 2) is the largest fullonica discovered in Pompeii.[36] Hypsaeus was a wealthy businessman as well as a major political figure in Pompeii.[37] His fullonica reused two houses, the larger of which (VI.8.20, 2) had a front entrance on the Via di Mercurio and a rear entry on the Via della Fullonica. The main washing area, with four large vats and six fulling stalls, was located at the rear of the building, under the northwest portico. Twelve square

29   Pirson 1997: 171.

30   The *Insula Aracoeli*, built against the rock face at the foot of the Capitoline Hill, is the best-preserved apartment building in Rome. It dates from the first century CE. Each of the ground-floor *tabernae* measures around 30 square metres, and above each was a *pergula*, accessed by an internal staircase. On the *Insula Aracoeli*, see Claridge 1998: 232–4; Oakes 2009: 94; Wallace-Hadrill 2003: 14–15.

31   Craftwork could take place in an unconverted, ordinary *domus*, as in the House of the Cabinet-Maker in Pompeii (I.10.7) discussed by Oakes (2009: 15–32). But such a house is not a workshop proper.

32   Moeller 1976: 41–3; cf. Flohr 2009: 179–81.

33   Moeller 1976: 42.

34   So Moeller 1976: 42.

35   Moeller 1976: 42. Flohr (2009: 179) thinks that the fullery was occupied and run by a family

36   Moeller 1976: 44–6 (followed in the main text); cf. Pirson 2007: 463–6.

37   Moeller 1976: 44; cf. CIL 4.200.

pillars of brick encompass the peristyle, where drying probably took place. The presence of a kitchen equipped with an oven and a flourmill show that at least some of the staff lived on site, probably in the upper area indicated by the remains of a stairway. Hypseaus himself almost certainly lived elsewhere.[38] At least some of the staff may have been his slaves (including women and children: see below). The fullonica of Marcus Vesonius Primus (VI.14.21-22, see Fig. 16) similarly takes up what was once an atrium-peristyle house (VI.14.22).[39] The establishment appears to have started out at the *taberna* at VI.14.21, later expanding to take over the large *domus* next door.[40] The proprietor, Primus, lived in the large house at VI.14.20, and like Hypseaus, he may have used his own slaves to staff the fullery. The main washing facilities were situated at the rear of the building. Two of the rooms off the atrium served as kitchens,[41] in which food would have been cooked for the workforce. An upper floor would have provided sleeping quarters for the workers.

The largest Roman workshops were large halls or large buildings with halls. The fullonica on the Via degli Augustali (V.8.3), in Ostia, was as big as all the excavated Pompeian combined.[42] The workshop consists of a major hall and two smaller rooms.[43] The original construction dates to the Trajanic or early Hadrianic period.[44] The fullery was installed in the building during the reign of Marcus Aurelius. There is no evidence of stairs to an upper level, or of any other quarters that might have served as living space, and so it seems likely that the staff did not live on site.[45] The hall was dominated by four very large basins, and there were 35 fulling stalls along the west, north and east walls.[46] Miko Flohr opines that between fifty and a hundred people worked in the building.[47] He thinks that the workforce was made up of hired workers rather than slave labour.

---

38   Moeller (1976: 46) thinks that 'a magnate of Hypsaeus' stature probably would have occupied a large and more imposing house'.
39   Moeller 1976: 46–9.
40   The *taberna* was originally independent from the atrium house: Flohr 2007: 8.
41   Moeller 1976: 47.
42   Flohr 2009: 181–3. The recently discovered fullonica at Casal Bertone in Rome was twice as large as the large Ostian fullonicae; see Flohr n.d.: 3.
43   Online: www.ostia-antica.org/regio5/7/7-3.htm.
44   Online: www.ostia-antica.org/regio5/7/7-3.htm.
45   Flohr 2009: 181.
46   Online: www.ostia-antica.org/regio5/7/7-3.htm.
47   Flohr n.d.: 14.

1.3. *Shops and Workshops as Possible Christian Meeting Places*

Shops and workshops are highly plausible gathering places of the early Christians, easily satisfying our criteria of availability, analogous usage, adequacy and advantageousness.

If, as the evidence suggests, early Christians were often small business folk and handworkers,[48] many of them would have worked and slept in *tabernae* doubling as living quarters. Such structures would thus have been among the most readily available spaces to groups of believers for their gatherings.

In terms of analogous usage, shops and workshops were places where private worship and intellectual/didactic activity could be conducted. Many of the Pompeian *lararia* documented by Boyce were found in *tabernae* and other workshops.[49] *Lararia* have also been discovered in many shops and workshops in Ostia.[50] The presence of shrines in these places testifies to the practice of 'private religion' in them. Workers' religious festivals, especially the Quinquatrus (the feast in honour of Minerva held from 19 to 23 March),[51] were apparently sometimes celebrated in workshops.[52]

As Ronald Hock has shown, shops and workshops were recognized settings for intellectual discourse.[53] Xenophon shows Socrates discussing philosophical matters in various shops and workshops, including a saddler's shop, a painter's studio and a corselet-maker's workshop.[54] According to Diogenes Laertius, Socrates often visited the workshop of Simon the shoemaker and engaged in learned conversation with him. Simon made notes of these conversations, and he is said to have been the first person to write Socratic dialogues.[55] Simon was idealized by some later Cynics and portrayed in some Cynic writings as routinely

---

48   Acts 18.3; 1 Cor. 9.6; 2 Tim. 4.14; *Did.* 12.3-4; Athenagoras 11; Origen, *C. Cels.* 3.55-56, 58. See further Fiensy 2002: 565, 574. On elite attitudes towards shopkeepers and artisans, see MacMahon 2003: 10–16.

49   Boyce 1939: 105–6.

50   See Bakker 1994: 58–9 (*lararia* in workshops), 84–9 (*lararia* in shops, bars and markets). For *lararia* in the *tabernae* of Roman Britain, see MacMahon 2003: 71–2.

51   On which see Ovid, *Fasti* 3.809-34.

52   This is indicated by Pliny the Elder's reference to a painting depicting the celebration of the Quinquatrus in a fullery: Pliny the Elder, *Nat. His.* 35.143; cf. Bakker 1994: 73. A painting depicting fullers celebrating the Quinquatrus adorned a wall in the fullonica of Primus in Pompeii: Moeller 1976: 48.

53   Hock 1979: 444–9; 1980: 37–41.

54   Xenophon, *Mem.* 4.2.1-20; 3.10.1-15. Cf. Hock 1979: 444.

55   Diogenes Laertius, 2.122-23.

discussing philosophy in his workshop.[56] He represented the 'workshop philosopher', and his example was occasionally followed by Cynics.[57] A sarcastic comment by Plutarch suggests that workshops were still in his day places where one might meet and talk with a philosopher.[58] Much of Paul's missionary activity probably took place in small workshops, with the apostle teaching and engaging in evangelistic conversation as he toiled at his trade.[59]

Shop premises, as noted in the previous chapter, were often used as accommodations for schools.[60] Libanius, the teacher of rhetoric, tells how he first taught in his house when he returned to Antioch from Nicomedia.[61] His only students were the fifteen he had brought with him, and he had no success in recruiting more. He was advised to set up school in a more visible location, and so he rented a shop on the edge of the forum. As he result, he doubled the number of his students. A popular location for schools was evidently shop/workshop *pergulae*.[62] The '*pergulae* of the masters at Rome' were undoubtedly spaces of a higher quality than the humble lofts of most urban *tabernae*. But the *pergulae* of common *tabernae* probably served the needs of many ordinary teachers, and teaching in such an environment would have been a step up from teaching in streets and at street corners (on which see Chapter 8).[63] A *taberna* (IX.8.2, known as the House of Potitus) on Pompeii's Decumanus Minor has been identified as the site of a grammatical (secondary) school (see Fig. 17).[64] The relatively small structure (25 square metres)

56   Hock 1980: 39.
57   Hock 1980: 40.
58   Plutarch, *Maxime cum princ.* 776B.
59   Hock (1979: 450) imagines Paul sitting in the workshop with his fellow-workers and customers, telling them to turn from idols to the true God (cf. 1 Thess. 1.9-10). Some of those who listened would want to know more, and from these workplace conversations some would eventually accept Paul's gospel.
60   Bonner 1977: 119–22; Yegül 1992: 178. Livy, in his narrative of the rape of Verginia, states that elementary schools were located in the Forum at Rome *in tabernis* (3.44.6). However, the alternative reading *in tabernaculis*, 'in booths', is generally preferred: see Bonner 1977: 119.
61   Libanius, *Or.* 1.102; cf. Bonner 1977: 119.
62   According to Suetonius (*Gramm.* 18), the grammarian Crassicius Pansa (on whom, see T.P. Wiseman 1985), before he achieved fame, taught in a *pergula*. It was said of Julius Saturninus (*S.H.A. Firmus, Sat.* 10) that he must have been a good rhetorician because he had attended 'the *pergulae* of the masters at Rome' (as Bonner [1977: 120] translates the Latin).
63   As well as shop/workshop *pergulae*, teaching also took place in *maeniana*, which were balcony rooms extending over an arcade: Bonner 1977: 121–2.
64   Bonner 1977: 120; García y García 2005: 68–78, from which the details in the main text are taken.

has two rooms: a front room with wide entrance and threshold, and a rear room. In the southeast corner of the rear room are the remains of steps to a *pergula*. The interior was decorated with paintings (a garden scene and two landscape scenes), and there was a fresco against a black background in which philosophers were depicted. Twelve figures were visible at the time of excavation, but it has been estimated that there were originally forty-four figures in all. The front room of the *taberna* functioned as a shop, but the *pergula* apparently served as a classroom.[65] A scholastic function is inferred from the subject of the frieze and also from certain graffiti, such as 'beaten' (*vapulo*) and 'beaten three times' (*III vapulo*). Laurentino García y García calculates that the *pergula* could contain up to 15 pupils.[66]

Tabernae would have been adequate settings for Christian assembly. Meeting could have been convened in the open-fronted shop/workshop room, or the back room if there was one, or across front and back rooms (if the opening between them permitted), with perhaps some of those present (children?) sitting above in the interior balcony. Of course, fixtures, raw materials and stock would have needed to be negotiated. Many crafts, though, did not require technical fixtures and fittings.[67] Businesses that were purely retail may have required a counter, but, as noted above, this need not have been a permanent fixture but simply a board resting on a trestle. Working materials and goods for sale could presumably have been moved around to create space. Some proprietors would have kept the bulk of their materials and stock in a warehouse storeroom (see below), rather than in the shop/workshop. *Tabernae* (aside from those functioning as *popinae*, on which see next chapter) generally lacked kitchen areas, but as MacMahon states, 'a degree of food preparation and cooking must have taken place' in them.[68] It is thus reasonable to imagine a simple fellowship meal being enjoyed in a *taberna* setting. Since there would have been no formal dining room, worshippers would have had to eat seated on stools, benches, working materials, or simply the floor. Given that they were sometimes used as pedagogical facilities, the *pergulae* of *tabernae* would have been appropriate for teaching. The situation depicted by Celsus was perhaps one in which teaching took place in the *pergula*, while work carried on in the shop/workshop below. The 'school of Tyrannus' of Acts 19.9-10, if these verses reflect a historical reality, could perhaps have been a *pergula*

65   Bonner 1977: 120.
66   García y García 2005: 77. Another Pompeian *taberna* (VII.12.14) may have been the site of a technical school: García y García 2005: 78–80.
67   MacMahon 2003: 57.
68   MacMahon 2003: 70.

classroom, which Paul leased, or acquired the use of, outside of normal teaching hours.

In terms of advantageousness, *tabernae* potentially offered more meeting space many tenement flats and other poorer urban accommodations could provide. The number of Christian worshippers that could meet in a *taberna* would vary according to the size and layout of the structure, but if Oakes is correct, a spacious *taberna* on the ground floor of an apartment block could have accommodated perhaps up to thirty persons.[69]

A workshop created out of a *domus* might have yielded even more meeting space/s, but large *domus*-workshops, as we have seen, tended to be owned by wealthy and prominent individuals. It is possible, though, that a Christian in a smaller urban centre like *Pompeii* might have controlled a modestly sized *domus*-workshop. Also, believers might have fellowshipped and worshipped in a large *domus*-workshop, like the fullonica of Hypsaeus, as slaves who laboured and lived in it.

A factory-style workshop, such as the fullonica on Ostia's Via degli Augustali (V.8.3), is not a feasible Christian meeting place. Aside from the difficulty of imagining Christians having use of such a place, the physical layout would not have been conducive to meeting.

It is important to note that women often worked in shops and workshops, especially textile industrial establishments. Paintings from the fullonica of Lucius Veranius Hypsaeus show three women and a girl performing finishing tasks (checking the work; folding clothes), while three boys are depicted treading in the fulling stalls.[70] At least two of the three shops/workshops mentioned by Celsus are ones in which women could be expected to be found working (especially the wooldresser's shop).[71] The use of workshops as Christian loci may thus have facilitated a greater involvement of women in Christian activities, including didactic activity.

2. Barns

2.1. *Evidence for Barns as Christian Meeting Places*
At the beginning of the final surviving section of the *Acts of Paul*, describing the apostle's martyrdom, we read of Paul's arrival in Rome from Corinth. In Rome, he is met by Luke and Titus.

---

69   Oakes 2009: 95.
70   Flohr 2009: 177.
71   Cf. MacDonald 1996: 111. MacDonald notes that in the passage in Celsus, women (with little children) have an active role in bringing prospective members to the various shops/workshops to receive Christian teaching.

> When Paul saw them he rejoiced and rented a barn outside Rome where
> he and the brethren taught the word of truth. He became famous and
> many souls were added to the Lord, so that it was noised about in Rome
> and a great many from the house of the emperor came to him and there
> was much joy (*Acts of Paul* 11.1).

One of the members of the emperor's household, the cupbearer
Patroclus, comes late to a meeting in the barn and cannot enter because
of the crowd. He sits at a high window and listens to Paul as he preaches.
But, due to the malevolence of Satan, he falls from the window and dies.
Paul has him brought back inside, and the young man is restored to life
(cf. Acts 20.9-12).[72]

This passage gives us the best-known example in the Apocryphal
Acts of the use of a non-house building as a meeting place. Over an
unspecified period, Paul teaches the word of God to large numbers in the
venue. Most, it seems, come as non-believers but are converted as they
listen to Paul; they then return as adherents to be built up in the faith.

The word translated 'barn' is ὅρριον, a transliteration of the Latin
horreum, which can refer to a barn, granary or any kind of building used
for storage.[73] The Latin word, often in the plural form *horrea*, came to be
associated particularly with a store building or complex of a special
design, with multiple rooms (see below). In our passage, it is fairly clear
that by ὅρριον a barn or barn-like building is in view. The building is a
large structure with an open-space interior, hall walls and a high window.
It is situated outside the city, as was typical of barns.

2.2. *Roman Barns*
Barns were mainly located in farms and estates outside of urban centres.
They were functional structures, comparatively easily constructed (requiring little anchorage) and dismantled (cf. Lk. 12.18). Most would have
been used for grain storage. As they were usually made of non-durable
materials (especially timber), few remnants of them have survived.

Some of the best archaeological evidence of barns comes from
Roman Britain. Traces of a Roman timber aisled barn were discovered
at Wakerley during excavations in 1972–75.[74] The barn was located in
a plot of land that was used for agricultural purposes throughout the
Roman period. The remains show two rows of eight large holes for posts,
which would have supported a roof, and a trench on at least three sides,

---

72 Patroclus returns to Nero's household and confesses his faith in Christ.
Patroclus' confession is what prompts Nero to persecute the church.
73 Rickman 1971: 1; LSJ; OLD: 804.
74 Jackson and Ambrose 1978: 139–40.

which would have held the external walls. The aisled barn would have measured 19.8 × 11.5 m and dates to a period between the mid-second and the mid-third century.

The remains of three distinct barns have been detected on the site of the Roman villa complex at Beddington, excavated during the 1980s.[75] The villa complex, in its earliest phase, dates to the late second century CE.[76] Two structures, Buildings 6 and 7, identified as barns, lie southeast of the villa and were among the early constructions.[77] Building 6 was aligned east-west and had 17 large postholes – two rows of eight and a further posthole at the centre of the east end – into which were inserted the main load-bearing posts. The barn measured at least 7 × 18.2 m. A roof may have projected beyond the posts and rested on exterior walls, making the barn an aisled structure like the Wakerley barn, but there is no specific evidence that the barn was aisled. Entrance was probably on the western and slightly shorter side. Building 7, aligned north-east, had seven pairs of large postholes and two smaller ones at the southern end. The minimum dimensions were 6.7 × 17.8 m, making it slightly narrower and shorter than Building 6. As with Building 6, the structure may have extended beyond the posts, forming a barn with a nave and two aisles. If the two barns had roofs projecting beyond the lines of the posts, the buildings could not have been contemporary (since they would have been too close to each other), in which case, Building 7 was probably built to replace Building 6. A third barn, Building 8, replaced Building 7 around 300 CE.[78] Like its forerunner, it was aligned north-south, but it was significantly larger (see Fig. 18). Remains of an exterior wall beyond the post-pads (not postholes as in the previous structures) show that the barn definitely consisted of a nave and two aisles. The structure measured 34 × 15.5 m.

The largest Roman barn detected in Britain is the Rivenhall barn, dating to the fourth century CE. It was an aisled barn, dividing internally into six main bays, and measured a massive 57 × 18 m.[79]

2.3. *Barns as Possible Christian Meeting Places*
Barns were more a feature of the countryside than built-up areas in the Roman world, but this need not have rendered them inaccessible to urban Christians. Many Roman towns and cities were close to farmlands. Rome

---

75   Howell 2005: 32–5, 40–4, 51–3.
76   Howell 2005: 51.
77   Howell 2005: 32–5.
78   Howell 2005: 40–4.
79   Rodwell and Rodwell 1985: 64.

itself was surrounded by 'a broad green belt' made up of small farms and private estates. Thus, 'a semirural environment was available within easy reach of the city's Forum, temples, and markets'.[80] Barns thus broadly meet the criterion of availability.

As regards adequacy, barns would have been suitable for large assemblies of Christians, such as an occasional gathering of all Christians in a locality (who would ordinarily have met in distinct groups). They would have sufficed for large preaching meetings (as in *Acts of Paul* 11.1), though many of those present would have had to sit on the floor, perhaps on mats. The setting would have been less than idyllic for meal meetings. Yet, sitting on mats to eat, which was regarded as appropriate for outdoor feasting,[81] may have been occasionally adopted for banquets in the large halls with no formal dining facilities (as we saw in the previous chapter, in connection with the Baccheion of the *Iobakchoi* in Athens). Meal meetings in barns would presumably have been of the *eranos* or 'bring and eat' type.[82]

Barns satisfy the criterion of advantageousness by having the capacity to accommodate a much larger number of people than could be contained in a house. Of all the non-house possibilities for meeting we are considering in these chapters, a barn would have provided early Christians with the greatest amount of indoor space for assembly. A barn with the dimensions of the timber aisled barn at Wakerley (224.25 square metres) could readily contain well over 200 persons. A storage building the size of the Rivenhall barn (970 square metres) could have accommodated around 1000 people![83]

3. *Warehouses*

3.1. *Evidence for Warehouses as Christian Meeting Places*
As noted above, the word ὅρριον in *Acts of Paul* 11.1 is a transliteration of *horreum*, which came to designate, often in the plural form *horrea*, a store building of a particular architectural form: a multiple-roomed

---

80   Stambaugh 1988: 191. The scenario depicted in the *Acts of Paul* in which a barn on the outskirts of the city could be hired for large Christian gatherings is, therefore, a realistic one.

81   This dining posture had an ancient pedigree: Burkert 1991: 18.

82   Lampe 1994: 38–9

83   It is tempting to wonder whether a tradition of meeting in aisled barns facilitated the acceptance of basilicas as church buildings. However, Hadman (1978: 187) suspects that aisled barns may have been 'largely a Romano-British phenomenon'.

warehouse. It was noted in Chapter 4 that one of the Roman buildings at the lowest level of constructions below the Church of S. Clemente in Rome is almost certainly a *horreum*, with rooms around a central quadrangle (see Fig. 19).[84] The building dates to the first century and was erected perhaps before the fire of 64 CE. The outer walls surround an internal space of around 45 × 35 m. There were at least eight rooms along the north and south sides and four rooms on the west side (the east side has been completely lost).[85] One of the rooms of the warehouse lies directly underneath the high altar of the church.[86] The room is known as 'the oratory of Clement'. Joan Petersen postulates that the warehouse 'is the original *Titulus Clementis*, where until the late second or early third century, worship was held in an ordinary room, which was subsequently set aside for the purpose, and later was much altered or destroyed when the basilica was built'.[87] According to Philip Esler, the room 'has a good claim to be the oldest extant interior space used for Christian worship'.[88] Unfortunately, there is no direct evidence of Christian usage of the room in question or the building in general.[89] Even so, the cell is at least suggestive of a type of space that could have been used for Christian meeting both in Rome and elsewhere.

3.2. *Roman Civil Warehouses*

Civil warehouses were, as Geoffrey Rickman puts it, 'part of the everyday life of the Roman world'.[90] The regionary catalogues of the fourth century CE list some 290 *horrea* for Rome.[91] *Horrea* served as storehouses for grain, wine and other commercial items. Some *horrea* acted as safe deposits, 'rentable by anyone who needed to store anything'.[92]

The characteristic feature of Roman civil warehouses was a row of long narrow rooms or cells, known as *cellae*.[93] Usually, rows of cells were arranged around a central quadrangle or on either side of a central

---

84   See Rickman 1971: 107–8. The alternative suggestion that it was a mint does not seem likely: White 1997: 224.

85   Rickman 1971: 108.

86   Esler 2003: 106.

87   Petersen 1973: 277.

88   Esler 2003: 384 n. 164.

89   Another level of construction separates the *horreum* from the basilica above. See White 1997: 225–7.

90   Rickman 1971: 1.

91   Claridge 1998: 55.

92   Claridge 1998: 55.

93   Rickman 1971: 148. Military *horrea*, by contrast, were long, narrow, rectangular buildings.

corridor,[94] but sometimes the rows were set out back-to-back, or a *horreum* might consist of only one row of *cellae*.[95] The external walls of *horrea* were normally very thick so as to give some protection from fire: in Pliny's day, it was recommended that *horrea* walls should be three feet wide.[96] The walls were made of heavy material, such as tufa blocks or bricks. Windows on the outer walls were narrow and placed high up, their shape and positioning reflecting the concern for security.[97] The fenestration served mainly to provide ventilation rather than illumination. Light entered into individual rooms mainly through cell doorways and windows above them.[98] Doorways consisted of thresholds on which two doors hung on pivots. *Horrea* often had at least one upper floor, reached by a ramp rather than a stairway, facilitating movement of heavy goods to higher levels.[99] *Horrea* used exclusively or mainly for grain storage had raised ground floors, or *suspensurae*, to reduce the effects of damp.[100] Warehouses varied considerably in size. The largest *horrea* in Ostia and Rome were extremely large. In Rome, the *Horrea Galbana* occupied some 225,000 square feet, and more than 140 cells were available for storage on the ground floor alone.[101]

While some *horrea* were in the possession of the state, most were owned by individuals or families and run as commercial enterprises.[102] Rickman believes that the rental of warehouse space was fundamental to the Roman economy.[103] The general pattern was 'that the owner let the whole building to a contractor, who sublet parts of it to individual depositors'.[104] Depositors would often be private merchants and traders. In Rickman's view, 'the renting and hiring of warehouse space must

---

94   Rickman 1971: 77.
95   Rickman 1971: 148.
96   Pliny the Elder, *Nat. His.* 18.301; cf. Rickmam 1971: 296.
97   Rickman 1971: 81.
98   Rickman 1971: 81.
99   Rickman 1971: 82.
100   Claridge 1998: 55. Rickman (1971: 293–7) argues that *suspensurae* were not introduced into masonry warehouses until the second century CE (though raised floors in wooden granaries or granaries with wooden floors were around much earlier [293]).
101   Rickman 1971: 5.
102   Rickman 1971: 195.
103   Rickman 1971: 209.
104   Rickman 1971: 209. The contractor evidently took responsibility for the protection of whatever was stored inside, and was liable in the event of loss of or damage to the goods (209). Later, it became more common for the warehouse owner also to be the manager (209).

have been the regular procedure for ordinary merchants in the practice of their trade'.[105]

The best-preserved remains of *horrea* are in Ostia. The largest of the Ostian *horrea* is the *Grandi Horrea* (see Fig. 20), which was originally built in the mid-first century CE but which underwent several phases of reconstruction.[106] It is situated between the Theatre to the east and the *Capitolium* to the west, just north of the Decumanus Maximus. As the remains stand, the structure occupies some 7200 square metres. The *Grandi Horrea* was a probably publicly owned storehouse. The existence of *suspensurae* in it, at least from the mid-second century, suggests that it was mainly used for the storage of foodstuffs, probably grain.[107] At the other end of the spectrum, the small and out-of-the-way *horreum* at IV.5.12, consists of only six rooms on either side of a wide corridor (see below)

A well-preserved Ostian warehouse is the misnamed *Piccolo Mercato* (I.8.1) or 'small market', which dates to around 120 CE (some restoration work was carried out in the north-eastern section of the building during the Severan period).[108] The main entrance, flanked by *tabernae* on either side, lies on the north end of the building, facing the Via dei Misuratori del Grano. The interior consists of a central courtyard with brick-pier porticos (see Fig. 21). The courtyard is divided in the middle by a passage, over which hung a roof resting on four central pillars. Facing into the courtyard are eleven rooms on the west side, ten on the east side, and seven on the south side. The rooms on the east and west are more or less exactly the same size: 11.85 × 5.3 m. The cells on the south are longer but slightly narrower, at 13.2 × 5.1 m. All the rooms have the same size of entrance (2.3–2.4 m). The rooms were barrel-vaulted and 7 m high. Above the room doorways were square windows, and high up on the back wall of each room were two slit windows, providing ventilation and extra light. A stairway at the northwest corner and another at the southeast corner show that there was at least one upper storey. The bottom steps of each stairway give way to a ramp. The ramps indicate that the upper level was also used for storage purposes.[109] It is unlikely that the warehouse was a granary;[110] it is not clear what commodities were stored in it.

---

105   Rickman 1971: 195.
106   Rickman 1971: 43–54.
107   Rickman 1971: 53.
108   What follows now in the main text uses the information given by Rickman 1971: 17-24. See also online: http://www.ostia-antica.org/regio1/8/8-1.htm.
109   Rickman 1971: 23.
110   Rickman 1971: 23.

The *Horrea Epagathiana et Epaphroditiana* (I.8.3) is the only Ostian building formally identified as *horrea*. It is designated as such by an inscription on a marble slab above the main doorway leading into the building.[111] From evidence that includes the materials used and the construction style, the warehouse has been dated to 145–150 CE. The monumental entrance, on the west side of the building, comprises an arched doorway framed by two columns supporting an architrave. To the right of the main entrance are four *tabernae,* the last of which has a doorway in its rear wall that gives entry into a large room in the south side of the *horrea.* Through the main doorway a corridor is entered that leads into a square porticoed courtyard. Halfway along the passage was a second large doorway, which could be barred on both sides. The floor of the courtyard has a black and white mosaic, with meander designs, a swastika, a panther and a tiger. An arcade with brick piers surrounds the courtyard. On all four sides are rooms of differing sizes. Two stairways, one at the northwest corner and the other at the southwest, give access to a second storey, which was of similar plan to the ground floor, with rooms opening to porticoes, looking down into the quadrangle below. Sophisticated locks both at the main doorways and on cell doorways suggest that valuable items were stored here. Rickman interprets the *horrea* as a 'safe deposit' warehouse in which ordinary individuals could hire a room to put valuables in storage.[112]

3.3. *Warehouses as Possible Christian Meeting Places*
Warehouse cells make good sense as early Christian meeting places on the grounds of availability, analogous usage, adequacy and advantageousness.

If cells in privately owned urban warehouses were commonly leased to traders and business folk and even to ordinary individuals for the storage of goods, they would probably have been available to local Christians. One could imagine a Christian group gathering in a *cella* rented for business purposes by a group member. Conceivably, a group of believers might collectively have hired a room in a *horreum* with one of them acting as named depositor. Access to the *cella* out of business hours admittedly may have been difficult (given the security surrounding these places) and may have required special permission, though a church group may have been able to come to an arrangement with the guard/s.

---

111   The account that follows in the main text is drawn from Rickman 1971: 30–8.
112   Rickman 1971: 37–8.

Dedicatory inscriptions discovered in the remains of the large ware-houses in Rome testify to the veneration of deities by workers in them.[113] It is not certain, though, that all the gods mentioned in the dedications were actually worshipped in the warehouses themselves.[114] However, that worship could and did take place in *horrea* is indicated by the existence of *lararia* in them. Again, Ostia has the best-preserved examples of shrines in warehouses.[115] The aforementioned *Grandi Horrea*, *Piccolo Mercato* and *Horrea Epagathiana et Epaphroditiana* all contain at least one *lararium*. The *Horrea dei Hortensius* has an elaborate *sacellum*, with an altar and podium.[116] The cult-room, which dates to the mid-third century, is situated in the northwest corner of the colonnade, near the entrance to the *horrea*. An inscription in the mosaic floor tells us that the shrine was built by L. Hortensius Heraclida, who was captain of the mili-tary fleet at Misenum, while the mosaic was paid for by a certain Julius Victorinus. The latter is identified as *sacerdos*, or 'priest', of the cult. As Bakker states, 'The presence of a *sacerdos* in the Horrea di Hortensius implies at least the idea of a group of people led by him during religious celebrations'.[117] Bakker thinks that the *sacellum* was used by devotees of Isis and Serapis, since these deities were worshipped by sailors of the Misenum fleet.[118]

That a warehouse cell could be used as cultic space is at least sug-gested by the mithreaum installed in one of the cells of the small Ostian *horreum* at IV.5.12 (see Fig. 22).[119] The warehouse, as noted above, consists of only six rooms and was built very early in the first century CE.[120] The mithraeum, known as the Mitreo delle Sette Porte (Mithraeum of the Seven Gates, IV.5.13), was set up in the southernmost room on the east side of the *horreum*. The room measures 7.05 × 5.80 m.[121] It is entered through a doorway around 2 m wide. The threshold has pivot

113   Rickman 1971: 312–15.
114   So Bakker 1994: 75.
115   See Bakker 1994: 68–71. A *sacellum* was nevertheless discovered in the *Horrea Agrippiana* in Rome. The shrine was set up by a *collegium* of *negotiantes* (merchants), who probably worshipped at it. See Ascough, Harland and Kloppen-borg 2012: 238–9.
116   See Bakker (1994: 70–1) for description and drawing.
117   Bakker 1994: 194.
118   Bakker 1994: 71.
119   For a description of the *horreum*, see Rickman 1971: 58–61.
120   Rickman 1971: 59.
121   The description of the mithreaum in the main text follows the information given at http://www.ostia-antica.org/regio4/5/5-13.htm. See the website for a plan of the mithrauem, including the mosaic floor.

holes for two doors. In the back wall, there is large arched wall-niche, which was painted blue with red spots. The middle section of the back was painted red. Along the sidewalls are benches, which are decorated with mosaic pictures on their vertical sides. The walls above the benches were garnished with garden imagery. The floor mosaic has a picture of seven gates (a large middle gate with three smaller gates on each side of it) at the entrance and a set of pictures, including a depiction of Jupiter, at the rear. The warehouse cell was transformed into a mithraeum sometime between 160 and 180 CE.[122] Whether the rest of the building continued to function as a *horreum* after the installation of the mithraeum is uncertain.

Another cell in another Ostian *horreum* (V.12.2) was similarly turned into a cultic room. The *horreum* dates to 120–125 CE, and the installation took place in the first half of the third century.[123] Along the walls are masonry benches, and on the floor is a mosaic with various inscriptions. Three steps on the bench at the east wall would have led up to an altar. One of the inscriptions suggests that the shrine was dedicated to Jupiter Sabazius; hence the room is known as the 'Sabezeum'. However, as Bakker points out, the room has characteristics of a mithraeum, and he wonders whether 'a shrine dedicated to Sabazius was later converted into a mithraeum'.[124]

As a space-type a warehouse cell would have been suitable as a meeting place. The lack of proper fenestration would have presented a problem, but oil lamps would have provided the customary level of artificial light. There would have been no cooking facilities to hand, so the communal meal would have had to be celebrated in an *eranos* style, with each participant contributing food to be shared by all. There was, though, at least the potential for the room to be set up with couches or makeshift couches for dining (if it was not heavily taken up with stored items).

A warehouse *cella* would have held an advantage over house space by potentially offering more space for meeting. One of the smaller east or west side rooms in the *Piccolo Mercato*, for example, in Ostia could easily accommodate 60 people (62.8 square metres). With no fixtures or furnishings, a vacant room could be made over to suit the group's needs. With no 'pagan' decorations, the room would have offered completely uncontested cultic space.

---

122   Rickman (1971: 61) dates it to 160–170 CE, but White (2012: 469) dates it to 170–80.

123   Online: http://www.ostia-antica.org/regio5/12/12-3.htm.

124   Online: http://www.ostia-antica.org/regio5/12/12-3.htm.

4. *Conclusion*

Literary references and/or ecclesiastical archaeology point to the use of shops and workshops, barns and warehouse cells as early Christian gathering places. All are locations in which Christians could credibly have met. Shops and small workshops, i.e., *tabernae*, were probably the abodes and workplaces of many urban Christians during the first two centuries and thus would have been among the most convenient meeting locales for Christian groups. They were typical sites of private cultic devotion as well as conventional settings for intellectual discussion and didactic activity. Although *tabernae* were not large, they would have given more space for meeting than many *insula* flats. Barns located on the outskirts of towns or cities would have been within reach of urban Christians. They potentially offered a large indoor meeting area and so would have been especially suitable for large gatherings of believers. Warehouse (*horrea*) cells were apparently hired out to business folk and others and so could have been available to early Christians to rent. Private worship evidently took place in warehouses. Ostia provides a couple of examples of a warehouse cell transformed into cultic space. A modest warehouse cell would have provided a good, if spartan, meeting area.

Chapter 7

COMMERCIAL HOSPITALITY AND LEISURE SPACE

This chapter looks at three other kinds of spaces identified or suggested in the sources as settings for early Christian meetings, and tries to show that they may genuinely have been places where Christians assembled. The space-types considered here are hotels and inns; rentable dining rooms; bathhouses.[1] The approach is the same as in the previous chapter. Thus, with each space-type, literary and archaeological evidence for use of it for Christian meetings is first highlighted. An account of the space-type, drawing on relevant archaeology, is next given. That the space-type may be regarded as a plausible setting for early Christian meetings is then argued (on the grounds of availability, analogous usage, adequacy and advantageousness). We begin, then, with hotels and inns.

1. *Hotels and Inns*

1.1. *Evidence for Hotels and Inns as Christian Meeting Places*
In *Acts of John* 60-61, John and those with him stop at an inn on their journey to Ephesus. John's friends insist that he takes the only bed in the room and that they sleep on the floor. But the bed is full of bugs, and at midnight the apostle can suffer them no longer and so commands them to keep their distance, to the amusement of his companions.[2] John falls

---

1   There is partial overlap between hotels and inns, on the one hand, and rentable dining rooms on the other, since hired dining rooms might be found in hotels and inns among other places (as might garden spaces for rent, on which see the next chapter). In discussing hotels and inns separately, I do so with their capacity as lodging houses providing overnight accommodation for paying guests specifically in view.

2   The reference to the bugs may be partly symbolic. Klauck (2008: 26) points out that the Greek word for bug, κόρις, is similar to that for girl, κόρη. Thus when John commands the bugs to leave the bed, he may be signalling that he can share no intimacy with females. Whatever the deeper meaning, the writer is evoking the reputation of hostelries for bedbugs.

asleep, and the others converse quietly in the room. When morning comes, John's companions awake and are astonished to find the bugs collected together at the door. When the apostle himself wakes up and sees that the bugs have been obedient to his command, he allows them to go back to the bed after he has risen from it. John teaches the others a lesson from the incident before they leave the inn and continue on their way to Ephesus.

In the Pseudo-Clementines, Peter and his companions frequently take lodgings at an inn (*Hom.* 6.26; *Rec.* 4.1; 7.2, 25; 9.38). At Antharadas, Peter instructs his fellow missionaries to go ahead of him to find lodgings 'at the inn nearest to the gate of the city', and to do this 'at every city', so that the band may not seem to be vagrants (*Rec.* 7.2). Peter and his co-travellers enjoy close fellowship with each other in the inns at which they stay. At the inn in Laodicea, Peter gives post-baptismal instruction to Clement's mother Mattidia, in the presence of Clement and her other sons (*Rec.* 7.38). The apostle initiates her into 'all the mysteries of religion in their order'. Afterwards, they all dine together and praise God.[3]

There is no archaeological evidence for hotels or inns as meeting places of believers. However, in a hotel building in Pompeii (VII.11.11-14, discussed below) was discovered a charcoal graffito apparently with the word '*Christianos*' (CIL 4.679). The scribble was found on an atrium wall but has vanished since 1864 and is known only from two conflicting copies made of it in 1862. The text clearly speaks of Christians, apparently in a polemical way, but there is no agreed reconstruction or interpretation of the wording.[4] Lampe states: 'Whoever made the scribble evidently had once had contact, direct or indirect, with Christians'.[5] It would not be unreasonable, in my opinion, to deduce that direct contact

---

3   In *Epitome of the Acts of Andrew* 21-22, Andrew stays at an inn in Patras until he is taken in by Lesbius the proconsul. In the *Acts of Thomas*, the apostle lodges at an inn for the duration of his brief visit to the royal city of Andrapolis (4, 16). An inn is the setting of a miracle, preaching and a mass conversion later in the narrative (51-59). A young man under conviction of sin confesses to the murder of a maiden at an inn. He had tried to persuade the girl, who worked at the inn, to enter into a chaste marriage with him, and when she refused, he slew her with a sword. Thomas and the young man go to the inn and find her lying dead. Thomas commands that her corpse is taken into the courtyard of the inn, and after prayer and the laying on of hands, she comes back to life. Recounting her experience in the realm of the dead, she tells of the punishments of Hell. Seizing the moment, Thomas urges those present to repent of their ways and believe in Christ Jesus. All the people believe and pledge their allegiance to Christ.
4   See the discussion in Giordano and Kahn 2001: 83–8.
5   Lampe 2003: 8.

was made in the hotel itself. The graffito would then bear witness to the presence of Christians in the hotel, whether as overnight guests passing through or as locals using the facilities of the hotel (renting a dining room? [see below]). However, neither scenario can be more than a speculative deduction.

1.2. *Roman Hotels and Inns*

Hotels and inns tended to be non-elite establishments. When members of the elite travelled, they could usually count on friends, acquaintances, and business associates to provide them with lodging.[6] Wealthy individuals who made frequent trips along the same route would often maintain lodgings along the way and have a house at their destination.[7] Inns and hotels generally catered for more 'ordinary' travellers,[8] such as merchants, traders and sailors,[9] though some were aimed at more affluent guests. Inns could be found at strategic points on major highways, in the open country and in towns and cities.[10] Urban inns and hotels clearly did good business: John DeFelice has identified at Pompeii no fewer than fifty-one businesses that provided overnight accommodation.[11]

Several Latin words are used in the literature to denote hospitality businesses offering lodgings, but the terms are not always employed in a clearly differentiated way.[12] DeFelice distinguishes between three main types of establishment.[13] A *hospitium*, sometimes also called a *deversorium*, was a large boarding house or hotel, with both short and long-term guests. A *caupona* was an inn, providing accommodation, food and drink, especially for travellers. A *stabulum* was a hotel that could receive horses and carts. *Stabula* had wide inclined entrances, allowing wagons to pass through, and tended to be situated at city gates.[14] Examples of all three can be found at Pompeii.

---

6   Casson 1974: 197–200; DeFelice 2007: 476.

7   Casson 1974: 197.

8   Meggitt (1998: 133–5) rightly emphasizes that it was not only the wealthy who travelled.

9   This was not necessarily the only option: one might find a room for rent in a house (CIL 2.4284; 4.4957; the latter is from the exterior of a Pompeian house), or simply sleep rough.

10   Casson 1974: 200–209.

11   DeFelice 2007: 483 n. 1.

12   Frier 1977: 30–4; DeFelice 2001: 18–21.

13   DeFelice 2001: 178. Cf. Kleberg 1957: 1–25.

14   For a sample survey of all three kinds of property, see Packer 1978. See also DeFelice's master list of hospitality businesses in Pompeii (DeFelice 2001: 176–306).

The House of Sallust (VI.2.4-5, 30-31) was an old Samnite house converted into a higher-end *hospitium* (see Fig. 23).[15] From the front door, the *fauces* led into the atrium. On the north and south sides of the atrium were bedrooms. Towards the rear were two open rooms (*alae*), one on either side of the court, which may have been sitting areas.[16] At the back (east side) of the atrium, and opening into it, was the *tablinium*, which had a large window through which could be viewed the garden behind. The size and positioning of the window enabled the back garden to be seen from the front door.[17] The garden area, overlooked by a colon-nade, measured 6 × 20 m (see Fig. 24), but a garden scene painted on the back wall had the effect of making the *hortus* seem bigger than it actually was.[18] In the north corner of the garden was a shaded *triclinium*,[19] and a hearth was located in the portico. As well as the outdoor *triclinium*, there were at least four internal dining rooms.[20] Moreover, there was a snack bar at the left of the entrance, accessible both from the *fauces* of the house, and from the street.[21] The hotel also incorporated a smaller house on the south side, which may have been either the private quarters of the hotel manager and his family,[22] or additional facilities for hotel guests.[23] The hotel had an upper storey, accessible from at least one staircase.[24]

The largest hotel found at Pompeii (VII.11.11-14, see Fig. 25) is located near the Forum, on a street just a couple of blocks away from the thriving Via dell'Abbondanza.[25] It was in this hotel that the graffito with

15　DeFelice 2001: 28–9, 237–9; Jashemski 1979: 168–70; L. Richardson 1988: 108–11; Stambaugh 1988: 163–4. DeFelice (2001: 238) notes that although the building is known as the House of Sallust (after an electoral notice painted on the front of the building recommending this person for office), on the basis of a seal found in the premises, it may have belonged to a certain A. Cossius Libanius.

16　Stambaugh 1988: 164.

17　Jashemski 1979: 168.

18　Jashemski 1979: 168.

19　Jashemski 1979: 168.

20　Stambaugh 1988: 164.

21　Jashemski 1979: 168. The outlet evidently sold food to passers-by on the street as well as to hotel guests. The snack shop had a counter with six *dolia* and a stove (DeFelice 2001: 238). A large marble slab behind the counter may have functioned as a table around which customers sat.

22　Jashemski 1979: 170.

23　Stambaugh 1988: 164.

24　DeFelice 2001: 238. The second storey was probably introduced when the large house was converted into a hotel.

25　DeFelice 2001: 278–9; Jashemski 1979: 171–2; Stambaugh 1988: 179–80.

the word '*Christianos*' was discovered. The *hospitium* could accommodate over fifty guests.[26] The hotel had two entrances, one at the north of
the building (VII.11.11), which was the main entrance, and the other on
the east side (VII.11.14). The north entrance led into the atrium, which
may have served as a reception area.[27] Two rooms on either side of the
fauces, opening into the atrium, were bedrooms.[28] On the east side of the
atrium were a kitchen, a bedroom and a stairway leading to the upper
floor.[29] The establishment had several dining rooms and a very large
walled garden. Along the north wall of the garden were three arbours,
and in the middle of the west wall was a large *lararium* with an arched
niche. As Stambaugh thinks, in good weather most meals were probably
eaten in the large garden, 'where fruit trees, flowers, and vegetables
provided pleasant surroundings for dining'; the arbours would have
provided shady enclosures for formal meals.[30] A *cella meretricia*, a
prostitute's quarters, was located at VII.11.12 (under the staircase to the
upper level of the hotel), but as DeFelice points out, this 'one room
business' does not communicate with the *hospitium* and so may not have
been a hotel amenity.[31]

The most famous Pompeian *caupona* is the *caupona* of Euxinus
(I.11.10-12, see Fig. 26), located in the Amphitheatre area (this *caupona*
is also an example of what Jashemski calls 'garden restaurants': see the
next chapter).[32] The open-fronted entrance room had an L-shaped
counter, from which food and drink were served to customers on the
street as well to those inside. A number of amphorae were found in the
counter room, one of which had on it a delivery address, which identified
the owner of the establishment as 'the *copo* [innkeeper], Euxinus'.
Behind the counter room were a dining room and two other larger rooms.
In addition, there were a small storeroom and a latrine. To the right of
the entrance room were two doors that led into an enclosed garden (see
Fig. 27). There was also an entrance into the garden directly from the
street. The large part of the garden, as Wilhelmina Jashemski has shown,

26   Jashemski 1979: 172.
27   Stambaugh 1988: 180.
28   DeFelice 2001: 278.
29   DeFelice 2001: 278.
30   Stambaugh 1988: 180.
31   On the *popina* (or *caupona*) next door (VII.11.13, which similarly has no
communication with the *cella*), there was a sign warning against loitering, perhaps to
discourage the prostitute's trade (see CIL 4.813). Cf. DeFelice 2007: 482.
32   DeFelice 2001: 203–4; Jashemski 1979: 172–6. I follow here Jashemski's
description.

was used as a vineyard. The rest probably served as an outdoor eating area. There is no sign of a *triclinium*, but Jashemski thinks that patrons probably ate at tables set up in booths and under trees.[33] Some could also have sat to eat on mats on the grass. The house next door to the *caupona* and which communicates with it was probably the dwelling of Euxinus and his family. A stairway in the northwest corner of the garden indicates the existence of an upper floor, where the guest bedrooms were no doubt located. The inn had a sign with a painting of phoenix and two peacocks. The invitation (CIL 4.985) read: *Phoenix Felix Et Tu*, which Jashemski translates as 'The phoenix is happy, and you will be too'.[34]

A good example of a *stabulum* is the lodging-house run by a certain Hermes (I.1.6-9) on the Via Stabiana.[35] The establishment receives its name from a picture and graffito on the south wall of the entrance passage. A man is shown pouring wine from an amphora into a *dolium*; the graffito above names him Hermes.[36] Presumably he was the proprietor of the *stabulum*.[37] A wide opening (I.1.8), closed by a wooden door divided into four slats, allowed carts to enter from the streets. To the left of the main entrance is a *popina* with an L-shaped counter, which probably sold food and drink to both hotel guests and passers-by. The room behind the counter room was probably a private dining room.[38] A *taberna* to the right of the main entrance was probably another small *popina*. Halfway along the entrance passage was a hearth and a cauldron for the supply of hot drinks. The passage led into a large courtyard. In the southwest corner of the court was a cistern, and a stairway to the upper level(s) was located at the northwest corner. Off the northeast corner was a latrine. Behind the courtyard was a stall for animals. The second storey had two parts: the first consisted of two independent flats, accessed from the door at I.8.7 on the street; the second, entered from the staircase in the courtyard, was an L-shaped balcony, which had at least five independent rooms extending above the ground-floor rooms at

---

33   Jashemski 1979: 175.

34   Jashemski 1979: 176. A representation of Priapus was apparently found next to the entrance of the inn, and underneath it was a graffito expressing a preference for blonde women over against brunettes, prompting Jashemski (175) to wonder whether Euxinus's inn was also a *lupanar*, i.e., brothel. But the evidence is insufficient to justify such a conclusion.

35   Packer 1978: 7–9. Cf. DeFelice 2001: 182–3; 2007: 477. I follow here Packer's description.

36   CIL 4.3355

37   Packer 1978: 8.

38   Packer 1978: 8.

I.8.7-10. The second floor had a latrine, which was located directly above the latrine on the ground floor.

In literature, inns and lodging houses receive bad publicity.[39] They are filthy,[40] plagued by bugs[41] and unsafe.[42] The literary sources, of course, express the views of the elite, but their comments and portrayals no doubt play on popular perceptions and real experiences. The literati, though, are not wholly negative about boarding houses. Epictetus knows of good and pleasant inns (*Diss.* 2.23.36).

It is often stated in the secondary literature that women who worked in inns were usually prostitutes,[43] but as DeFelice has shown, the evidence for this, at least in Pompeii, is very slight. While light-hearted amorous scribbles can be found on the walls of many inns and other hospitality businesses in the city, courser graffiti (of the *futuo* type) occur in a much small number of establishments, mainly the well-known brothels.[44] Sexual activity undoubtedly took place in inns and hotels, but this does not mean that they doubled up as bordellos.

A revealing account of life in an inn is given by Petronius in *Satyr.* 91-99.[45] Encolpius rents a room in a lodging house, referred to both as a *deversorium* (81.3; 82.4) and as a *stabulum* (97.1). The room, called a *cella* (94.4-7; 95.3, 5, 7), is one of a number in the building (97.7). It is sparsely furnished with only a bed (94.8-9) and a large wooden candle-stick (95.6). There is some kind of table, on which food may be spread (93.4), though this may have been brought in along with the food. The door of the room can be locked (94.7-8). Food is cooked and served within the *deversorium* (90.7; 92.1; 95.1; 96.4). Particularly interesting is the fact that guests can have the food delivered to their rooms (95.1). Encolpius orders dinner beforehand (90.7; 92.1), and the courses are brought to his room (92.13; 95.1). The owner of the establishment is a certain Marcus Mannicius, but it is run by a manager called Bagartes (96.4). Staff include a female housekeeper who attends to orders for dinner (90.7; 92.1).[46] There are kitchen staff (95.8) and slaves (96.6). Some of the residents, such as the old woman with a pet dog (95.8) and

---

39   DeFelice 2007: 476.

40   Livy 45.22.2

41   Pliny the Elder, *Nat. His.* 9.154 (or 71).

42   Petronius, *Satyr.* 95; Apuleius, *Met.* 1.7-17, 21-23.

43   Casson 1974: 204.

44   DeFelice 2007: 482.

45   Rowell 1957; cf. Frier 1977: 31–2; Stambaugh 1988: 182. The location is a city in Campania, probably Puteoli.

46   Cf. the old woman at 79.6 who lets guests in at night.

the resident (*deversitor*) who brings in part of the meal ordered by Encolpius (95.1-3), seem to be long-term lodgers.[47]

That some inns and hotels in towns and cities could accommodate long-term residents as well as travellers is clear from Ulpian.[48] Those who lived in such establishments were generally poorer urban-dwellers. Rent was probably paid on a weekly or daily basis.[49]

1.3. *Hotels and Inns as Possible Christian Meeting Places*
Hotels and inns pass the tests of availability, analogous usage, adequacy and advantageousness to count as plausible early Christian meeting places.[50] As commonplace establishments, used mainly by non-elites, they would have been available to believers. Christian journeyers, especially missionaries, must sometimes have stayed at an inn, for example, when making an overnight break of journey, or when visiting places where they had no Christian contacts. It is likely that Paul found lodging at an inn sometimes, especially when making 'a stopover on a journey to a still more distant city'.[51] Moreover, believers may have lived in lodging houses as long-term guests. In *Acts of Peter* 4, two women residing in 'the hospice [i.e. lodging-house] of the Bithynians' are among the faithful remnant of Roman Christians who have not been led astray by Simon the sorcerer. They were evidently not in transit. A hostelry (in its capacity as a boarding house) could thus have served as a place of worship either for Christians who were travelling together or for believers who were longer-term residents in it. A Christian could conceivably have been the owner or manager of an inn.[52] We read of a Christian innkeeper in *Acts of Peter* 6. When Peter lands at Puteoli, he is introduced by Theon, the captain of the ship on which he had been sailing (and whom Peter had baptized), to Ariston, the proprietor of the inn where Theon normally stays in the port. Ariston has been eagerly waiting the arrival of Peter, having received a vision in which he was told that the apostle would come.

---

47   He berates them over their wild behaviour in the room and accuses them of intending to abscond during the night without settling their bill.

48   *Dig.* 47.5.1.6; Frier 1977: 33; Scobie 1986: 402.

49   Scobie 1986: 402.

50   Cf. Osiek and MacDonald (2006: 31): 'might some of the earliest meeting places for believers have been rooms in inns that had been rented by itinerant leaders?'

51   Hock 1980: 29.

52   As well as providing accommodation for travelling Christians or a home for more long-term believing residents, a believing innkeeper could have acted as the host of a local group of Christians, offering them meeting space.

The presence of *lararia* in inns and hotels in both Pompeii and Ostia shows that private worship occurred in such places.[53] In all of the Pompeian establishments discussed above, at least one *lararium* has been discovered.[54] The *caupona* of Euxinus, according to Jashemski, offered 'plentiful provision' for worship.[55] There was a *lararium* painting in the counter room. In the rear wall of the garden was an *aedicula lararium*, in front of which stood a masonry altar. In the northeast corner of the garden was another altar, a self-standing one, with a shelf in the back of it for sacrificial apparatus. Ashes from the last offering were found on this altar when it was excavated. Since Euxinus lived in the house next door, the altars were for the use of overnight guests. Such altars were, as Jashemski puts it, 'the Pompeian equivalent...of today's Gideon Bible'.[56] Pious travellers often carried with them a figurine of the family god, so that they could make offering to it as opportunity permitted.[57] The gods honoured at altars in shrines in guesthouses would have varied with guests.[58]

Guestrooms in inns and hotels tended to be very small, accommodating one to four people.[59] Nevertheless, a good-sized bedroom would still have given adequate space for a handful of Christian travellers or long-term residents to worship together. Perhaps the bed could have been put up against the wall to create more room (cf. *Satyr.* 95.1). Since food could be taken in the bedroom, it might have been possible to enjoy a small Eucharistic meal there. It may have been possible for believers who were overnight guests or Christians who were longer-term residents to dine and worship in private in a dining room or a garden area.

As for advantageousness, hotels and inns would have allowed Christians travelling together to worship together when they were away from their homes and their regular meeting places.

---

53   For Pompeii, see list in Boyce 1937: 106. Particularly noteworthy is the *sacellum* or cult-room in the *caupona* at VI.1.1: Boyce 1937: 43 n. 132. The cult-room is located in the northeast corner of the building. It is a rectangular, windowless room measuring 1.8 × 2 m, 'with red walls and low benches running around three of the sides'. The niche is on the wall directly opposite the door. In front of the niche stood a masonry altar. On Ostia, see Bakker 1994: 90–1.

54   On the House of Sallust, see Boyce 1937: 44 (no. 139); on the hotel at VII.11.11-14, see Boyce 1937: 69 (no. 310); on the *stabulum* of Hermes, see Boyce 1937: 21 n. 2.

55   So Jashemski 1979: 120.

56   Jashemski 1979: 120.

57   Apuleius, *Apol.* 63; Plutarch, *Sulla* 29.6. Cf. Jashemski 1979: 120.

58   Jashemski 1979: 120.

59   Rowell 1957: 222. But some establishments had larger flats.

2. Rented Dining Rooms

2.1. *Evidence for Rented Dining Rooms as Christian Meeting Places*
As we saw in Chapter 2, Mark may be suggesting that the upstairs room
in which the Last Supper took place was a rentable dining room (Mk
14.14-15). Commercially available dining spaces could be found in
popinae, which were small restaurants frequented primarily by the non-
elite.[60] The use of *popinae* as Christian meeting places is suggested by
Suetonius. In *Life of Nero* 16.2, the historian tells us that Nero tried to
place restrictions on *popinae*, and in the very next sentence he states that
the emperor inflicted punishment on the Christians and suppressed other
groups (charioteers and pantomime actors and their followers). The
connection could be taken to imply that *popinae* were places frequented
by Christians and other undesirable groups. The *Historia Augusta*
(*S.H.A. Sev. Alex.* 49.6), cited in Chapter 3, indicates that Christians and
popinarii tussled over a certain property, with the Emperor Severus
Alexander intervening in the Christians' favour. The property is likely to
have been some kind of restaurant building. The Christians may have
been drawn to it because they were accustomed to meeting in such a
space.[61]

2.2. *Rentable Dining Rooms in the Roman World*
It is well known that dining rooms attached to temples were available for
hire for dinner parties. Many associations, as we have seen, used temple
dining rooms as their meeting places. However, temples did not have the
monopoly on rentable dining rooms in the Roman world.

As we have just seen, dining rooms could be found in hotels and inns.
These were not only amenities for overnight guests and lodgers; they
would also have been available to local customers for social dining. A
Pompeian *caupona*, known as the Inn of Sittius (VII.1.44-45, see Figs.
25 and 28), proudly advertised on its sign lodging and a *triclinium* with

---

60   As Meggitt (1998: 110) has rightly observed, Roman elites may from time to
time have 'enjoyed the thrill of rubbing shoulders with their clientele' in such establishments. Despite trying to suppress them, Nero apparently enjoyed going to the
popinae at night (Suetonius, *Nero* 26.1). The Emperors Verus and Commodus are
said to have had a *popina* installed in their palaces (*S.H.A., Verus* 4.5; *Comm.* 2.7).
61   Note again White's (1990: 114) point that the kind of edifices which the
Christians took over and transformed into church buildings are likely to have been
the same kinds of buildings that they had been in the habit of using as meeting
venues.

three couches.[62] The small inn is situated opposite the large hotel at VI.11.11-14, on the other side of the street.[63] There was a counter room at VII.1.44 and guest rooms at VII.1.45. The *triclinium* was probably the room behind the counter room. The advertisement of a *triclinium* was undoubtedly aimed at locals as well as travellers.

Small dining rooms were also obtainable in *popinae*.[64] These eating-houses were extremely popular. DeFelice has identified 94 such establishments in Pompeii.[65] Architecturally, *popinae* (or at least those known from Pompeii and elsewhere in Italy) are *tabernae*, with wide entrances leading to the street. The front room usually contained a counter, about 1.8 to 2.44 m long, with a pot of hot water, and shelves with food along the back wall.[66] The most basic type of *popina* had only one room; it functioned as a simple snack bar.[67] Customers would stand to eat and drink either inside the *popina* or in the street.[68] Larger *popinae*, though, had space for more private dining.[69] The *popina* at V.2.13 in Pompeii (see Fig. 29), which opened into the Via di Nola, had a small dining room, measuring c. 3.5 × 4 m, behind the main counter room.[70] Of similar plan is the structure at VI.14.35-36 (see Fig. 30), the so-called Inn of Salvius.[71] The secluded back room measures c. 4 × 4m. The most elaborate *popinae* offered guests several dining rooms. The *popina* at V.1.13 (see Fig. 31) had a dining room leading off the main shop room,

62   *Hospitium hic locatur triclinium cum tribus lectis* (CIL 4.807). That Sittius calls his place a *hospitium* shows that the terms *hospitium* and *caupona* were often interchangeable; cf. DeFelice 2001: 262.

63   DeFelice 2001: 262; Stambaugh 1988: 180–2.

64   The term *taberna* is sometimes applied to these establishments both in Roman literature and in modern scholarship (DeFelice 2001: 20). The words *popina* and *taberna* are used synonymously in *S.H.A., Had.* 16.4. To avoid confusion, I will stick with the word *popina* when referring to eating-places, and continue to use *taberna* with reference to the architecture in which *popinae* and many other small businesses were set.

65   DeFelice 2007: 483 n. 1.

66   DeFelice 2007: 475.

67   Sometimes a single-room *popina* is called by archaeologists a *thermopolium*. However, this term is not widely attested in the literature. DeFelice (2001: 20) points out that the term does not appear in ancient literature after the early second century BCE.

68   Casson 1974: 212.

69   Casson 1974: 212.

70   Packer 1978: 32–3.

71   Packer 1978: 33–6.

and another dining room, a more secluded one, behind that.[72] There was additionally a large open court that could also have been used for dining.

The quality of food served in *popinae* would not have been high (Horace refers to them 'greasy spoons'), but like today's fast-food restaurants, they catered to popular tastes. Sometimes, more sophisticated victuals were on offer (including goose liver pate, pork, cheese and pickled vegetables).[73] Foods were sometimes put on display in a bid to attract customers.

Seneca associates *popinae* with brothels and characterizes them as iniquitous spaces:

> Pleasure is something lowly, servile, weak, and perishable, whose haunt and abode are the brothel and the tavern (*popina*). Virtue you will find in the temple, in the forum, in the senate-house – you will find her standing in front of the city walls, dusty and stained, and with calloused hands (*De vita beata* 7.3).[74]

However, as DeFelice points out, this passage represents the values of an elite minority, and one cannot conclude from it that *popinae* were dens of iniquity.[75] Although Seneca links *popinae* with brothels, aside from amorous scribbles on the walls, there is little positively to indicate that sexual activity regularly occurred in such places.[76]

During the first century CE, emperors passed laws restricting the sale and/or display of certain foods and drink in *popinae*.[77] As Stambaugh states, 'There are many unresolved questions about the significance of these laws'.[78] At least partly, it seems, the restrictions were introduced to make eating-houses and drinking dens less attractive as association meeting places (cf. Dio Cassius 60.6.7), given the emperors' fear of associations.[79] The fact that the legislation had to be repeated seems to

72   Packer 1978: 37–43.
73   DeFelice 2001: 32.
74   Cf. *Ep.* 51.4.
75   DeFelice 2007: 479–80.
76   DeFelice 2007: 482.
77   Tiberius (Suetonius, *Tib.* 34) forbade the sale and display of baked products in *popinae*. Claudius (Suetonius, *Claud.* 38) at first relaxed restrictions imposed on *popinae* but subsequently issued an edict prohibiting the sale of meat and hot water in them (Dio Cassius 60.7.7). Despite patronizing the *popinae*, Nero renewed the ban on them (Suetonius, *Nero* 16; Dio Cassius 62.14.2), allowing only vegetables to be sold in them. Vespasian (Dio Cassius 65.10.3) similarly prohibited the sale of cooked meats in such establishments.
78   Stambaugh 1988: 365.
79   Hermansen 1981: 170.

suggest that it was not very successful. After Vespasian, there is no further legislation. As DeFelice points out, the prohibitions apparently had little effect on the many hospitality businesses in Pompeii.[80] He concludes that such establishments 'were perhaps never really excluded as gathering places for any length of time'.[81]

In *cauponae* and *popinae* customers often had to eat sitting at a table (Martial, *Ep.* 5.70.2-4). Two Pompeian inns have frescoes showing guests seated at a table.[82] But as we have seen, even a humble inn might have a *triclinium* proper, and larger and better-class establishments often had at least one.[83]

Business premises that were not formally hospitality establishments might also offer a dining room for rent. Mary Beard observes that the *triclinium* in the Bakery of the Chaste Lovers is so large that it must have been used by people other than the baker and his family. She thinks it likely that it was hired to groups for their dinner parties:

> Though not a restaurant in the modern sense of the word, this was probably a place where people paid to eat – with food either cooked in the kitchen adjacent or brought in from outside. It was not exactly glamorous surroundings. You would have reached the dining room either via the stable or by going past the bread oven and flour mills. But the room's decor was elegant enough, and it could certainly have accommodated more people than could easily be squeezed into the average living quarters of the poor.[84]

Beard suspects that such an arrangement may have been quite common, at least in Pompeii.

Rentable dining rooms could also be attached to private houses. Lawrence Richardson thinks the banquet hall and other facilities of

---

80   DeFelice 2001: 34. Hermansen (1981: 201), though, thinks that the prohi-bitions were enforced in Ostia. He points to the difference between Pompeii and Ostia in terms of bar counters.

81   DeFelice 2001: 34.

82   Frescos decorating the south wall of the rear room of the Caupona della Via di Mercurio (VI.10.1) show guests seated on stools. One depicts four patrons seated around a small round table, with food hanging on racks above them. Online: http://pompeiiinpictures.com/pompeiiinpictures/R6/6%2010%2001.htm. A fresco on the north wall of the counter room in the Inn of Salvius (VI.14.35-36) is divided into four scenes. In one scene, two customers seated on stools reach out their right hands to receive a cup of wine from a barmaid. In another, two men are seated on stools playing dice at a table. Online: http://www.pompeiiinpictures.eu/r6/6%2014%2036.htm. See further Balch 2012: 207–9; Weissenrieder 2012: 72–3.

83   DeFelice 2001: 32.

84   Beard 2008: 176.

Pompeii's Villa Imperiale could have been 'hired for an evening by a *collegium* or *sodalicum* that had no clubhouse of its own'.[85] Papyri from Oxyrhynchus, albeit dating to a later period than the first two centuries CE, bear witness to the rental of συμπόσια.[86] A συμπόσιον was a dining room in a private property.[87] Such dining rooms or *sumposia* may have been structurally linked to houses, but they seem to have functioned as separate units.[88] According to Richard Alston, some of the private invitations to dinner parties known from Oxyrhynchus, which appear to be to houses may have been 'to the dining rooms associated with those houses and not to the houses themselves'.[89]

2.3. *Rented Dining Rooms as Possible Christian Meeting Places*

Rentable dining rooms were probably widely available in the Roman world. Such rooms were commonly used for family and club dining. Basic dining rooms, such as those in low-end inns and *popinae*, would have been within economic reach of most early Christians. While a better-off believer might have acted as host, covering the cost of the meal and the hire of the room for the evening, one can also imagine a scenario in which each group member contributed more or less equally to the expenses.

Numerous associations, we have seen, met in temple dining rooms. Many other *collegia* met in dining space in inns and restaurants. Scribbles on the wall of an inn (V.2.4) on Via di Nola in Pompeii indicate that an association of fullers celebrated a festive event here.[90] Graffiti suggest that a Pompeian association of copyists or bookmakers used the dining facilities of the large hospitality business at I.2.24-26 for their banquets.[91]

Rentable dining rooms would certainly have been suitable in practical terms for meal meetings. However, it is extremely difficult to imagine believers engaging in Christian worship within the grounds of a 'pagan' temple (cf. 1 Cor. 8.10-13; 10.14-22).[92] Yet, dining halls that were the property of a temple were not always situated within the temple's

85   L. Richardson 1988: 197, 218–20.
86   See *P. Oxy.* 1129; 3203; 3600; 4832.
87   Alston 1997: 36.
88   Alston 1997: 36.
89   Alston 1997: 36.
90   Jashemski 1979: 179.
91   Jashemski 1979: 179. The building at I.2.24-26 was either a *hospitium* (DeFelice 2001: 186) or 'a restaurant with facilities for overnight guests' (Packer 1978: 12). It had two spacious internal dining rooms and also a large garden *triclinium*. See the description in Packer 1978: 12–18.
92   Cf. Dunn 2009: 602.

precincts. In Roman Tebtunis in Egypt, for example, dining rooms (*deipneteria*) operated by the Temple of Soknebtuinis were located on the street (the *dromos*) leading to the temple and not within the temple complex itself.[93] A dining room that was under the control of a temple but that was sited outside the temple compound might have appeared to some Christian groups an acceptable environment for their worship. *Popinae* may also seem unfitting locales for Christian meetings. Yet, as noted above, their reputation as dens of vice was probably much exaggerated, and while many *popinae* would have been busy and noisy places, ambiences no doubt varied. Presumably Christian worshippers would have avoided the more raucous *popinae*. A back room closed off from the main 'bar' area might have given a tolerable level of privacy. A rentable dining room attached to a bakery or a house would clearly have been a more felicitous setting. It is possible that a group of believers might have been able to lease a συμπόσιον (or the local equivalent) on a medium or long-term basis, which would have given them a relatively fixed and stable meeting place. Standard rentable dining rooms would have accommodated up to a dozen diners, and dining rooms in *popinae* may have held even fewer.[94] For larger groups, larger restaurant buildings and banquet halls would have been required.[95]

The advantage of meeting in a rentable dining room over against a small tenement flat would be the ability to worship in a setting properly equipped for dining. Most *tabernae* lacked a dining room and even a kitchen. Thus, even a group of Christians customarily meeting in shop or workshop space might have elected to meet, from time to time, in a proper dining facility.

3. *Bathhouses*

3.1. *Evidence for Bathhouses as Christian Meeting Places*
As we saw in Chapter 3, Justin's response in the *Martyrdom of Justin* to Rusticus' question about the meeting place of his group in Rome could be read as indicating that his school was located *within* the bathhouse above which he was staying rather than in his living quarters. In the Syriac version of the *Acts of Thomas*, the baptism of King Gundaphorus and his brother Gad takes place in a bathhouse (26-27):

93   Bagnall and Rathbone 2004: 149.
94   Dunbabin 2003: 95–6.
95   See Appendix 1 on the Roman Cellar Building in Corinth, which, if a restaurant, could have accommodated perhaps up to forty persons.

And the king gave orders that the bath should be closed for seven days
and that no man should bathe in it. And when the seven days were done,
on the eighth day they three entered in the bath by night that Judas might
baptise them. And many lamps were lighted in the bath.[96]

Thomas leads the two into the bathhouse and anoints them with oil.[97] He
baptizes them, and as they come out of the water, a young man (probably
Christ) appears to them holding a lighted holder, which shines brightly.
The Eucharist follows in the morning, and Thomas preaches a sermon.

Clear-cut historical evidence for Christian meeting in a bathhouse
comes from a later period. In the early fifth century, when John Chrysostom was exiled from Constantinople, his followers, having been
expelled from the church, celebrated Easter in the public baths.[98]

Possible archaeological evidence for the use of a bathhouse as a
Christian meeting place meeting is offered by the Church of S. Pudenziana in Rome (see Fig. 32), which incorporates as its core the basilica of
a *thermae* or bathing establishment.[99] Brick stamps found in situ suggest
that the bathhouse was built after 139 CE, perhaps in the middle of the
second century.[100] The bathhouse basilica was an oblong hall.[101] The
central nave was about 9 m wide and 27 m long, with curved ends. There
were six columns along each long side, and two at each curved end.
Arches spanned the spaces between the columns: seven on each long side
and three in each of the ends. The arches opened into vaulted ambula-
tories, approximately 4 m in breadth, surrounding the nave on all four
sides.[102] Along each long wall were seven windows, five of which survive on the north side and four on the south.[103] Originally the floor of the
nave of the basilica contained bath tanks, but in a subsequent renovation
the tanks were filled in and the nave was paved with mosaics featuring
marine creatures.[104] The structure of the bathhouse basilica was preserved
when the building was converted into a church edifice towards the end of

96   Translation from Klijn 2003: 75.
97   In the Greek text, baptism precedes the anointing.
98   Sozomen 8.21. Cf. Palladius, *Dialogue* 9; Socrates, *Ecclesiastical History*
6.18. Palladius reports that the catechumens were baptized. I owe these references to
Siri Sande
99   *CBCR* 3.277–302.
100   *CBCR* 3.288, 299.
101   *CBCR* 3.288, 297.
102   *CBCR* 3.291.
103   *CBCR* 3.290
104   *CBCR* 3.297.

the fourth century.[105] In the first phase of development, the western curved end of the basilica was turned into an apse with a mosaic.[106] The eastern end was turned into the main entrance, the curved end being replaced by lateral arches.[107] A façade was also created. In a second campaign of construction, in the sixth century,[108] the existing clerestory walls with their windows were built. The church building underwent substantial remodelling in the Romanesque era and again in the late sixteenth century.[109] An inscription in the apse mosaic indicates that the first phase of construction, which transformed the bathing complex into a church building, began in 387 or 390 and terminated in 398.[110] An epitaph that is no longer extant, but that was read and copied in the late sixteenth century, suggested that the *thermae* was already in use as the meeting place of a congregation – the *ecclesia Pudentiana* – in 384, i.e., *before the building was converted into an ecclesiastical edifice.*[111] Krautheimer points out that the Church of S. Pudenziana is 'the only instance surviving in Rome of the adoption by a Christian congregation of a Roman secular basilica – a *thermae* basilica in this case'.[112]

3.2. *Roman Bathhouses*

A practice borrowed from the Greeks, bathing in specially equipped bathhouses 'became the single most characteristic feature of Roman culture'.[113] According to Garrett Fagan, the Roman bathing habit grew steadily in the first century BCE and rose dramatically in the first century CE.[114] The Regionary Catalogues indicate that by the end of the fourth century, the number of baths in the city of Rome, excluding the grand imperial bathing centres, stood at 856.[115]

---

105   *CBCR* 3.297–301.
106   *CBCR* 3.293.
107   *CBCR* 3.294.
108   Krautheimer dates it 536–537.
109   *CBCR* 3.301
110   *CBCR* 3.279
111   *CBCR* 3.279. According to a legend recorded in the *Acta Pudentis* and found in the *Liber Pontificalis*, Pope Pius I dedicated a church to S. Pudentiana in the Baths of Novatianus at the request of her sister. However, one cannot be sure of the historical value of the story.
112   *CBCR* 3.301. The Church of S. Demetrius in Thessalonica was also partially built over a Roman bathhouse: Ferguson 2009: 830.
113   Claridge 1998: 54.
114   Fagan 1999: 74.
115   Yegül 1992: 30.

In ancient literature, Roman bathhouses are referred to interchangeably as *balnea* and *thermae*.[116] In scholarship on Roman baths, *thermae* is
used to refer to the large bathing complexes (especially the imperial
baths of Nero, Titus, Trajan, etc.), while *balneum/balnea* is applied to
smaller-scale bathhouses. Only the smaller *balnea* are credible as
Christian meeting places in the first two centuries. They were privately
owned establishments, but open to the public, while city authorities
owned and ran the large *thermae*.

Thermae were grand civic structures, often designed to display axial
symmetry.[117] *Balneae*, on the other hand, tended to be 'shaped by rudi-
mentary factors, such as economy and structural efficacy' and were
'susceptible to peculiarities of planning in response to a wide variety of
local conditions and accidents'.[118] The majority of *balneae* were asym-
metrical structures. A common type, sometimes called the 'Pompeian
type', involved a division into a bathing suite, with a row of parallel
rectangular rooms, and a colonnaded palaestra or exercise court.[119] The
design of the *balneum* known as the *Balnea Surae* exemplifies the type.[120]

The bathing zone typically consisted of a sequence of cold, tepid and
hot rooms, referred to as *frigidarium*, *tepidarium* and *caldarium* respectively.[121] A suite of bathing rooms would usually also include an
apodyterium, or changing room.

The Sarno Baths at Pompeii provide a good archaeological illustration
of a smaller city bathhouse. The complex has been studied in detail by
Ann Olga Koloski-Ostrow.[122] The Sarno Baths occupied the lower levels
of a multi-storeyed building, which was built against the southern cliff of
the city (see Fig. 33). The building comprises five surviving storeys
(there is evidence of a sixth storey, which was presumably made of
wood, above the highest extant level).[123] The whole complex contained
well over a hundred rooms (96 of which survive).[124] Luxury apartments

116   Yegül 2010: 48.
117   Yegül 1992: 3.
118   Yegül 1992: 66.
119   Yegül 1992: 66.
120   Yegül 1992: 66.
121   Yegül 1992: 3. It is usually assumed that the 'correct' bathing procedure
would have been to move through progressively hotter rooms and to end with a cold
plunge in the pool of the *frigidarium*, but as Beard (2008: 243) states, 'All kinds of
different pathways would have been possible'.
122   Koloski-Ostrow 1990; 2007: 239–40.
123   See Koloski-Ostrow 2007: 239–40.
124   Koloski-Ostrow 1990: 82.

took up the top tier, level 1 (and no doubt the lost one above it). The next level down, level 2, was apparently a service area, and the level below that, level 3 (see Fig. 34), contained further apartments. An extremely large room (room 84, c. 10 × 6 m) and other rooms (84, 87 [a *triclinium*]) on level 3 appear to have functioned as communal rooms, or a lounge area.[125] Koloski-Ostrow thinks that certain privileged bathhouse clients may have had special access to these rooms.[126]

The bathing zone, rooms 48-54, is concentrated on the west side of level 4 (see Fig. 35). The bathing rooms present 'a well-ordered block',[127] consisting of vestibule (48), *apodyterium* (50), *praefurnium* or furnace room (49), *tepidarium* (51), *caldarium* (52) and *frigidarium* (53) with plunge pool (54). The chambers were interconnected, allowing several possibilities for circulation.[128] The rooms had large windows, and at one level up, they were well positioned to receive the light of the sun as it passed across the southern sky. The bathing area would have enjoyed the warmth of the sun for much of the day throughout the year.

The *frigidarium*, room 53, is a rectangular room, which can be entered from both the vestibule and the *apodyterium*. On the southeast corner of the chamber, a door leads into corridor 55. At the north end of the room, there is a cold plunge pool, which is separated from the rest of the room by a low parapet. The main area of room 53 is divided by a brick arch. The *frigidarium* was elaborately decorated.[129] The walls and ceiling contain the best-preserved paintings in the whole building. A painting of a seated river god (taken to be Sarno, the river closest to Pompeii) occupies the central section of the north wall of the basin (54). The river god is flanked by caryatids and birds. A painting on the east wall portrays a warrior pouring water from a jug upon the head of a youth. On the ceiling above the east wall are two erotic mythological scenes: the myth of Hylas and that of Ganymede, both common in bathhouse decor.[130] Around the basin is a band depicting a Nilotic scene with pygmies.

A row of seven cubicles, rooms 56-62, runs southeast from the bathing suite. Each room measures 2.5–3.0 × 4m and has a low barrel-vaulted ceiling. It has been suggested that these cubicles served as brothels, but there is no clear evidence for this suggestion (in the form of graffiti or

125   Koloski-Ostrow 1990: 85.
126   Koloski-Ostrow 1990: 95–6.
127   Koloski-Ostrow 1990: 95.
128   Koloski-Ostrow 1990: 100.
129   Koloski-Ostrow 1990: 73–8.
130   Koloski-Ostrow 1990: 78.

erotic paintings). Koloski-Ostrow thinks that the rooms served, at least partly, as private changing rooms for more affluent bathers.[131]

The Sarno Baths lacked the typical *palaestra*. The siting of the building on a hillside no doubt made the inclusion of an exercise court impractical. The baths were accessible directly from the street, which indicates that they served the general public as well as those living in the apartments above. They were undergoing renovation at the time of the eruption, suggesting that they were not in service at the time.[132]

Bathing establishments were important foci of social life in towns and cities in the Roman world. As Nielsen puts it,

> Here one could meet friends, find dinner guests and wangle an invitation to dinner… Much of the life of the town went on in the baths, whose social importance can hardly be overestimated.[133]

As well as bathing, a range of secondary activities went on in bathhouses, especially the larger *thermae*, including sports, games and various entertainments (provided by jugglers, musicians, mime artists, etc.).[134] One might also eat and drink in the baths. It seems to have been quite common for people to enjoy a light snack in the baths before the evening meal.[135] Food and drink could be purchased in *popinae* located outside and brought into the bathhouse. Food items were also sold by hawkers who operated inside the baths.[136] Prostitutes evidently frequented certain baths,[137] but again one should not assume that prostitution was endemic in bathhouses. Like the Greek gymnasia, it is likely that large Roman bathing centres offered facilities for learning. Philosophers and rhetors 'probably met their students in exedrae and lecture rooms' in large bathing complexes.[138]

3.3. *Bathhouses as Possible Christian Meeting Places*
Bathhouses were virtually a *sine qua non* of Roman towns and cities. In Pompeii, there were at least nine bathing establishments available for public use.[139] In Ostia, three or four *thermae* and around twenty smaller

131   Koloski-Ostrow 1990: 95.
132   Koloski-Ostrow 2007: 238.
133   Nielsen 1990: 146.
134   Nielsen 1990: 144–6; Yegül 2010: 14–20.
135   Martial, *Ep.* 12.19. A graffito (CIL 4.10677) found in the Suburban Baths at Pompeii indicates that eating took place there.
136   Yegül 2010: 19.
137   Martial, *Ep.* 3.93.14; *Dig.* 3.2.4.2; cf. Nielsen 1990: 145.
138   Yegül 2010: 126; cf. Yegül 1992: 178
139   See Koloski-Ostrow 2007: 224.

balnea are known.[140] During the first two centuries, Christians apparently had no qualms about visiting the baths.[141] In *Apol.* 42, Tertullian explains that Christians are no different from other people in going to the Forum, the baths and the markets; he says that he himself uses the baths (at a decent and appropriate hour) for health reasons.[142] Since baths functioned as social centres, a bathhouse would have been a good place for local Christians to meet up informally (probably males with males and females with females).[143] A bathing establishment could hardly have served as a Christian worship setting during service hours. However, baths usually closed around dusk.[144] Thus, a room in a *balneum* would potentially have been available to a Christian group in the evening (or very early in the morning). Access to a bathhouse out of hours would have had to be by special arrangement with the *balneator*, who was responsible for running it.[145] This would no doubt have involved a monetary transaction (unless

140　Meiggs 1973: 406–20.

141　Ward 1992: 125–6. The letter written by representatives of the churches at Lyons and Vienne describing their suffering mentions, as one of the first actions taken against them, their exclusion from the baths (*H.E.* 5.1.5), implying that the Gallic Christians had been in the habit of frequenting them. Irenaeus (*Adv. Haer.* 3.3.4) tells of how the apostle John went to the baths at Ephesus and rushed out without bathing when he learned that Cerinthus was there. The *Acts of Andrew* has the apostle performing two exorcisms in a public bathhouse in Corinth (Gregory of Tours' *Epitome of the Acts of Andrew* 27). After driving out the demons, he bathes.

142　This raises the question of how Christians negotiated mixed bathing. Ward (1992) thinks that mixed bathing was universally practiced in this period and that Christians were indifferent towards it. More likely, as Fagan argues (1999: 27), practices varied from region to region and establishment to establishment. In Fagan's view, to a certain extent, whether or not one bathed in a mixed bathing environment was a matter of choice. Clement of Alexandria (*Paed.* 3.5. 9) is critical both of ostentation at the baths and the practice of men undressing before women and vice versa. He does not, however, prohibit Christians from going to the baths; he allows them to bathe for the sake of health and cleanliness but counsels against bathing for pleasure's sake and bathing too frequently. See Ward 1992: 142–3, and 143–6 for later Christian polemic against bathing in mixed company and bathing as a luxurious activity.

143　Members of an association might arrange to meet up in the baths before going to their banquet. The society of Diana and Antinous met in the baths before banqueting: see Smith 2003: 128.

144　Night-time bathing was rare. Usually, public baths were closed by imperial or municipal order before dusk. Alexander Severus is said to have donated oil for the lighting of baths so that they could be kept open at night (*S.H.A., Alex. Sev.* 24.6). However, the normal hours of opening were reinstated again by Emperor Tacitus so as to avoid nocturnal disturbances (*S.H.A., Tac.* 10.2). See Yegül 2010: 12.

145　Nielsen 1990: 127–8.

the *balneator* was himself a believer, or sympathetic to Christianity). Each member of the group could have contributed to the cost. Bath entrance fees were usually low and were not a significant source of revenue. Allowing a Christian group to use bathhouse space for their meetings may have been seen as a good way of making a little extra income.

As noted above, it is likely that teaching and other intellectual activities were carried out in some baths. Libraries and classrooms were common in the larger Greek gymnasia,[146] and it is probable that they featured in the imperial *thermae* in Rome.[147] The large Forum Baths at Ostia, which occupy a total area of 3200 square metres,[148] contain a series of rooms and halls that have been interpreted as lecture halls and classrooms.[149] There is no explicit evidence for classrooms in the smaller *balnea* of the Roman world, but since smaller bathing centres often tried to replicate on a smaller scale the amenities available in the larger *thermae*,[150] it is reasonable to suppose that some of the more substantial neighbourhood *balnea* might have had areas for intellectual pursuits. As noted in Chapter 3, the Baths of Sura in Rome are called a γυμνάσιον by Dio Cassius (68.15.3), which suggests teaching that went on there.

Religious activity did not, as a rule, take place in bathing complexes. However, a private religious cult requiring water for ritual purposes might conduct its water ritual/s in a public bath. Apuleius (*Met.* 11.23) tells how Lucius, prior to his initiation into the cult of Isis, was taken by the priest to the nearest public baths (*ad proximus balneas*) in Cenchraea to undergo purification.[151] A group of devotees escorted him from the temple of Isis to the baths. When he arrived at the bathhouse, he first took a normal bath. Then, having sought the blessing of the gods, the priest ritually sprinkled him with water, thus purifying him. Lucius and the group then returned to the temple.

In terms of adequacy, it has often been noted that baths would have been suitable for baptism.[152] Evidence indicates that natural bodies of water were the preferred setting for baptism in the first two centuries

146   When he was a teacher of rhetoric in Nicomedia, Libanius was allowed to hold classes anywhere, even in the baths (*Or.* 1.55). See Cribiore 2001: 34.
147   There is at least evidence for the existence of libraries in the imperial thermae: see Yegül 1992: 178–9.
148   Online: http://www.ostia-antica.org/regio1/12/12-6.htm.
149   Hermansen 1981: 84–5.
150   Cf. Fagan 1999: 66.
151   Ordinarily, sanctuaries of Isis and Sarapis would have included water facilities: see Wild 1981.
152   Nielsen 1990: 145.

(see the next chapter), but when a sea or river was not easily accessible, a bathhouse seems an obvious alternative, if Christians could gain use of it. A chamber in a bathhouse, such as the *frigidarium*, would also have been appropriate for Christian worship meetings. A *frigidarium* could take a variety of forms but was most commonly rectangular in shape, with a vaulted roof, and with a pool located at one end of the room, and sometimes with pools at both ends.[153] It was usually the largest and most finely decorated room in the baths. Because of its size, it was often used as a social room.[154] It could thus serve quite satisfactorily as a Christian meeting room.[155] The *frigidarium* in the Sarno baths (roughly 9 × 4 m, divided in middle by an arch) could have comfortably accommodated up to 40 persons. Food could be brought in for a communal meal. The décor of *frigidaria* and other bath rooms, with pagan religious scenes and sometimes erotic scenes, may not have been conducive to Christian worship, but as Balch has shown, such scenes often adorned the walls of ordinary houses.[156] A skilful preacher could have woven the scenes into a sermon.[157] Of course, the room would have had to be illuminated with oil lamps, but so would any indoor space at night.

The advantage of a bathhouse chamber as a meeting place would have been twofold: the capacity to hold larger numbers of people than most urban dwellings in large cities could contain; the provision of on-site facilities for baptism.

4. *Conclusion*

Evidence indicates or suggests the use of hotels and inns, rented dining rooms and bathhouses as early Christian meeting venues. As with *tabernae*, barns and warehouse cells, these space-types may be considered genuine spatial possibilities for early Christian gatherings. Hotels and inns largely catered to non-elite guests and so were socially accessible to early Christians. Lodging houses would have offered meeting spaces for Christians travelling together or Christians who were longer-term residents in them. Believers might have fellowshipped together in a guestroom or perhaps occasionally in a communal area of the hostelry. Rentable dining rooms could be found in hospitality and other small

153   Nielsen 1990: 153.
154   Nielsen 1990: 154.
155   So Sande 1999: 15.
156   Balch 2008.
157   Cf. Balch 2008: 84–108.

businesses as well as in private houses. They were rented out for private dinners and family celebrations and would often have been used by associations which had no meeting places of their own. As they were specially equipped for dining, they would have been appropriate for Christian meal meetings. Spaces in neighbourhood bathhouses would potentially have been available (for a fee) for Christian use out of business hours. It is likely that *balnea* were sometimes used for baptism, and a bathing chamber such as the *frigidarium* would have provided serviceable space for a worship gathering.

Chapter 8

OUTDOOR SPACES AND BURIAL PLACES

As Stambaugh points out, 'Roman cities tended to conduct their activities outdoors – parades and promenades of course, but also trials,
political meetings, elections, funerals, plays, buying and selling'.[1] Dining
too was 'always more pleasant' in the open air than indoors. Given this
'characteristic' preference for the open air, and the weather conditions to
encourage it, it seems reasonable to suppose that outdoor spaces might
be among the earliest Christian meeting places.[2] In this chapter, guided
as before by the literary evidence, we consider four possible contexts for
meeting outdoors: gardens; watersides; urban open space; burial sites.

1. *Gardens*

1.1. *Evidence for Gardens as Christian Meeting Places*
As was noted in Chapter 2, in Jn 18.2, we learn that the garden of Jesus'
arrest was a place where he met regularly with his disciples (cf. Lk.
22.39).[3]

In the Pseudo-Clementines, in the intermezzo in Tyre as recounted in
the *Homilies* (4.1–7.5), a tranquil garden is the setting of a theological/
philosophical discussion.[4] When Clement agrees to debate with Appion,
one of the latter's entourage (around thirty men) suggests that they all go
to his garden outside the city (4.10):

---

1   Stambaugh 1988: 198.
2   The open air has sometimes been suggested as a likely/possible early Christian
meeting place: e.g. Dunn 1996: 286; G.F. Snyder 2003: 128. G.F. Snyder (2003:
128) thinks that the meeting described by Pliny in *Ep.* 117 is an open-air meeting,
but this is not explicitly indicated in the text.
3   See p.48, above.
4   As noted by Klauck 2008: 206.

> Accordingly they went forth, and sat down in a place where there were
> pure streams of cool water, and a green shade of all sorts of trees. There I
> sat pleasantly, and the others round about me…

Clement delivers a long discourse, and Appion promises to reply the next
day (4.24-25). The following day, Clement returns to the garden, where
Appion's friends and others are already gathered, but Appion himself
fails to show (5.1). Clement nevertheless engages in discussion with
those who have turned up. On the third day, Clement and his companions
go back to the garden, where Appion is waiting with two of his companions and 'many other learned men' (6.1). Appion and Clement debate
until news of Peter's arrival in Tyre causes the discussion to break up
(6.26).

When Peter arrives in Tripolis, he stays with Maro (*Rec.* 4.1-2). The
apostle asks Maro where there is a suitable place to address the crowds.
Maro replies:

> I have a very spacious hall which can hold more than five hundred men,
> and there is also a garden within the house; or if it please you to be in
> some public place, all would prefer it, for there is nobody who does not
> desire at least to see your face (*Rec.* 4.6).

Peter views the hall and then goes into the garden. At that moment, the
crowds rush into the house, breaking through to the garden. Peter mounts
a pillar near the garden wall and addresses the multitude (4.7). After
giving his speech, he dismisses the crowd, but invites them to return the
next day. He then orders couches to be spread in the shaded part of the
garden, where he dines with his inner circle. Peter's companions sit
according to their rank, and he converses with them concerning the
miracles of Christ, until night falls, at which time they all retire to their
bedchambers (4.37). Early the next morning Peter proceeds to the garden
where many are already assembled, and he teaches them (5.1). At the end
of the discourse, he lays hands on those who are ill or oppressed by
demons. When the crowd leaves, Peter washes himself in waters running
through the garden. Again, he commands that the couches be spread on
the ground, and they recline in order (5.36):

> And thus, having taken food and given thanks to God after the manner of
> the Hebrews, as there was yet some portion of the day remaining, he
> ordered us to question him on any matters that we pleased. And although
> we were with him twenty in all, he explained to every one whatever he
> pleased to ask of him; the particulars of which I set down in books and
> sent to you some time ago. And when evening came we entered with him
> into the lodging, and went to sleep, each one in his own place.

The following day Peter repeats the procedure, teaching the crowds assembled in the garden, and then, after the crowds have gone, dining and conversing with his companions in the garden till bedtime. The pattern continues for three months (6.15).

1.2. *Roman Gardens*

If Pompeii was broadly representative of Roman urban centres, green spaces were plentiful in and around them. By means of pioneering garden archaeology, Jashemski identified remains of approximately 626 gardens in Pompeii, Herculaneum and the surrounding area.[5] Some were attached to large public buildings, such as baths and temples. Some were in or connected to private structures such as houses, *tabernae* and larger industrial premises. Others (including vineyards and orchards) were independent or semi-independent configurations.

In the previous chapter, we saw that hospitality businesses often had a garden area where customers could dine and relax. Thus the *hospitium* known as the House of Sallust, the large hotel at VII.11.11-14, and the *caupona* of Euxinus in Pompeii all had gardens equipped or suitable for outdoor dining and socializing. The latter is an example of what Jashemski calls a 'garden restaurant'. Jashemski states that 'The garden restaurants and inns in Pompeii are many'.[6] A large number were located in the area around the Amphitheatre and the Great Palaestra. The large garden restaurant at II.3.7/9 (see Fig. 36), which was originally part of the garden of the House of Venus Marina but which had been separated from it, was strategically positioned directly across from the Palaestra.[7] A vineyard opposite the Amphitheatre contained two triclinia, one at the entrance and another further within.[8] Jashemski states of this place: 'the unknown vintner must have enjoyed a rushing business when the games were held'.[9] A very large garden (II.9.6/7) to the west of the Amphitheatre contains the most elaborate garden *triclinium* so far discovered in Pompeii.[10] The garden was linked to a building that was probably a *caupona*.[11] The *triclinium* was covered by a pergola supported by four large columns (see Fig. 37). In front of the *triclinium* were two richly decorated fountains facing each other. Balch reckons that if only a

---

5 Jashemski 2007: 487.
6 Jashemski 1979: 177.
7 Jashemski 1979: 176; 1993: 85
8 Jashemski 1979: 176.
9 Jashemski 1979: 176.
10 Jashemski 1979: 176; 1993: 97.
11 Jashemski 1979: 176.

quarter of this garden were open to customers, a crowd of around 220 could have been accommodated.[12] On a somewhat smaller scale was the garden restaurant at II.8.2-3.[13] Customers could be served in the counter or room or in an attractive garden at the rear. The garden measured c. 25 × 8 m. A *triclinium* was built against the north wall at the entrance into the garden. A hearth in the south wall of the garden would have been used to cook food served there. A small *caupona* next door (II.8.4-5) had a little garden with six small *triclinia*, three on each side facing each other.[14] The masonry couches of these *triclinia* were so small that they were probably used as seats rather than for reclining.

1.3. *Gardens as Possible Christian Meeting Places*

Gardens used for commercial dining 'were apparently available for hire for public or semipublic festivities'.[15] As non-elite venues, such gardens would have been within the economic grasp of a Christian group, especially if each member contributed towards the cost of hire for an evening's meeting. The regular or occasional use of an ordinary grove or vineyard (without dining facilities) on the edge of a town or city might have been obtainable for a modest fee. It is possible that a church member owned or rented a sizeable garden that could have been used for gatherings. In Pompeii, a large garden (c. 21 × 27 m) was attached to a humble *taberna* (I.20.5, see Fig. 28).[16] The *taberna* had a front room and two rear rooms, and a stairway in the second room led to mezzanine (what was sold and/or made in the shop/workshop cannot be deter-mined). The garden was entered only through a door on the west side of the *taberna*; it was thus clearly under the control of the family occupy-ing the *taberna*.[17] There were walls on all sides. The walled garden, excavated by Jashemski in 1971–72, was 'intensively planted in trees, vines, and vegetables' and 'enabled the family to produce their own wine and fruit'.[18] It is likely that a surplus, especially of wine, was produced and sold by the proprietor for profit. Broken amphorae were discovered along the top of the north wall to deter thieves. There were two unplanted areas within the garden, one on the east side and the other, the larger, at the rear. The former was a working area (as indicated by object finds); the latter apparently served a recreational purpose. Objects discovered,

12   Balch 2012: 227. He measures the garden as a whole at c. 35 × 35 m.
13   Jashemski 1979: 177–78; 1993: 92.
14   Jashemski 1979: 178; 1993: 92.
15   Dunbabin 1991: 125.
16   Jashemski 1979: 188–94.
17   Jashemski 1979: 188.
18   Jashemski 1979: 193.

including a tripod for cooking and fragments of pottery and dishes, indicate that meals were prepared and eaten here. Animal bones and teeth were probably the remnants of meals. Lamps were also discovered in this area, suggesting that 'the family lingered in the cool of the garden after dark'.[19] An open area like this would have given good meeting space.

Gardens were natural locations for the practice of private religion.[20] Many of the *lararia* discovered in Pompeian houses, *tabernae*, inns, etc., were found in the garden area/s of these buildings.[21] As noted in the previous chapter, the *caupona* of Euxinus contained two altars, apparently for the use of patrons. A modest peristyle garden in Pompeii (II.1.12) was the meeting place of a cult of Sabazius, one of the most popular mystery cults in the Roman world.[22] The garden was entered through a wide vestibule.[23] A masonry altar stood in front of a large room at the rear of the garden that had been turned into a *sacellum*. The cult-room was closed by a shutter. To the left of the *sacellum* were two store-rooms, and to the right were two cubicles in which cult objects were discovered. Two of these objects were near life-size bronze hands, recognizable as mantic hands associated with the worship of Sabazius. A seated figure of Sabazius rests in the palm of one of the hands. Excavations indicated the existence of a row of four trees at the side of the altar, which would have provided shade, while leaving 'plenty of room for the worshippers who attended the sacrifices'.[24]

Gardens had acquired a reputation as places suited to the teaching and learning of philosophy. Diogenes states of Plato that 'he pursued philosophy at first in the Academy, then in the garden by the Kolonos as Alexander says in his *Diadochai*, καθ' 'Ηράκλειτον'.[25] The school of Epicurus, of course, was set in a garden.[26] The philosophical associations of gardens were still reverberant in the Roman imperial era, as seen

19   Jashemski 1979: 193.
20   On religion in the gardens of Pompeii, see Jashemski 1979: 115–40.
21   Jashemski (1979: 121) regards statues of the gods discovered in Pompeian gardens as further evidence of worship in them.
22   Clement of Alexandria (*Protrep.* 2.162) describes the initiation into the mysteries of Sabazius.
23   For a full description of the garden, see Jashemski 1979: 135–7; cf. 1993: 76. Descriptive details in the main text are taken from Jashemski.
24   Jashemski 1993: 76.
25   Diogenes 3.5; cf. Cicero, *Fin.* 5.1-2; Apuleius 1.100; see Wycherley 1962: 3.
26   Wycherley 1962: 15. His garden, like Plato's, was apparently a little one (Cicero, *Fin* 5.3); according to Apollodoros, whom Diogenes (10.10) quotes, it cost him only eighty minae. Cicero (*Fin.* 1.65) seems to indicate that Epicurus' house was his base of operation. The house and garden were probably adjacent properties: so Wycherley 1962: 16.

from the garden scenes depicted in the Pompeian *taberna*-school at IX.8.2.[27]

Gardens were also conventional sites for collegial dining. At Parma, an *eques Romanus* bequeathed a cultivated garden to his *sodales* that they might spend the return on the land on an annual feast to be held in the garden itself.[28] Commercial hospitality gardens were probably often rented out to associations that had no clubhouse of their own.[29]

A garden would have been a very suitable setting for a Christian meeting. It was appropriate for worship, teaching, and eating and drinking. If there was no *triclinium*, which would only have accommodated a fraction of the congregation in any case, believers could recline or sit on cushions, which were perfectly acceptable for outdoor dining.

A garden could potentially offer a great deal more space for meeting than could the interior of a house. A garden would also have been a much more pleasant place to meet in warm weather. A completely walled garden would have given privacy to the meeting within it (though a garden that was partially open or that could easily be viewed by passers-by would have offered less freedom from the attention of others: see Appendix 1).

Gardens are thus highly plausible candidates as early Christian meeting places, satisfying our criteria of availability, analogous usage, adequacy and advantageousness.

2. Watersides

2.1. Evidence for Watersides as Christian Meeting Places
The seaside (or more correctly lakeside), as we have seen, is a recurring setting of Jesus' teaching in the Synoptic Gospels, especially Mark (Mk 2.13; 3.9; 4.1). The two mass feedings in Mark also take place near the sea (Mk 6.32-45; 8.1-10). In John's Gospel, Jesus' final post-resurrection meeting with his disciples takes the form of a 'picnic breakfast' on the shore (Jn 21). In the book of Acts, Paul's farewell meeting with the Ephesian elders in Miletus appears to be located at the harbour (Acts 20.36-38). In a subsequent episode in Acts, Paul and the believers at Tyre pray at the beach, before the apostle boards the ship for Ptolemais (21.5).

---

27   Also, the famous mosaic from the villa of T. Siminius Stephanus, Pompeii, depicts Plato and his students. Plato is seated under a tree, suggesting a garden. See Balch 2012: 222.
28   Donahue 2004: 39.
29   Dunbabin 2003: 95.

In *Acts of Peter* 3, Paul is escorted to the harbour by a great crowd, which includes women, a nobleman, and a senator. The threat of a storm postpones his departure. Paul sends the brothers back to Rome to tell the believers who had remained in the city that if they wish to hear him speak, they can come to the harbour. A large number make their way. At the harbour, Paul strengthens them over a period of three days. On the fourth day, they pray with Paul until he boards ship. In the *Epitome of the Acts of Andrew*, Andrew walks with Lesbius to the shore at Patras. They sit down, with others, on the sand, and Andrew proceeds to teach them (24). In the *Clementine Recognitions*, Peter and his entourage go in the morning to the harbour to bathe in the sea. Having bathed, they find a secluded spot to pray. They return to the same place for the purpose of prayer the next morning (8.37).[30]

In early Christian narrative texts, baptism is frequently depicted as taking place in open bodies of water outdoors.[31] In the Synoptic Gospels, Jesus is baptized in the Jordan River (Mk 1.9-11 par.). The Fourth Gospel locates John the Baptist's baptizing activity on the east bank of the Jordan (Jn 1.28; 3.26; 10.40) and also at Aenon, where 'water was abundant' (3.23). In the book of Acts, the Ethiopian eunuch is baptized in a body of water along the road from Jerusalem to Gaza (Acts 8.36-38). The *Acts of Paul* contains the famous story of Paul's baptism of a lion. The baptism occurs in 'a great river'.[32] In *Acts of Peter* 5, during the voyage from Caesarea to Puteoli, Peter baptizes the ship's captain, Theon, in the sea. The baptism takes place when the ship reaches calm waters in the Adriatic. Peter and Theon go down into the water by rope, Theon receives baptism, and the two go back up into the boat. In the *Epitome of the Acts of Andrew*, Andrew finds a sick man 'full of ulcers and worms' lying on the shore in Patras (33). The apostle commands the man in Christ's name to rise and follow him. He does so, and the two go into the sea. We read that 'the apostle washed him in the name of the Trinity'. The healed man then runs naked through city proclaiming God. In the *Acts of Thomas*, the apostle rescues a beautiful woman tormented by a demon (42-50). She asks for the seal, which the apostle confers upon her. In the Syriac text, we are told that Thomas 'went to a river which was close by there, and baptised her in the name of the Father and the Son and the Spirit of holiness, and many were baptised with

---

30 The philosophical debate with the old man, who turns out to be Clement's father, takes place at 'a quiet recess near the harbour' (*Rec.* 8.3).

31 Jensen 2010: 129–32.

32 See the Coptic fragment Schneemelcher 1992: 263–5.

her' (49).[33] The baptism of Mygdonia takes place in a spring (121). In the Pseudo-Clementines, at the end of Peter's three-month period of ministry at Tripolis, Clement receives baptism 'in the fountains which adjoin the sea' (*Rec.* 6.15; cf. *Hom.* 11.35). At the same location, Peter baptizes those 'who had fully received the faith of the Lord', and celebrates a post-baptismal Eucharist with them there. Clement's mother, Mattidia, is baptized in the sea at Laodicea (*Rec.* 7.38; *Hom.* 14.1). The baptism takes place early in the morning in a sheltered spot between two rocks so that she may be baptized 'without attracting observation' (*Hom.* 14.1).

The *Didache* teaches that baptism should ideally be administered in 'running water' (7.1), by which is meant flowing water, as in springs, streams, rivers and seas.[34] According to Tertullian (*De Bapt.* 4.3), 'it makes no difference whether a man be washed in a sea or a pool, a stream or a fount, a lake or a trough'. The range of options presumes that baptism often takes place in open bodies of water.[35] The *Apostolic Tradition* (21.1-2, as represented by the *Testamentum Domini*) dictates that baptism should take place in 'pure and flowing' water. A natural body of water – sea, river, lake – would thus seem to have been the most regular and desirable setting for baptism in the early period.[36]

2.2. *Watersides as Possible Christian Meeting Places*

Watersides in general terms meet the criterion of availability. Many ancient cities were built near bodies of waters. Urban Christians would thus often have lived in close proximity to a sea, river or lake.

Watersides also satisfy as potential Christian meeting places on the grounds of analogous usage. Watersides were popular picnic spots. In Homer's *Odyssey*, Nausicaa and her handmaids enjoy a picnic meal prepared by her mother, as they wait by the river for their washing to dry.[37] For Lucretius (*de rerum* 2.29-31), one of life's pleasures was 'to lounge with friends in the soft grass beside a river of water, underneath a big tree's boughs, and merrily to refresh our frames, with no vast outlay'. Pliny (*Ep.* 4.30) speaks of dining often by a natural spring in Comum,

---

33   Translation from Klijn 2003: 123.

34   In the absence of running water, 'cold' or 'warm' water can be used, and if neither is available, then water may poured over the head of the baptisand (*Did.* 7.2-3). By 'cold' water, standing water, as in ponds and lakes, is probably in view, and by 'warm' water, stored water (in a bath or mikveh) may be in mind. Cf. Ferguson 2009: 204.

35   Jensen 2010: 130.

36   Cf. Jensen 2010: 130.

37   Homer, *Od.* 6.76-8, 97-9. Cf. Burton 1998: 153.

which ran through an artificial grotto. Waterside picnics are frequently depicted in Roman art.[38]

Watersides were appropriate sites for philosophizing. The setting of Plato's dialogue *Phaedrus* is the river Ilissos on the outskirts of Athens. Socrates reclines with Phaedrus on the riverbank, and the two engage in philosophical discussion. Religious festivals often took place at open water. The feast of the Roman goddess Anna Perenna on the Ides (15th) of March was celebrated on the banks of the Tiber.[39] In his description of the festival, Ovid tells how couples, some in the open air, others in the shelter of tents or makeshift huts, would drink wine and pray. As we saw in Chapter 5, there is good evidence to indicate that watersides were customary Jewish meeting places.[40]

Watersides would have been adequate locales for Christian assembly. They were suitable for prayer, teaching and (picnic) dining. With regard to advantageousness, like gardens, they were *loci amoeni*. Moreover, they offered potentially unrestricted meeting space. Meetings by water would have been open to public view, though presumably Christian groups would have chosen a secluded waterside spot outside the town or city.

3. *Urban Open Spaces*

3.1. *Evidence for Urban Open Spaces as Christian Meeting Places*
In all four Gospels, but especially in the Fourth Gospel, Jesus teaches in the precincts of the Jerusalem temple. On one occasion in John's Gospel, he is shown debating with the Jewish leaders in Solomon's Portico (Jn 10.23-42). In the book of Acts, the temple is the setting for Peter's early preaching (explicitly in Acts 3.1–4.3) and the place where members of the growing community of believers come together (2.46; 5.42). Solomon's Portico is identified as the specific area of the temple in which believers regularly gather (5.12). Paul's claim in Acts 20.20 to have taught the Ephesians 'publicly', it was argued in Chapter 2, is probably to be understood as indicating his use of urban open space, most likely the marketplace, as a teaching locale during his founding mission in Ephesus.[41]

---

38   Dunbabin 1991: 134.
39   Ovid, *Fasti* 3. See Donahue 2004: 58.
40   Thus, they might have been favoured particularly by Jewish-Christian groups.
41   Celsus (Origen, *C. Cels.* 3.50, 52) indicates that Christians evangelized in the marketplaces ('We see those who display their secret lore in the market-places'). Later, Cyprian tells us that he preaches 'openly, and publicly, and in the very market-place' (*ad Demetr.* 13).

3.2. *Urban Open Spaces as Possible Christian Meeting Places*
Urban open space – streets, forum, city gates, etc. – was freely available
and accessible space. Urban Christians, like all other urbanites, frequented
marketplaces.[42] Christians would no doubt have sometimes clustered
informally in streets and squares (unless local hostility towards them
made that unwise). Lucian (*Double Indictment* 6) complains that 'the
public walks are full of people assembling in companies and battalions'.

Urban open spaces were established pedagogical sites. Elementary
teaching often took place in the streets. According to Livy (6.25.8-9),
when Camilius entered Tusculum, he found 'the shops with their shutters
off and all their wares exposed, the craftsmen all busy at their respective
trades, the schools buzzing with the voices of the scholars, crowds in the
street'. Dio Chrysostom (*Or.* 20.9) tells how 'The elementary teachers sit
in the streets with their pupils, and nothing hinders them in this great
throng from teaching and learning'.[43] Another conventional locale for
primary teaching was a *trivium* or *quadrivium*, a place where three or
four streets met. It was at such a spot that Dionysius II was forced to
teach when he came to Corinth, after his exile from Syracuse.[44] Horace
(*Ep.* 1.20), addressing his first book of *Epistles*, as it is about to be published, wonders whether it will end up being used as elementary reading
material for boys 'at the ends of the streets' (*extremis in vicis*), i.e., at the
trivium or *quadrivium*. As Bonner points out, the *trivium* was hardly a
salubrious teaching venue:

> It was a place of noise and bustle, where friends met and gossiped, and
> rowdies argued and exchanged abuse; it was frequented by quacks
> peddling their wares, parasites angling for an invitation, vagabonds,
> fortune-tellers, and itinerant musicians.[45]

42   Tertullian, *Apol.* 42; Eusebius, *H.E.* 5.1.5. Christian references among the
recently discovered (in 2003) graffiti of the basement level of the basilica in the
agora of Smyrna offer epigraphic evidence of the presence of Christians in public
city space. On the graffiti, see Bagnall 2010: 7–26. The graffiti date to a period from
the late first/early second century to the third quarter of the second century (8). The
graffito that is most clearly Christian in character (collocating 'lord' and 'faith'), in
Bagnall's view (22), should be dated before 125 CE. The basilica basement contained
shops, a long corridor and naves with pillars and arches (8) and may have served as
an extension of the forum (24).

43   See Bonner 1972: 516. A teacher who plied his trade in such circumstances
was known as a *chamaididaskalos* or 'ground-teacher', a term equated in the
glossaries with *ludi magister*.

44   *Justinus* 21.5. Cf. Bonner 1977: 166.

45   Bonner 1977: 117. Quintilian refers disdainfully to *trivialis scientia*, knowledge acquired at the *trivium* (cf. the English words 'trivia' and 'trivial').

Elementary teaching also went on in public arcades and porticos. A famous painting discovered in the atrium of the *Praedia* of Julia Felix in Pompeii, depicts a teaching scene in a portico. A boy, held in position by two of his schoolmates, is shown receiving a beating. Three pupils sit on a bench with books or tablets on their laps. Behind are passers-by who have stopped to look at what the boys are reading. The schoolmaster stands at the side. The location is thought to be the Pompeian Forum portico near the temple of Apollo.[46] Another wall painting of the same series shows a street teacher sitting on a bench in front of a column, with a book open, and a young boy gazing up at him.

Porticoes, among other urban public places, were also typical settings for higher education.[47] Justin locates his dialogue with Trypho in the colonnades of Xystus in Ephesus.[48] According to Vitruvius (5.11.2), stoas typically have recesses or exedrae where philosophers and rhetoricians may teach (5.11.2). One would not normally expect to see a teacher of advanced learning holding classes in streets and street corners, but as Rafaela Cribiore notes, 'teachers of advanced education were at the mercy of the available accommodations and had to provide for themselves as much as the humble primary teachers'.[49]

Christians could not claim the elite public teaching spaces occupied by philosophers and rhetors.[50] Thus, a Christian missionary would not be able to set up pitch in the exedra of a colonnade in the forum. However, it would surely have been possible for a Christian teacher to sit in the street, on a street corner, or at the corner of the marketplace with a small group of disciples.

46 García y García 2005: 59.
47 The Stoa was a traditional site of teaching in Athens. Tradition places Socrates in stoas (Pseudo-Plato, *Theages* 121a; Xenophon, *Oecon.* 7.1; Pseudo-Plato, *Eryxias* 392a; see Wycherley 1961: 158). The stoa was a preferred didactic location for Cynics and especially Stoics. Zeno chose the Painted Stoa at Athens as the site for his school (Wycherley 1953: 33). Alciphron (depicting life in Athens in the fourth century BCE, but writing around 200 CE) portrays a fisherman who is trying to sell his catch listening to a philosopher declaim in the Stoa (1.3.2). A thief seeking a place to consume his stolen food enters the Painted Stoa at a time 'when it was not infested by any chattering philosophers' (3.53.2). Lucian in *Zeus Tragoedus* depicts a philosophical debate between Damis the Epicurean and Timocles the Stoic in the Painted Stoa, with a large audience gathered around (4-5, 16-18, 35-51).
48 Justin, *Trypho* 1.1; 9.3. Cf. Telbe 2009: 118.
49 Cribiore 2001: 34.
50 Alexander 1994: 81.

Such non-elite urban open spaces, of course, would not have been suitable for prayer, worship or the Eucharistic meal. They only come into question as possible Christian meeting places as venues for small-group teaching, and they would have fulfilled that function quite adequately.

The advantage of such sites as teaching spots, over against the more private environment of houses and dwellings, is that they would have offered a better opportunity for recruitment. Whether at elementary or higher level, teaching a group of students in open public view drew in curious onlookers.[51] As Rihll states, 'When teaching took place in public spaces, anyone in or moving through the area could, in principle, form the audience, for as much of the presentation as they liked'.[52] The presence of onlookers (though not hecklers) was usually welcomed since it was a means of gaining new students. Giving Christian instruction to insiders in public places where outsiders would also be present would thus been an indirect (and less confrontational) way of proselytizing.[53]

4. *Burial Sites*

4.1. *Evidence for Burial Sites as Early Christian Meeting Places*
In *Acts of Paul* 3.23-27, Paul fasts with Onesiphorus, his wife and children 'in a new tomb' over a period of six days. Thecla finds Paul at the tomb. As she enters, she hears Paul praying that she might be saved from the fire. She responds with a prayer of thanksgiving for her deliverance. When Paul stands up and sees her, he in turn thanks God for the speedy answer to his prayer. The text continues:

> And there was great love in the tomb as Paul and Onesiphorus and the others all rejoiced. And they had five loaves and vegetables and water, and they rejoiced in the holy works of Christ (*Acts of Paul* 3.25).

The account of John's second stay in Ephesus in the *Acts of John* (62-86) is taken up with events surrounding Drusiana, the wife of Andronicus, and much of the story is set in her tomb. Drusiana dies in the presence of John (64) and is entombed. Callimachus, who has fallen in love with

---

51   Galen presumes a context in which philosophers teach in public and can be interrupted by listeners and passers-by (*On the Passions and Errors of the Soul* 3-5).

52   Rihll 2003: 173.

53   Alexander (1994: 81) argues that the two-tier pattern of instruction we find in Hellenistic schools, with instruction given to insiders, with the expectation that outsiders would also be present, would have been replicated in the early churches, though she thinks this would have taken place privately in houses.

Drusiana, bribes Fortunatus, the steward of Andronicus, to let him into the tomb so that he may have sexual intercourse with her corpse. As he is about to perform the heinous act, a serpent suddenly appears and kills Fortunatus; it then pins down Callimachus, who soon dies too. John and the brethren arrive at the tomb at dawn so that they can break bread there (72). When they enter the sepulchre, they are greeted by an angel, who tells John that he is to raise Drusiana. The angel disappears, and they discover the bodies of Callimachus and Fortunatus (73). Andronicus works out what has happened and informs John. The apostle raises Callimachus (75-76), who also undergoes a spiritual renewal (78). Drusiana and Fortunatus are then brought back to life (80-83), but the latter runs from the tomb and quickly dies again. John celebrates the Eucharist in the tomb, and when all have partaken of it, they leave the sepulchre (86). The extent to which action in this long stretch of the narrative takes place in the tomb strongly suggests to Kathleen Corley 'the author's familiarity with tombs as a venue for Christian gatherings'.[54]

There is archaeological evidence from the later third and early fourth centuries for Christian dining at burial sites. A *triclia*, a walled structure used for banquets, was discovered in the catacomb area underneath the Church of S. Sebastiano in Rome. Many graffiti (around 222) are scribbled on the walls,[55] especially the east wall. The graffiti are clearly Christian and date between 260 and 320 CE.[56] A number make mention of a *refrigerium* or funerary banquet. Evidently *refrigeria* were eaten here for deceased members of the family. Peter and Paul are frequently invoked in prayers for the family dead. A number of frescoes depicting Christian banquets are to be found in the Catacombs of SS. Marcellino e Pietro.[57] These paintings date to the late third or early fourth century. The meals portrayed are almost certainly funerary meals (though probably with Eucharistic features). Banqueters are shown dining *stibadium* (or sigma)-style, seated in a semi-circle. Female figures are prominent in eight of the paintings. The words *Agape* and *Irene* appear in seven of them.[58] These words may have been spoken as part of a funerary toast.[59]

---

54   Corley 2010: 60. Corley (61–2) takes the dance hymn of 94–96 as a hymn that 'would have been composed more specifically for early Christian worship in funerary contexts rather than as a more general dance accompanied by song'.

55   G.F. Snyder 2003: 251–8.

56   G.F. Snyder 2003: 256.

57   Tulloch 2006.

58   Tulloch 2006: 174.

59   Tulloch 2006: 186–91.

A funerary epitaph of a Christian woman (Aelia Secundula), dating to 299 CE, gives an account of a Christian funerary banquet.[60] It describes the setting up of a stone table, the placement of food and drink on it, and the recounting of stories about the deceased until 'a late hour'.[61]

4.2. *Tombs and Tombside Dining Facilities in the Roman World*

Burial sites were generally situated outside towns and cities.[62] Tombs often lined roads leading to city gates. At Pompeii, monumental and humble tombs (along with luxurious villas and small *tabernae*) can be seen along the road leading out of/into the Porta de Ercolano, known as the Street of the Tombs.[63] Tombs have also been discovered outside other Pompeian gates (Porta di Nocera, Porta del Vesuvio, Porta di Nola and Porta di Stabia).[64] At Ostia, many tombs have been excavated along the ancient roads leading to the Porta Romana and the Porta Laurentina. A large necropolis, the Isola Sacra Necropolis, was discovered along the road that ran between Portus and Ostia.[65]

Roman tomb structures varied enormously. Pompeii provides examples of a number of tomb-types paralleled at other sites: multi-storey *aedicula* tombs; podium tombs supporting a circular structure; tombs with an altar on a podium; tombs with a prominent niche in the façade; tombs with multiple niches for funeral urns to be stored.[66] The tombs of the poor were simply urns buried in the ground marked by epitaphs cut into city walls. A set of funerary inscriptions appears on a stretch of Pompeii's city walls between the Sarno Gate and the Nola Gate.[67] These appear to be linked to cinerary urns found nearby.

The tomb was the traditional site of the various funerary meals called for by Roman domestic religion.[68] A meal was celebrated on the day of burial (*silicernium*) and then on the ninth day after the funeral (*cena novendalis*). The latter signalled the end of the formal period of mourning.

60   Jensen 2008: 124–5.
61   Jensen 2008: 125–6.
62   Cremation, it seems, was the standard Roman burial practice in the first century CE, but from the second century onward, inhumation became more common: Stambaugh 1988: 196.
63   Jashemski 1979: 141.
64   Jashemski 1979: 141.
65   Jashemski 1979: 141.
66   Cormack 2007: 588–9. A tomb-type distinctive to Pompeii is the *schola* tomb, which is a semicircular bench supporting a large column: Cormack 2007: 586. For a detailed review of Roman tomb-types, see Toynbee 1971: 101–244.
67   CIL 10.8349-61. See Cooley and Cooley 2004: 154.
68   Jensen 2008.

Another funerary meal could take place on the fortieth day after death. After that, meals were held annually on the deceased's birthday (*dies natalis*) and during the festival for the commemoration of ancestors (the *parentalia*), from 13 to 21 February.

Some tombs were equipped with dining facilities. The tomb of Gnaeus Vibrius Saturninus (see Fig. 29), on the Street of Tombs in Pompeii was an unroofed enclosure (though perhaps it was originally roofed) with a masonry *triclinium* much like the outdoor *triclinia* found in many domestic gardens in the city.[69] There was a table in the middle, and in front of the table was a small altar for offerings to the deceased. The walls of the enclosure were decorated with plants, animals and birds. Fixed *triclinia*, together with ovens and wells for food preparations, have also been found in Ostia.[70] Fixed dining facilities, though, were not necessary for tombside feasting. The funerary banquet was essentially a picnic, so a table and chairs could be brought to the tomb, or diners might sit on the ground on mats or cushions (or on a large sigma cushion).[71]

4.3. *Burial Sites as Possible Christian Meeting Places*
Burial sites may be posited as places where early believers met for the specific purpose of funerary dining, remembering and commemorating departed members of the believing community. The plausibility of tombsides as sites of early Christian gathering can be established with complete ease: tombsides were plainly available to non-elite urban Christians as gathering spots, they were conventional sites for funerary feasting,[72] and they were adequate for this purpose. The criterion of advantageousness does not come to play since tombside dining obviously took place at tombs and not in houses.

Gathering at tombs was a well-established Christian custom by the 'Constantinian turn'.[73] Ramsay MacMullen argues that in the fourth century more Christians could be found at burial sites eating and drinking in memory of the dead than in formal church buildings! By the time

69   Jashemski 1979: 142.
70   Jashemski 1979: 142.
71   See Dunbabin 1991: 128–9.
72   Funerary associations would often have their formal meeting places at burial sites. The meeting place of the College of Aesculapius and Hygieia, a burial club, was located in a cemetery area, between the first and second milestones of the Appian Way. The meeting place consisted of 'a chapel with a vine trellis' containing a statue of Aesculapius and 'a roofed terrace' for dining (Smith 2003: 104).
73   Cf. the decree of the deputy prefect at the trial of bishop of Alexandria (257 CE): 'it shall in no wise be permitted either to you or to any others to hold assemblies or to enter the cemeteries, as they are called' (Eusebius, *H.E.* 7.11.10).

of Augustine, Christian funerary banqueting had begun to attract the disfavour of church leaders. Augustine himself sought to transform funerary meals at cemeteries into pious celebrations within church buildings.[74] Since the Christian practice of 'dining with the dead' was a continuation of a 'pagan' funerary custom, it is highly likely that a habit of meeting at the graves of deceased church members was formed early on. The *Acts of John* provides evidence for the practice in the second century.[75]

Some Christian funerary meals in the second century may have involved a Eucharistic celebration (as indicated in the *Acts of John*). Judging from the funerary meal scenes depicted in the Catacombs of SS. Marcellino e Pietro, women could have taken the lead role at tombside gatherings.

5. *Conclusion*

Given the Mediterranean climate, outdoor spaces would have been natural meeting spots for early Christians. Sources identify or point to four specific outdoor locales as early Christian meeting places: gardens, watersides, urban open space and tombsides (which were often open to the air). All are spatial contexts in which Christian meetings could indeed have taken place. Gardens were used for private religion, philosophizing and collegial dining. A group of Christians could have chartered a rentable garden with dining facilities, or a member of a believing community could have possessed a garden suitable for communal meeting. An enclosed garden would have offered sizeable meeting space, pleasant surroundings and a degree of privacy (if completely walled). Watersides were accessible places. They were popular sites for picnics and established sites for intellectual discussion. They were sometimes used as gathering places by Jewish groups. Watersides, it seems, were regularly used for baptisms, and it seems reasonable to conclude that Christian worship was also sometimes conducted there. Non-elite urban open spaces – streets, street corners, the marketplace – were plainly accessible to Christians and would have been appropriate for outdoor teaching, which may also have sometimes drawn in outsiders. Gravesites were

---

74   Jensen 2008: 141.

75   In *De Monog.* 10.4-5, Tertullian assumes that Christian widows make annual offerings to commemorate the death of their husbands. In *De Corona* 3, he ranks offerings for departed loved ones alongside baptism and Eucharist as mainline Christian rituals. Cf. Jensen 2008: 121–2.

well-established Christian gathering places by the Constantinian turn, and it is highly likely that Christians were engaging in tombside dining in the pre-200 CE period. Tombsides were the standard locale for funerary feasting. Christian funerary meals may often have had a Eucharistic element.

CONCLUSION

This study has directly challenged the received wisdom that the earliest Christian meeting places were 'almost exclusively' houses. The book has had two main aims: (1) to show that while there is indeed good evidence for houses as Christian meeting places in the first two centuries, it is not as extensive or exclusive as usually thought; (2) to identify, on the basis of explicit literary evidence and sometimes archaeological evidence, a number of other kinds of space that could plausibly have served as Christian meeting venues in the alleged 'house church' age.

Part I sought to meet the first aim. In Chapter 1, it was shown that much of the claimed evidence for 'house churches' in the New Testament epistles falls below the level of explicit evidence. Direct evidence within the epistles for houses as Christian meeting places, it was seen, is limited to the four occurrences of the expression ἡ κατ᾽ οἶκον ἐκκλησία, or 'the church at the home', in the Pauline corpus, two of which likely refer to groups located in *tabernae* rather than in houses proper. Moreover, it was pointed out that there is some New Testament epistolary evidence for gatherings in places other than believers' homes (Rom. 16.14-15; 1 Cor. 11.22, 34). Chapter 2 dealt with the Gospels and Acts. Gospel references to Jesus teaching and dining in a house, it was stressed, do not constitute direct evidence of 'house churches'. Even taken as correlative evidence, such references do not point to a Christian practice of meeting 'almost exclusively' in houses, since Jesus teaches and ministers in a range of locations in the Gospels and by no means in houses alone. 'House churches' are thought by some to be almost omnipresent in Acts. It was demonstrated, though, that while some passages indubitably show house meetings and houses as gathering places, in many other passages, the alleged reference to a house church or house churches is either debatable or no more than a speculative inference. Furthermore, it was noted that a variety of spaces serve as settings of mission and meeting in the book. Chapter 3 covered the literary evidence from 100 to 313 CE. Explicit evidence for unaltered houses as meeting venues, it was shown, is virtually confined to references and passages in the Apocryphal Acts. The data in the Apocryphal Acts are not insubstantial; they clearly indicate that houses were significant among early Christian assembly places in the period. But these writings, along with other literary sources, it was seen, also point to the use of various non-house locations as meeting places. While the literary sources testify to the existence of dedicated church buildings (in some places) in the third and early fourth centuries, we saw that there is little explicit evidence for these being adapted houses. Chapter 4 assessed the archaeological evidence. It was shown that the Christian building at Dura Europos is the only secure case of a house-turned-church dating to the *ante-pacem* era. On its own, it hardly bears witness to a general Christian practice of adapting houses into church buildings. If the structures underlying the titular churches of Rome tell us anything about early Christian meeting places, they sustain a scenario in which Christians met in a variety of settings and not only houses. Chapter 5 dealt with the comparative evidence. It emerged that claimed analogies to 'house churches' simply presuppose that early Christian meeting places were almost invariably houses. The full range of comparative data (the multiple contexts of private religion; the diversity of settings in which teaching could take place; the varied nature of collegial meeting places; evidence for watersides as sometime Jewish gathering sites), it was argued, comport with a wider understanding of Christian meeting venues. In sum, then, the literary, archaeological and comparative evidence does not suffice to uphold the AEH consensus, and a significant portion of the evidence runs against it.

Part II strove to meet the second objective. In Chapters 6 to 8, various possibilities for non-house meeting spaces were identified and explored. Chapter 6 considered retail, industrial and storage spaces (shops and workshops, barns and warehouses). Chapter 7 examined commercial hospitality and leisure spaces (hotels and inns, rented dining rooms and bathhouses). Chapter 8 gave attention to outdoor spaces and burial places (gardens, watersides, urban open spaces and burial sites). The discussion of each space-type in these chapters followed a set pattern. First, specific literary and/or archaeological evidence for the space-type as a place of Christian meeting was highlighted. Then, where appropriate, a description of the space-type was given, drawing on examples from (mainly Pompeian and Ostian) archaeology. Finally, a case was made for seeing the space-type as a plausible setting for early Christian meetings (whether regular or occasional meetings), employing (at least three of) the criteria of availability, analogous usage, adequacy and advantageousness. The thrust of these chapters was that numerous non-house spaces directly indicated or suggested by the literature and/or by ecclesiastical archaeology as early Christian gathering sites could credibly have served as such places.[1]

This study thus concludes that the consensus view that Christians of the first two centuries gathered 'almost exclusively' in houses is a severely restricted viewpoint. To be preferred (and more consistent with the actual evidence) is a wider perspective, which acknowledges the importance of houses as Christian meeting places during this period but insists that Christian groups could plausibly have met in a variety of other available places too.

As was seen in the Introduction, the conviction that early Christians met nearly always in the houses of church members has been foundational for scholarly work on the social formation of the early churches, the origins and early development of ecclesiastical architecture, early Christian worship, and the early 'house church'. The challenge to the AEH consensus mounted in this book thus has significant ramifications for these areas of study.

The dominant model of early ecclesial formation, it has been noted, is the household model, according to which the household unit formed the nucleus of a Christian assembly, and the material house served as its meeting space. Other research has questioned the extent to which households converted *en bloc* to Christianity, pointing to evidence indicating that conversion often cut through and divided households.[2] By questioning the extent to which nascent Christian groups met in houses, the present study further problematizes the household model. There is no doubt that some early churches were created out of existing households, but the view that household conversion, coupled with the conversion of house space to ecclesial space, was 'the natural or even necessary way'[3] in which Christianity established itself in a new environment is unjustifiably totalizing. Fresh research is needed into other ways in which early Christian assemblies may have been formed.

The firm consensus within scholarship on early church architecture, as we have seen, is that the first church buildings, which have come to be labeled *domus ecclesiae*, were adaptations of the houses in which

1   I fully acknowledge the role that informed imagination has played in my attempt to reconstruct the possibilities, and I welcome criticism and correction from those who have a better understanding of spatial realities in the Roman world of the first two centuries CE.

2   Barclay 1997: 73–5; Barton 1994.

3   Judge 1960: 36 (cited earlier on p.50).

Christians were in the habit of gathering. An initial 'house-church' phase of assembly is the bedrock of this reconstruction. In the light of this study, it may be contended that the earliest phase of Christian meeting is better characterized as the 'available space' stage, in which, to borrow and paraphrase Justin's reply to Rusticus, Christians met 'wherever was chosen and was possible for each group'. This broadened view of the earliest Christian meeting places actually fits with White's understanding of the classification *domus ecclesiae*: '*any building* specifically adapted or renovated'[4] for ecclesial use (italics mine). White's wide definition of the category recognizes, in principle at least, that the first private structures physically adapted into church buildings need not have been exclusively houses.[5]

It is widely accepted, as was noted in the Introduction, that worship in the early church often took place in the context of a meal. The prominence of meal meetings in early Christianity is in turn connected with the assumed fact the early Christians met almost always in houses. This study does not dispute that communal meals were central to the worship of the early Christians. It does, however, contest the assumed inherent connection between meals and houses. Scholarship on early Christian worship needs to give greater consideration to the variety of contexts in which worshipful dining might have occurred, reflecting on how different spatial settings may have differently affected the dynamics of dining and worship.

The implications of the present work for study of the early 'house church' are major. The foregoing research, showing, on the one hand, that use of houses as early Christian meeting places is much less frequently documented than is usually thought, and examining, on the other, the evidence and possibilities for non-house meeting places, argues against the general labeling of early churches as 'house churches'. Going ever further, I would question whether the term 'house churches' should be used at all for early Christian groups, even those that did customarily meet in houses. First, the term is not found in the ancient literary sources. The relatively rare phrase ἡ κατ' οἶκον ἐκκλησία is not really an equivalent since the word οἶκος within it can have a broader meaning than 'house'. In two instances of the expression, the οἶκος in view is likely to have been a workshop dwelling. Moreover, the prepositional construction κατ' οἶκον functions locationally and not adjectivally, unlike 'house' in

4   White 1990: 21.
5   It should be clear, then, that I am in basic agreement with White's threefold schematization of ecclesiastical architectural origins. What I am calling for is an expanded understanding of the first and second phases.

'house church'. Second, the term 'house church/churches' is deeply associated with the modern house church movement, and in applying it to early churches, it is difficult to avoid thereby implying that they are homologous with house churches of modern times. I would go as far as to suggest that the category 'house church/churches' should be dropped altogether from New Testament and Early Christian studies. Discussion and exploration of house settings of early Christian assembly should rather form part of a wider and richer scholarly discourse on ecclesial space in early Christianity.

It is my hope that this book will clear the way for such discourse and stimulate further and deeper research into the non-house possibilities for early Christian meeting.

Appendix 1

THE SETTING OF THE CORINTHIAN COMMUNAL MEAL

As was argued in Chapter 1, the rhetorical questions of 1 Cor. 11.22 and the injunction of 11.34 render it doubtful that the Corinthian communal meal happened in the home of a church member. A hired dining venue would be a plausible alternative. Local archaeology provides a structure that can help us envision such a setting.

The Roman Cellar Building lies on the southwest corner of the Roman forum. It was first discovered in 1960 and excavated in 1976 (see Fig. 29).[1] The excavation uncovered the northern part of the building, revealing three ground-floor rooms and a deep cellar. The cellar measures 3.06 × 7.82 m and runs the full width of the north side of the building.[2] A rectangular stairwell gives access to the basement, at the southeast corner. A door from the stairwell opens through the south wall of the cellar. Near the centre of the south wall is the shaft of a well. This well (Well 76-2) apparently belonged to an earlier structure dating to before 146 CE.[3] At the west end of the cellar, there lie two wide, round pits. Three smaller pits run along the north wall of the cellar, and another well (Well 60-1), which seems to have been used for drainage, is located at the east wall. Although the basement is well preserved, the design of the ground floor is less easy to establish. The northernmost room, referred to as room 1, lies above the cellar. It is the largest of the three ground-floor rooms excavated. The floor of room 1 was originally supported on wooden beams that also formed the ceiling of the basement.[4] To the southwest of room 1 lies a room, identified as room 2, which is almost square. Here a large deposit of pottery was found. Rooms 1 and 2 were probably connected by a doorway.[5] The south-eastern room, room 3, contains the stairway leading down to the cellar. Room 3 was apparently entered from room 1.[6]

1   Robinson 1962.
2   Williams 1977: 59.
3   Williams 1977: 59, 61.
4   Slanc 1986: 274.
5   Wright 1980: 137.
6   Slane 1986: 273.

Deposits from the well at the east wall of the cellar (Well 60-1), the floor of room 2 and the basement and stairwell, analyzed by Kathleen Warner Slane, elucidate the history of the building.[7] According to Slane, the well fill dates to 'the last decade before Christ and perhaps the first few years of the new era', which was probably the time of the building's construction. The floor deposit from room 2 dates to the Tiberian period. The building appears to have suffered minor damage in an earthquake in 22/23 CE. The consequent repairs involved the raising of the floor level of room 2 (hence the floor deposit). The cellar deposit dates to the third quarter of the first century CE. The basement and stairwell were filled in as a result of damage sustained during a further earthquake in the reign of Vespasian in the 70s CE. The alteration was probably made to stabilize the building. The structure continued in use until the fourth century.

The Roman Cellar Building is not a house; its size and position indicate that it was a building open to the public.[8] The floor deposit found in room 2 consisted of the remnants of plates for eating, large serving platters, drinking cups, cooking pots and pans and other kitchenware.[9] The large quantity of material connected with the preparation and serving of food leads Slane to conclude that the Cellar Building, in its earliest phase, was 'most likely to be a restaurant or a tavern'.[10]

If both rooms 1 and 2 were used for dining,[11] the building could accommodate around 40 diners: 25 or so persons in room 1; 12-15 persons in room 3. A figure of this order has often been suggested as the size (or base size) of the Corinthian congregation.[12]

If we imagine the Corinthians holding their common meal in an environment like this, they would have been divided between two dining areas, one larger than the other. Spatial divisions among diners at an association banquet were not unusual. The guildhall of the carpenters at Ostia, for example, had four distinct dining rooms, all of which were

---

7   Slane 1986: 317.

8   Wright 1980: 174

9   Wright 1980: 173–4.

10   Wright 1980: 174. Walbank (1997: 123), however, thinks the building was 'a formal dining-place for a *collegium*'. It is possible, though, that an association might occasionally rent out its dining facilities (when they were not in use for its own banquets) to increase revenue.

11   As we have seen, Pompeiian *popinae* often have more than one dining area: Dunbabin 2003: 93. Slane, however, takes room 2 to be a pantry (Wright 1980: 174).

12   E.g. Dunn 1995: 171; Murphy-O'Connor 1995; Witherington 1995: 32. As Caragounis (2009: 413) points out, the phrase ἡ ἐκκλησία ὅλη in 1 Cor. 14.23 does not require the attendance of every single member of the community; 'the overwhelming majority would satisfy the phrase.'

probably in operation in times of banquets.[13] It is possible that a division of the Corinthians into two dining areas would have been made on socioeconomic grounds, with the more socially distinguished members of the church dining in the smaller and perhaps nicer room. However, the Cellar Building itself offers no archaeological basis for speculation along this line. If the Corinthian believers were split between two rooms for the meal, presumably they would have tried to assemble in the larger salon for plenary worship. The room would no doubt have had to be cleared of non-fixed furnishings. Most of those assembled would have had to sit on the floor (perhaps on mats). Interestingly, as Balch point outs,[14] Paul presumes that the congregants were seated during communal worship (1 Cor. 14.30). A gathering of around forty persons in a room the size of room 1 of the Cellar Building would have involved uncomfortable over-crowding, so we may have to reckon with an overspill into the second room.

It must be emphasized that there is no evidence whatsoever that Paul's church at Corinth ever gathered in the Roman Cellar Building. More-over, while there is evidence to suggest that the structure may have served as a dining establishment before the earthquake of 22/23 CE, we do not know how the building was used after this date. I appeal to the Roman Cellar Building simply as a near-contemporary, local example of a type of non-domestic dining space in which the Corinthian common meal might be located.

As noted above, it is unlikely that the Roman Cellar Building could have accommodated more than around 40 diners (though additional dining space might have been available in the unexcavated southern part of the building). Significantly larger numbers have been proposed for the church at Corinth at the time of Paul's Corinthian correspondence. Craig De Vos, for example, thinks that the community at this time would have run to around 100 persons,[15] and Richard Hays suggests a number between 150 and 200 (though Hays recognizes that 'these figures are on the high side').[16] A Christian community of such figures would have required a much larger dining hall.[17] In warmer months, though, an

---

13   Smith 2003: 103.
14   Osiek and Balch 1997: 203.
15   De Vos 1999: 204.
16   Hays 1997: 7. Caragounis (2009: 413) thinks in terms of 'hundreds of members'.
17   Caragounis (2009: 414) suggests that the Corinthian Christians could have rented one of the (excavated) civic basilicas, a suggestion also made by Finney (2011: 63–8). A barn would perhaps be more plausible.

enclosed or semi-enclosed garden suitable for dining would be a plausible locale. It is possible that the Corinthians, whatever the size of the
congregation, varied the location of the communal meal, sometimes
meeting in indoor dining space and sometimes, in good weather, dining
outdoors.

A semi-public setting such as a partially walled garden could perhaps
help to explain Paul's prohibition of women's speech in 1 Cor. 14.34-35,
if these verses come genuinely from him. A mixed meeting in a setting
that allowed proceedings to be seen by passers-by could be subject to the
expectations of a public ἐκκλησία. As Cornelia Crocker points out,

> Read within the setting of a public assembly in antiquity, this passage
> indeed reflects the proper thing to do, since only men were full partici-
> pants while women were no more than silent observers.[18]

18   Crocker 2004: 153; cf. Weissenrieder 2012: 97–8.

Appendix 2

FIGURES

The author and publisher gratefully acknowledge the permission granted to reproduce the copyright material in this book. Every effort has been made to trace copyright holders and to obtain their permission for the use of copyright material. The publisher apologizes for any errors or omissions in the details appearing below and would be grateful if notified of any corrections that should be incorporated in future reprints or editions of this book.

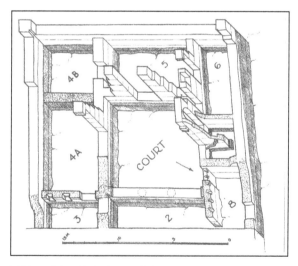

Figure 1. Plan of the Christian Building at Dura Europos before adaptation, from C.H. Kraeling, *The Christian Building* (The Excavations at Dura-Europos. Final Report 8.2; New Haven: Dura-Europos Publications, 1967), p.8. Reprinted with permission of Yale University Press.

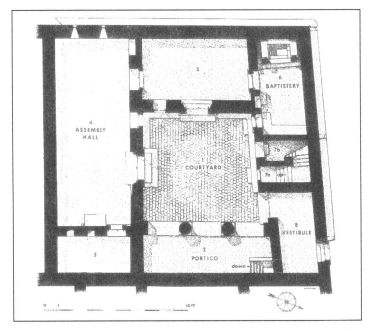

Figure 2. Plan of the Christian Building at Dura Europos, from C.H. Kraeling, *The Christian Building* (The Excavations at Dura-Europos. Final Report 8.2; New Haven: Dura-Europos Publications, 1967), p.4. Reprinted with permission of Yale University Press.

Figure 3. The Church of SS. Giovanni e Paolo, Rome. Author's photograph.

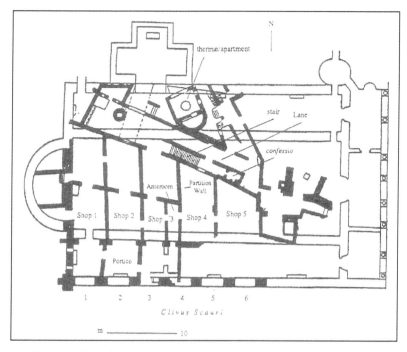

Figure 4. Plan of SS. Giovanni e Paolo, Rome (Based on Krautheimer, *Corpus Basilicarum*, I, pl. 36 and Snyder, *Ante Pacem*, Fig. 15), from B.B. Blue, 'Acts and the House Church', in D.W.J. Gill and C. Gempf (eds.) *The Book of Acts in its Graeco-Roman Setting* (The Book of Acts in its First Century Setting 2; Grand Rapids: Eerdmans, 1994), pp.119–222 (221). Reprinted with permission of Eerdmans.

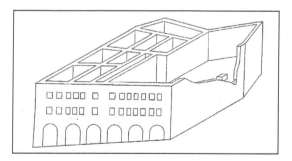

Figure 5. Isometric Reconstruction of SS. Giovanni e Paolo, Rome, from R. Krautheimer, 'The Beginning of Christian Architecture', *Review of Religion* 3 (1939), pp.127–48 (130).

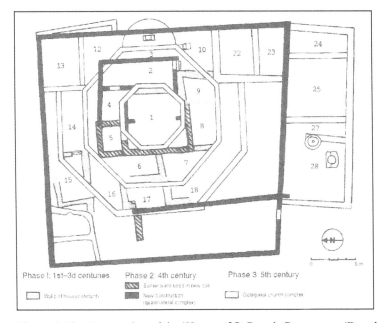

Figure 6. Plan Restoration of the 'House of St Peter', Capernaum (Based on V. Corbo), from L.M. White, *The Social Origins of Christian Architecture*, Vol. 2. *Texts and Monuments of the Christian Domus Ecclesiae in its Environment* (Harvard Theological Studies 42; Valley Forge, PA: Trinity Press International, 1997), p.156. Reprinted with permission of Bloomsbury Publishing.

Figure 7. The Chapel and Deep Room, Lullingstone Villa, Kent (UK). Author's photograph.

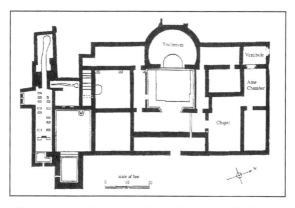

Figure 8. Plan of the Lullingstone Villa c. 350–425 A.D. (Based on G.W. Meates, *Lullingstone Roman Villa* [1962], p. 25), from B.B. Blue, 'Acts and the House Church', in D.W.J. Gill and C. Gempf (eds.), *The Book of Acts in its Graeco-Roman Setting* (The Book of Acts in its First Century Setting 2; Grand Rapids: Eerdmans, 1994), pp.119–222 (214). Reprinted with permission of Eerdmans.

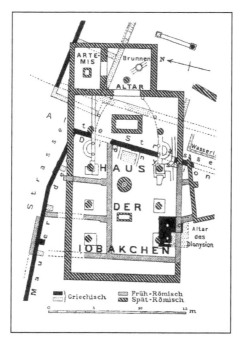

Figure 9. Plan of the Meeting Hall of the *Iobakchoi* at Athens, from W. Judeich, *Topograpihe von Athen* (Handbuch der Altertumswissenschaft; Munich: Beck, 1931). p.291.

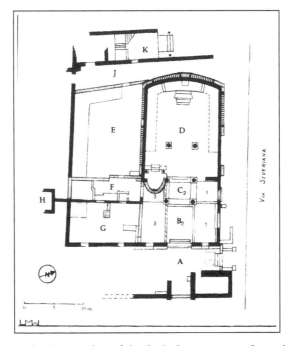

Figure 10. Plan Restoration of the Ostia Synagogue, c. Second–Fourth Centuries, from L.M. White, *The Social Origins of Christian Architecture*. Vol. 2, *Texts and Monuments of the Christian Domus Ecclesiae in its Environment* (Harvard Theological Studies 42; Valley Forge, PA: Trinity Press International), p.380. Reprinted with permission of Bloomsbury Publishing.

Figure 11. Shop (VI.6.20-21) of the Panaficio dei Cristiani, Pompeii. Author's photograph. Printed with permission of the Ministero dei Beni e delle Attività Culturali e del Turismo—Soprintendenza speciale per Pompei, Ercolano e Stabia. Reproduction or duplication of this image by any means is prohibited.

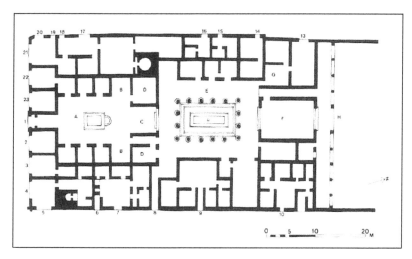

Figure 12. Plan of the *Insula Arriana Polliana*, Pompeii, from J.E. Stambaugh, *The Ancient Roman City* (Baltimore, MD: The Johns Hopkins University Press, 1988), p.166, Figure 13. © 1988 The Johns Hopkins University Press. Reprinted with permission of The Johns Hopkins University Press.

Figure 13. Elevation of the *Insula Aracoeli* (Apartment block beside Aracoeli steps), Rome, from A. Claridge, *Rome: An Oxford Archaeological Guide* (Oxford: Oxford University Press), p.233. Line drawing by A. Claridge. Reprinted with permission of Oxford University Press.

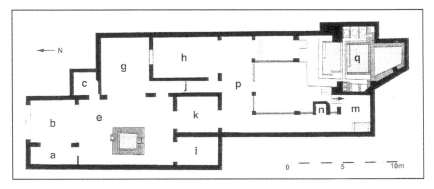

Figure 14. Plan of the Fullery of Stephanus (I.6.7), Pompeii, from M. Flohr, 'The Social World of Roman Fullonicae', in M. Driessen, S. Heeren, J. Hendriks, F. Kemmers, and R. Visser (eds.), *TRAC* 2008 (Oxford: Oxbrow Books): 173–85 (179) (after Spinazzola 1953). Reprinted with permission of Miko Flohr.

Figure 15. The inside of the Fullery of Stephanus, Pompeii. Author's photograph. Printed with permission of the Ministero dei Beni e delle Attività Culturali e del Turismo—Soprintendenza speciale per Pompei, Ercolano e Stabia. Reproduction or duplication of this image by any means is prohibited.

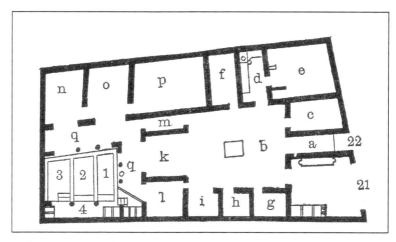

Figure 16. Plan of the Fullery of Primus (VI.14.21-22), Pompeii, from W.O. Moeller, *The Wool Trade of Ancient Pompeii* (Leiden: Brill, 1976), p.45.

Figure 17. *Taberna* IX.8.2, Pompeii. Author's photograph. Printed with permission of the Ministero dei Beni e delle Attività Culturali e del Turismo—Soprintendenza speciale per Pompei, Ercolano e Stabia. Reproduction or duplication of this image by any means is prohibited.

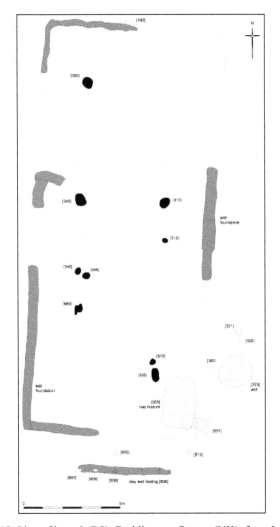

Figure 18. Plan of barn 8 (B8), Beddington, Surrey (UK), from I. Howell. (ed.), *Prehistoric Landscape to Roman Villa: Excavations at Beddington, Surrey, 1981–7* (Museum of London Archaeology Service Monograph 26; London: Museum of London Archaeology Service, 2005), p.41. Reprinted with permission of Museum of London Archaeology.

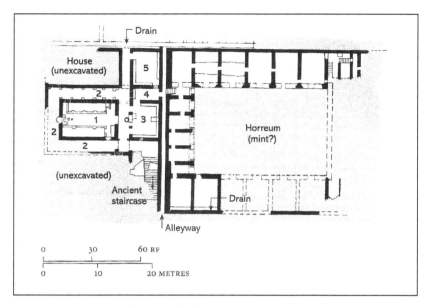

Figure 19. Plan of Roman buildings at lowest level of S. Clemente, Rome, from A. Claridge, *Rome: An Oxford Archaeological Guide* (Oxford: Oxford University Press, 1998), p.285. Line drawing by S. Gibson. Reprinted with permission of Oxford University Press.

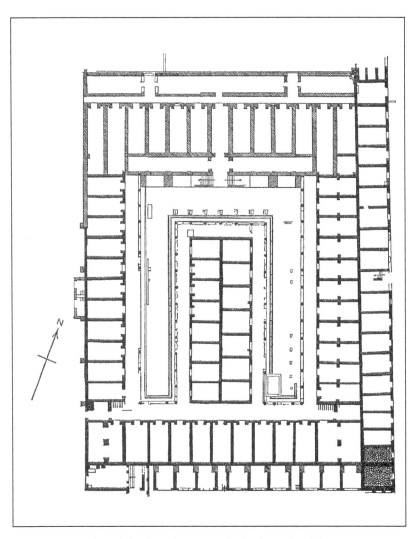

Figure 20. Plan of the *Grandi Horrea*, Ostia, from G. Rickman, *Roman Granaries and Store Buildings* (London: Cambridge University Press, 1971), p.44. Reprinted with permission of Mrs Anna Rickman.

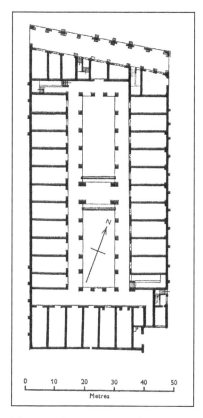

Figure 21. Plan of the *Piccolo Mercato*, Ostia, from G. Rickman, *Roman Granaries and Store Buildings* (London: Cambridge University Press, 1971), p.18. Reprinted with permission of Mrs Anna Rickman.

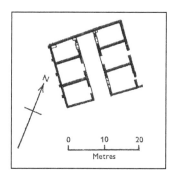

Figure 22. Plan of *Horrea* IV.5.12, Ostia, from G. Rickman, *Roman Granaries and Store Buildings* (London: Cambridge University Press, 1971), p.59. Reprinted with permission of Mrs Anna Rickman.

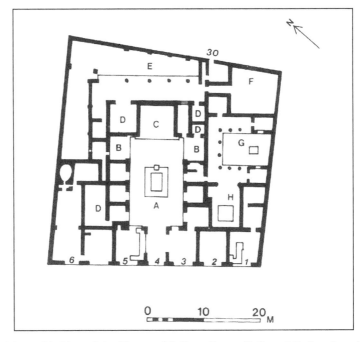

Figure 23. Plan of the House of Sallust, Pompeii, from J.E. Stambaugh, *The Ancient Roman City* (Baltimore, MD: The John Hopkins University Press, 1988), p.163, Figure 12. © 1988 The Johns Hopkins University Press. Reprinted with permission of The Johns Hopkins University Press.

Figure 24. The rear garden of the House of Sallust, Pompeii. Author's photograph. Printed with permission of the Ministero dei Beni e delle Attività Culturali e del Turismo—Soprintendenza speciale per Pompei, Ercolano e Stabia. Reproduction or duplication of this image by any means is prohibited.

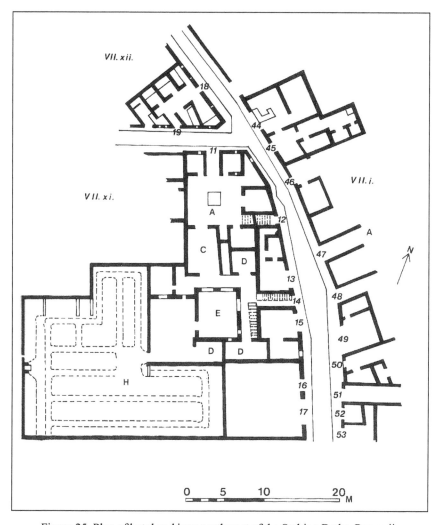

Figure 25. Plan of hotel and inns northwest of the Stabian Baths, Pompeii, from J.E. Stambaugh, *The Ancient Roman City* (Baltimore, MD: The Johns Hopkins University Press, 1988), p.181, Figure 20. © 1988 The Johns Hopkins University Press. Reprinted with permission of The Johns Hopkins University Press.

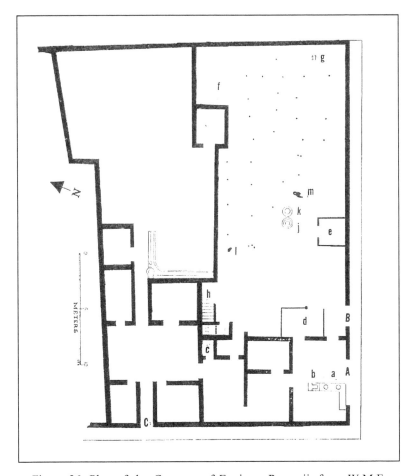

Figure 26. Plan of the *Caupona* of Euxinus, Pompeii, from W.M.F. Jashemski, *The Gardens of Pompeii: Herculaneum and the Villas Destroyed by Vesuvius* (New Rochelle, NY: Caratzas Bros., 1979), p.174. Courtesy of Aristide D. Caratzas, Publisher.

Figure 27. The garden of the *Caupona* of Euxinus, Pompeii. Author's photograph. Figure 28. The Inn of Sittius, Pompeii. Author's photograph. Printed with permission of the Ministero dei Beni e delle Attività Culturali e del Turismo—Soprintendenza speciale per Pompei, Ercolano e Stabia. Reproduction or duplication of this image by any means is prohibited.

Figure 28. The Inn of Sittius, Pompeii. Author's photograph. Printed with permission of the Ministero dei Beni e delle Attività Culturali e del Turismo—Soprintendenza speciale per Pompei, Ercolano e Stabia. Reproduction or duplication of this image by any means is prohibited.

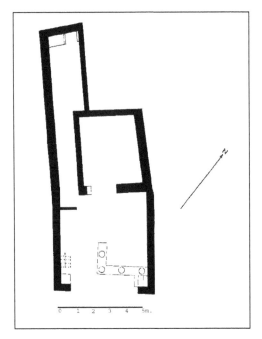

Figure 29. Plan of *popina* V.2.13, Pompeii, adapted from J.E. Packer, 'Inns at Pompeii: A Short Survey', *Cronache Pompeiane* 4 (1978), pp.5–53 (35).

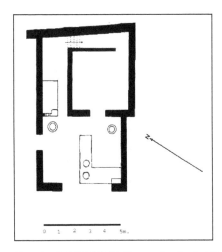

Figure 30. Plan of *popina* VI.14.35-36, Pompeii, adapted from J.E. Packer, 'Inns at Pompeii: A Short Survey', *Cronache Pompeiane* 4 (1978), pp.5–53 (38).

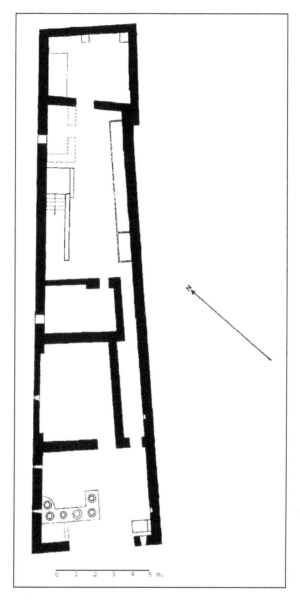

Figure 31. Plan of *popina* V.1.13, Pompeii, adapted from J.E. Packer, 'Inns at Pompeii: A Short Survey', *Cronache Pompeiane* 4 (1978), pp.5–53 (39).

Figure 32. The Church of S. Pudenziana, Rome. Author's photograph.

Figure 33. The Sarno Bath Complex, Pompeii. Author's photograph. Printed with permission of the Ministero dei Beni e delle Attività Culturali e del Turismo—Soprintendenza speciale per Pompei, Ercolano e Stabia. Reproduction or duplication of this image by any means is prohibited.

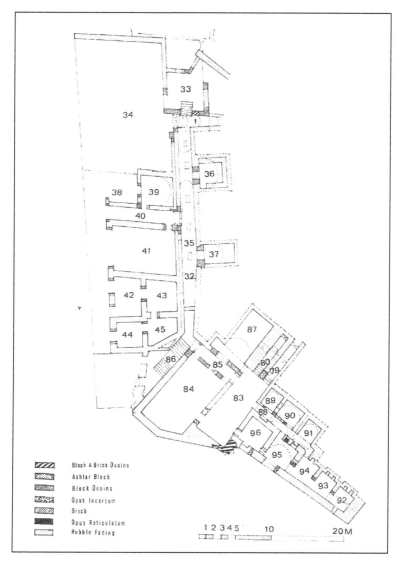

Figure 34. The Sarno Bath Complex, level 3, from A.O. Koloski-Ostrow, *The Sarno Bath Complex: Architecture in Pompeii's Last Years* (Monograph Series of the Italian Superintendency; Rome: L'Erma di Bretschneider, 1990). Reprinted with permission of L'Erma di Bretschneider.

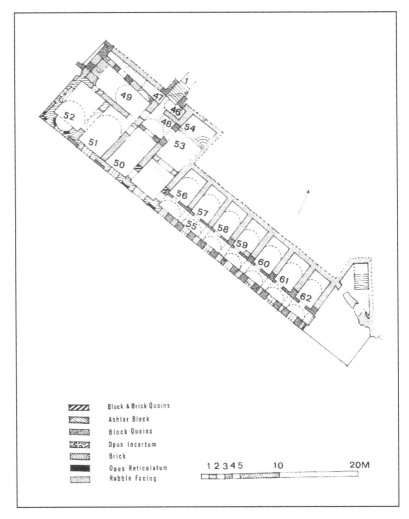

Figure 35. The Sarno Bath Complex, level 4, from A.O. Koloski-Ostrow, *The Sarno Bath Complex: Architecture in Pompeii's Last Years* (Monograph Series of the Italian Superintendency; Rome: L'Erma di Bretschneider, 1990). Reprinted with permission of L'Erma di Bretschneider.

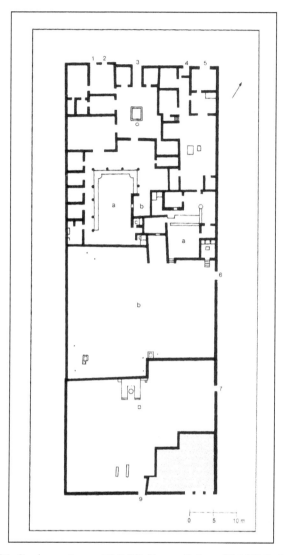

Figure 36. Garden restaurant II.3.7/9, Pompeii, from W.M.F. Jashemski, *The Gardens of Pompeii: Herculaneum and the Villas Destroyed by Vesuvius.* Vol. 2, *Appendices* (New Rochelle, NY: Aristide D. Caratzas Pub, 1993), p.84. Courtesy of Aristide D. Caratzas, Publisher

Figure 37. Garden *triclinium* at II.9.6/7, Pompeii. Author's photograph. Printed with permission of the Ministero dei Beni e delle Attività Culturali e del Turismo—Soprintendenza speciale per Pompei, Ercolano e Stabia. Reproduction or duplication of this image by any means is prohibited.

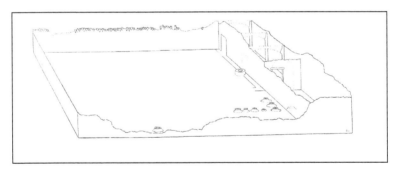

Figure 38. *Taberna* with large garden (I.20.5), Pompeii, from W.M.F. Jashemski, *The Gardens of Pompeii: Herculaneum and the Villas Destroyed by Vesuvius* (New Rochelle, NY: Caratzas Bros., 1979), p.191. Courtesy of Aristide D. Caratzas, Publisher.

Figure 39. Tomb *triclinium* of Gnaeus Vibrius Saturninus, Pompeii, from W.M.F. Jashemski, *The Gardens of Pompeii: Herculaneum and the Villas Destroyed by Vesuvius* (New Rochelle, NY: Caratzas Bros., 1979), p.153. Courtesy of Aristide D. Caratzas, Publisher.

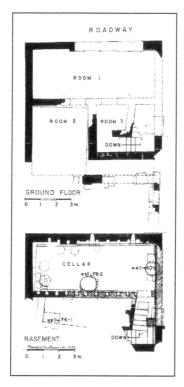

Figure 40. Plan of the Roman Cellar Building, Corinth, from K.S. Wright, 'A Tiberian Pottery Deposit from Corinth', *Hesperia* 49 (1980), pp.135–177 (136). Courtesy of the Trustees of the American School of Classical Studies at Athens.

BIBLIOGRAPHY

Texts and Translations

Biblical quotations in the present work follow the NRSV translations, with occasional modification. Greek and Roman sources and translations are generally from the LCL. The LCL has additionally been used for Philo, Josephus and Eusebius, *Historia Ecclesiastica*. Some citations follow White 1997 (indicated in the footnotes). Other texts and translations used in this work are:

Chadwick, H. (trans.)
    1953   *Origen: Contra Celsum* (Cambridge: Cambridge University Press).
Danby, H. (trans.)
    1933   *The Mishnah: Translated from the Hebrew with Introduction and Brief Explanatory Notes* (Oxford: Clarendon).
Elliott, J.K. (ed.)
    2009   *The Apocryphal New Testament: A Collection of Apocryphal Christian Literature in an English Translation* (repr.; Oxford: Clarendon [1993]).
Glover, T.R., and G.H. Rendall (trans.)
    1931   *Tertullian: Apology, de Spectaculis, Minucius Felix* (LCL; London: Heinemann).
Grenfell, B.P., A. Hunt et al.
  1898–2009 *The Oxyrhynchus Papyri* (London: Egypt Exploration Fund).
Harkins, P.W. (trans.)
    1963   *Galen on the Passions and Errors of the Soul* (with an Introduction and Interpretation by Walther Riese; Ohio: Ohio State University Press).
Holmes, M.W. (ed.)
    2007   *The Apostolic Fathers: Greek Texts and English Translations* (Grand Rapids: Baker Academic, 3rd edn).
Klijn, A.F.J.
    2003   *The Acts of Thomas: Introduction, Text, and Commentary* (Leiden: Brill, 2dn edn).
Kloppenborg, J.S, and R.S. Ascough
    2011   *Greco-Roman Associations: Texts, Translations, and Commentary*. Vol. 1, *Attica, Central Greece, Macedonia, Thrace* (Berlin: de Gruyter).
Lawlor, H.J, and J.E.L. Oulton (trans.)
    1927   *The Ecclesiastical History and the Martyrs of Palestine by Eusebius* (with introduction and notes; London: SPCK).
Lipsius, R.A., and M. Bonnet (eds.)
  1891–1903 *Acta Apostolorum Apocrypha* (3 vols.; Leipzig: Mendelssohn).

Moore, H. (trans.)
    1921   *The Dialogue of Palladius Concerning the Life of Chrysostom* (London: SPCK; New York: Macmillan)

Mommsen, T., and P. Krueger (eds.)
    1985   *The Digest of Justinian* (trans. A. Watson; 4 vols.; Philadelphia: University of Philadelphia Press).

Musurillo, H.
    1972   *The Acts of the Christian Martyrs: Introduction, Texts and Translations* (Oxford: Clarendon).

Rahlfs, A. (ed.)
    1993   *Septuaginta* (Stuttgart: Deutsche Bibelgesellschaft).

Rehm, B., and F. Paschke (eds.)
    1965   *Die Pseudoklementinen* (2 vols.; Berlin: Akademie-Verlag).

Roberts, A., and J. Donaldson (eds.)
    1994   *The Ante-Nicene Fathers* (10 vols.; Peabody, MA: Hendrickson).

Schaff, P., and H. Wace (eds.)
  1890–1900 *A Select Library of Nicene and Post-Nicene Fathers of the Christian Church* (14 vols.; New York: The Christian Literature Company).

Schneemelcher, W. (ed.)
    1992   *New Testament Apocrypha.* Vol. 2, *Writings Related to the Apostles; Apocalypses and Related Subjects* (Louisville, KY: Westminster John Knox).

Scott, S.P. (trans. and ed.)
    1973   *The Civil Law, including the Twelve Tables, the Institutes of Gaius, the Rules of Ulpian, the Opinions of Paulus, the Enactments of Justinian, the Constitutions of Leo* (7 vols.; repr.; Cincinnati: Central Trust Company [1932]).

Selby, J.S. (trans.)
    1853   *Justin, Cornelius Nepos, and Eutropius* (London: H.G. Bohn).

Stählin, O.
  1905–1909 *Clemens Alexandrinus* (Die Griechischen christlichen Schriftsteller der ersten Jahrhunderte; Leipzig: Hinrichs).

Williams, F.
    1987–94   *The Panarion of Epiphanius of Salamis* (3 vols.; Leiden: Brill).

Secondary Sources

Achtemeier, P.J.
    1996   *1 Peter* (Hermeneia; Minneapolis, MN: Fortress).

Adams, E.
    2008   'The Ancient Church at Megiddo: The Discovery and an Assessment of its Significance', *ExpTim* 120: 62–9.
    2012   'Placing the Corinthian Communal Meal', in C. Osiek and A.C. Niang (eds.), *Text, Image, and Christians in the Graeco-Roman World: A Festschrift in Honor of David Lee Balch* (Princeton Theological Monograph Series; Eugene, OR: Wipf & Stock): 22–37.

Alexander, L.A.
    1994   'Paul and the Hellenistic Schools: The Evidence of Galen', in T. Engberg-
            Pedersen (ed.), *Paul in his Hellenistic Context* (SNTW; Edinburgh: T. &
            T. Clark): 60–83.
    2002   ' "Foolishness to the Greeks": Jews and Christians in the Public Life of the
            Empire', in G. Clark and T. Rajak (eds.), *Philosophy and Power in the
            Graeco-Roman World: Essays in Honour of Miriam T. Griffin* (Oxford:
            Oxford University Press): 229–49.
Alikin, V.A.
    2010   *The Earliest History of the Christian Gathering: Origin, Development and
            Content of the Christian Gathering in the First to Third Centuries* (Supple-
            ments to Vigilae Christianae 102; Leiden: Brill).
Allison, P.M.
    2007   'Domestic Spaces and Activities', in J.J. Dobbins and P.W. Foss (eds.),
            The World of Pompeii (London: Routledge): 269–78.
Alston, R.
    1997   'Houses and Households in Roman Egypt', in A. Wallace-Hadrill and R.
            Laurence (eds.), *Domestic Space in the Roman World: Pompeii and
            Beyond* (Portsmouth, RI: Journal of Roman Archaeology): 25–39.
Apollonj-Getti, B.M.
    1978   'Problemi relativi alle origini dell'architettura paleocristiana', in *Atti del IX
            Congresso internazionale di archeologia cristiana, Roma 21–27 settembre
            1975* (2 vols.; Rome: Pontificio Istituto di archeologia Cristiana), I:
            491–511.
Ascough, R.S.
    1998   *What Are They Saying About the Formation of the Pauline Churches?*
            (New York: Paulist).
    2003   *Paul's Macedonian Associations: The Social Context of Philippians and
            1 Thessalonians* (WUNT II/161; Tübingen: Mohr Siebeck).
    2009   *Lydia: Paul's Cosmopolitan Hostess: Paul's Social Network: Brothers and
            Sisters in Faith* (Collegeville, PA: Liturgical).
Ascough, R.S., P.A. Harland, and J.S. Kloppenborg
    2012   *Associations in the Greco-Roman World: A Sourcebook* (Waco, TX:
            Baylor University Press).
Aune, D.E.
    1997   *Revelation 1–5* (WBC 52A; Waco, TX: Word).
Bagnall, R.S.
    2010   *Everyday Writing in the Graeco-Roman East* (Berkeley: University of
            California Press).
Bagnall, R.S., and D.W. Rathbone
    2004   *Egypt from Alexander to the Early Christians: An Archaeological and
            Historical Guide* (London: British Museum Press; Los Angeles: Getty).
Bakker, J.
    1994   *Living and Working with the Gods: Studies of Evidence for Private
            Religion and its Material Environment in the City of Ostia (100–500 AD)*
            (Amsterdam: J.C. Gieben).

Balch, D.L.
1981　*Let Wives Be Submissive: The Domestic Code in 1 Peter* (Chico, CA: Scholars Press).
2004　'Rich Pompeiian Houses, Shops for Rent, and the Huge Apartment Building in Herculaneum as Typical Spaces for Pauline House Churches', *JSNT* 27: 27–47.
2008　*Roman Domestic Art and Early House Churches* (WUNT I/228; Tübingen: Mohr Siebeck).
2012　'The Church Sitting in a Garden (1 Cor 14:30: Rom 16:23; Mark 39–40: 8:6; John 6:3, 10; Acts 1:15; 2:1-2)', in D.L. Balch and A. Weissenrieder (eds.), *Contested Spaces: Houses and Temples in Roman Antiquity and the New Testament* (WUNT I/285; Tübingen: Mohr Siebeck): 201–35.
Banks, R.
1980　*Paul's Idea of Community: The Early House Churches in their Cultural Setting* (Peabody, MA: Hendrickson).
Barclay, J.M.G.
1997　'The Family as Bearer of Religion in Judaism and Early Christianity', in H. Moxnes (ed.), *Constructing Early Christian Families: Family as Social Reality and Metaphor* (London: Routledge): 66–80.
Barnard, L.
1984　'The "Cross of Herculaneum" Reconsidered', in W. Weinrich (ed.), *The New Testament Age: Essays in Honor of Bo Reicke* (Macon, GA: Mercer University Press): 15–27.
Barrett, C.K.
1994　*A Critical and Exegetical Commentary on the Acts of the Apostles*. Vol. 1, *Preliminary Introduction and Commentary on Acts I–XIV* (ICC; Edinburgh: T. & T. Clark).
1998　*A Critical and Exegetical Commentary on the Acts of the Apostles*. Vol. 2, *Introduction and Commentary on Acts XV–XXVIII* (ICC; Edinburgh: T. & T. Clark).
Barth, M., and H. Blanke
2000　*The Letter to Philemon* (ECC; Grand Rapids: Eerdmans).
Barton, S.C.
1986　'Paul's Sense of Place: An Anthropological Approach to Community Formation in Corinth', *NTS* 32: 225–46.
1994　*Discipleship and Family Ties in Mark and Matthew* (SNTSMS 80; Cambridge: Cambridge University Press).
Bauckham, R.
1998　'For Whom Were Gospels Written?', in R. Bauckham (ed.), *The Gospels for All Christians: Rethinking the Gospel Audiences* (Edinburgh: T. & T. Clark): 9–48.
Beard, M.
2008　*Pompeii: The Life of a Roman Town* (London: Profile Books).
Best, E.
1981　*Following Jesus: Discipleship in the Gospel of Mark* (Sheffield: JSOT).
Binder, D.B.
1999　*Into the Temple Courts: The Place of the Synagogues in the Second Temple Period* (SBLDS 169; Atlanta: SBL).

Blue, B.B.
 1994   'Acts and the House Church', in D.W.J. Gill and C. Gempf (eds.), *The Book of Acts in its Graeco-Roman Setting* (The Book of Acts in its First Century Setting 2; Grand Rapids: Eerdmans): 119–222.

Bobertz, C.A.
 1993   'The Role of Patron in the Cena Dominica of Hippolytus Apostolic Tradition', *JTS* 44.1: 170–84.

Bock, D.L.
 2007   *Acts* (BECNT; Grand Rapids: Baker Academic).

Bockmuehl, M.
 1997   *The Epistle to the Philippians* (BNTC; London: A. & C. Black).

Bodel, J.
 2008   'Cicero's Minerva, Penates, and the Mother of the Lares: An Outline of Roman Domestic Religion', in J. Bodel and S.M. Olyan (eds.), *Household and Family Religion in Antiquity* (Oxford: Blackwell): 248–75.

Boedeker, D.
 2008   'Family Matters: Domestic Religion in Classical Greece', in J. Bodel and S.M. Olyan (eds.), *Household and Family Religion in Antiquity* (Oxford: Blackwell): 229–47.

Boëthius, A.
 1934   'Remarks on the Development of Domestic Architecture in Rome', *AJA* 38: 158–70.

Bollmann, B.
 1998   *Römische Vereinshäuser: Untersuchungen zu den Scholae der römischen Berufs-, Kult- und Augustalen-Kollegien in Italien* (Mainz: P. von Zabern).

Bonner, S.F.
 1972   'The Street Teacher: An Educational Scene in Horace', *AJP* 93: 509–28.
 1977   *Education in Ancient Rome: From the Elder Cato to the Younger Pliny* (London: Methuen).

Bowes, K.
 2008a   *Private Worship, Public Values, and Religious Change in Late Antiquity* (Cambridge: Cambridge University Press).
 2008b   'Early Christian Archaeology: A State of the Field', *Religion Compass* 2.4: 575–619.

Boyce, G.K.
 1937   'Corpus of the Lararia of Pompeii', *Memoirs of the American Academy in Rome* 14.

Bradshaw, P.F.
 2004   *Eucharistic Origins* (Oxford: Oxford University Press).

Bradshaw, P.F., M.E. Johnson, and L.E. Phillips
 2002   *The Apostolic Tradition: A Commentary* (Hermeneia; Augsburg: Fortress).

Branick, V.
 1989   *The House Church in the Writings of Paul* (Wilmington, DE: Michael Glazier).

Brenk, B.
 1995   'Microstoria sotto la chiesa dei SS. Giovanni e Paolo: La cristianizzazione di una casa privata', *Rivista dell'Istituto Nazionale di Archeologia e Storia dell'Arte* 18: 169–205.

Brothers, A.J.
  1996   'Urban Housing', in I.M. Barton (ed.), *Roman Domestic Buildings* (Exeter: University of Exeter Press): 33–63.
Bruce, F.F.
  1951   *The Acts of the Apostles: The Greek Text* (London: Tyndale, 2nd edn).
Burkert, W.
  1991   'Oriental Symposia: Contrasts and Parallels', in W.J. Slater (ed.), *Dining in a Classical Context* (Ann Arbour: University of Michigan Press): 7–25.
Burton, J.
  1998   'Women's Commensality in the Ancient Greek World', *Greece and Rome* 45: 143–65.
Button, M.B., and F.J. Van Rensburg
  2003   'The "House Churches" in Corinth', *Neotestamentica* 37: 1–28.
Campbell, R.A.
  1994   *The Elders: Seniority within Earliest Christianity* (SNTW; Edinburgh: T. & T. Clark).
  2007   Review of R.W. Gehring, *House Church and Mission: The Importance of Household Structures in Early Christianity* (Peabody, MA: Hendrickson), *JTS* 58.2: 666–71.
Caragounis, C.C.
  2009   'A House Church in Corinth: An Inquiry into the Structure of Early Corinthian Christianity', in C.J. Belezos (ed.), *Saint Paul and Corinth: 1950 Years since of the Writing of the Epistles to the Corinthians* (2 vols.; Athens: Psichogios), I:365–418.
Casson, L.
  1974   *Travel in the Ancient World* (London: George Allen & Unwin).
Catto, S.K.
  2004   'Does προσευχὰς ποιεῖσθαι in Josephus' *Antiquities of the Jews* Mean "Build Places of Prayer"?' *JSJ* 35: 159–68.
  2007   *Reconstructing the First-Century Synagogue: A Critical Analysis of Current Research* (LNTS 363; London: T&T Clark International).
Claridge, A.
  1998   *Rome: An Oxford Archaeological Guide* (Oxford: Oxford University Press).
Cooley, A., and M.G.L. Cooley
  2004   *Pompeii: A Sourcebook* (London: Routledge).
Corbett, G.U.S.
  1957   'Investigations at "Julianos" Church' at Umm-el-Jemal', *Papers of the British School at Rome* 25: 39–66.
Corbo, V.
  1969   *The House of St. Peter at Capharnaum: A Preliminary Report of the First Two Campaigns of Excavations, April 16–June 19, Sept. 12–Nov. 26, 1968* (Jerusalem: Franciscan).
Corley, K.
  2010   *Maranatha: Women's Funerary Rituals and Christian Origins* (Minneapolis, MN: Fortress).
Cormack, S.
  2007   'The Tombs at Pompeii', in J.J. Dobbins and P.W. Foss (eds.), *The World of Pompeii* (London: Routledge): 585–606.

Corwin, V.
    1960   *St. Ignatius and Christianity in Antioch* (New Haven: Yale University
            Press).
Cotterell, P., and M. Turner
    1989   *Linguistics and Biblical Interpretation* (Downers Grove, IL: InterVarsity).
Cox, C.E.
    1998   'The Reading of the Personal Letter as the Background for the Reading
            of Scriptures in the Early Church', in A.J. Malherbe, F.W. Norris, and
            J.W. Thompson (eds.), *The Early Church in its Context: Essays in Honor
            of Everett Ferguson* (NovTSup 90; Leiden: Brill): 74–91.
Crawford, J.S.
    1990   *The Byzantine Shops at Sardis* (Cambridge, MA: Harvard University
            Press).
    1999   'Jews, Christians and Polytheists in Late-Antique Sardis', in S.J. Fine
            (ed.), *Jews, Christians and Polytheists in the Ancient Synagogue: Cultural
            Interaction During the Greco-Roman Period* (London: Routledge): 190–
            200.
Cribiore, R.
    2001   *Gymnastics of the Mind: Greek Education in Hellenistic and Roman Egypt*
            (Princeton, NJ: Princeton University Press).
Crocker, C.C.
    2004   *Reading 1 Corinthians in the Twenty-First Century* (London: T&T Clark
            International).
Crosby, M.H.
    1988   *House of Disciples: Church, Economics, and Justice in Matthew*
            (Maryknoll, NY: Orbis).
Davies, J.G.
    1968   *The Secular Use of Church Buildings* (London: SCM).
Dearn, A.
    2004   'The Abitinian Martyrs and the Outbreak of the Donatist Schism', *JEH* 55:
            1–18.
de la Bédoyere, G.
    2001   *The Buildings of Roman Britain* (Stroud: Tempus).
DeFelice, J.
    2001   *Roman Hospitality: The Professional Women of Pompeii* (Warren Center,
            PA: Shangri-La Publications).
    2007   'Inns and Taverns', in J.J. Dobbins and P.W. Foss (eds.), *The World of
            Pompeii* (London: Routledge): 474–86.
Den Boer, W.
    1950   'Gynaeconitis: A Centre of Christian Propaganda', *VC* 4: 61–4.
De Vos, C.
    1999   *Church and Community Conflicts: The Relationships of the Thessalonian,
            Corinthian, and Philippian Churches with their Wider Civic Communities*
            (SBLDS 168; Atlanta: Scholars Press).
Dix, G.
    2005   *The Shape of the Liturgy (New Edition)* (London: Continuum).

Doig, A.
  2008   *Liturgy and Architecture from the Early Church to the Middle Ages*
            (Aldershot: Ashgate Publishing).
Donahue, J.F.
  2004   *The Roman Community at Table during the Principate* (Ann Arbor:
            University of Michigan Press).
Dunbabin, K.M.D.
  1991   'Triclinium and Stibadium', in J. Slater (ed.), *Dining in a Classical
            Context* (Ann Arbor: University of Michigan Press): 121–48.
  2003   *The Roman Banquet: Images of Conviviality* (Cambridge: Cambridge
            University Press).
Dunn, J.D.G.
  1988   *Romans 9–16* (WBC 38B; Dallas, TX: Word).
  1995   *1 Corinthians* (Sheffield: Sheffield Academic).
  1996   *The Epistle to the Colossians and to Philemon: A Commentary on the
            Greek Text* (NIGTC; Grand Rapids: Eerdmans).
  2009   *Beginning from Jerusalem* (Christianity in the Making 2; Grand Rapids:
            Eerdmans).
Elliott, J.H.
  1981   *A Home for the Homeless: A Sociological Exegesis of 1 Peter, its Situation
            and Strategy* (Philadelphia: Fortress).
  1991   'Temple versus Household in Luke–Acts: A Contrast in Social Institu-
            tions', in J.H. Neyrey (eds.), *The Social World of Luke–Acts* (Peabody,
            MA: Hendrickson): 211–40.
  2000   *1 Peter: A New Translation with Introduction and Commentary* (AB 37B;
            New York: Doubleday).
Esler, P.F.
  2003   *Conflict and Identity in Romans: The Social Setting of Paul's Letter*
            (Minneapolis, MN: Fortress).
Fagan, G.G.
  1999   *Bathing in Public in the Roman World* (Ann Arbour: The University of
            Michigan Press).
Ferguson, E.
  2009   *Baptism in the Early Church: History, Theology, and Liturgy in the First
            Five Centuries* (Grand Rapids: Eerdmans).
Fiensy, D.A.
  2002   'What Would You Do for a Living?', in A.J. Blasi, P.A. Turcotte, and J.
            Duhaime (eds.), *Handbook of Early Christianity: Social Science
            Approaches* (Walnut Creek, CA: AltaMira): 555–74.
Filson, F.V.
  1939   'The Significance of the Early House Churches', *JBL* 58: 105–12.
Finger, R.H.
  2007   *Roman House Churches for Today: A Practical Guide for Small Groups*
            (Grand Rapids: Eerdmans).
Finney, M.T.
  2011   *Honour and Conflict in the Ancient World: I Corinthians in its Greco-
            Roman Social Setting* (London: T&T Clark International).

Fitzmyer, J.A.
    1998   *The Acts of the Apostles: A New Translation with Introduction and Commentary* (AB 31; New York: Doubleday).

Flohr, M.
    2008   'Cleaning the Laundries II: Report of the 2007 Campaign', *Fasti OnLine Documents & Research* 111: 1–13.
    2009   'The Social World of Roman *Fullonicae*', in M. Driessen, S. Heeren, J. Hendriks, F. Kemmers, and R.Visser (eds.), *TRAC 2008* (Oxford: Oxbow Books): 173–85.
    n.d.   'Where to Go from Here? Work, Economy and Society in the Roman World Beyond the Fullonicae of Italy', unpublished paper.

Fotopoulous, J.
    2003   *Food Offered to Idols in Roman Corinth: A Social-Rhetorical Reconsideration of 1 Corinthians 8:1–11:1* (WUNT II/151: Tübingen: Mohr Siebeck).

Frier, B.W.
    1977   'The Rental Market in Early Imperial Rome', *JRS* 67: 27–37.
    1980   *Landlords and Tenants in Imperial Rome* (Princeton, NJ: Princeton University Press).

Friesen, S.J.
    2004   'Poverty in Pauline Studies: Beyond the So-called New Consensus', *JSNT* 26: 323–61.
    2010   'The Wrong Erastus: Ideology, Archaeology, and Exegesis', in S.J. Friesen, D.N. Schowalter, and J.C. Walters (eds.), *Corinth in Context: Comparative Studies on Religion and Society* (Leiden: Brill): 231–56.

Fulford, M.
    2003   *Lullingstone Roman Villa* (London: English Heritage).

Gamble, H., Jr
    1977   *The Textual History of the Letter to the Romans: A Study in the Textual and Literary Criticism* (Grand Rapids: Eerdmans).

García y García, L.
    2005   *Pupils, Teachers and Schools in Pompeii: Childhood, Youth and Culture in the Roman Era* (Rome: Bardi).

Gehring, R.W.
    2004   *House Church and Mission: The Importance of Household Structures in Early Christianity* (Peabody, MA: Hendrickson).

Gielen, M.
    1986   'Zur Interpretation der paulinischen Formel η κατ' οἶκον εκκλησία', *ZNW* 77: 109–25.

Giordano, C., and I. Kahn
    2001   *The Jews in Pompeii, Herculaneum, Stabiae and in the Cities of Campania Felix* (3rd edn revised and enlarged by L. García y García; trans. W.F. Jashemski; Rome: Bardi).

Goodrich, J.K.
    2010   'Erastus, *Quaestor* of Corinth: The Administrative Rank of ο οικονόμος τῆς πόλεως (Rom 16.23) in an Achaean Colony', *NTS* 56: 90–115.
    2011   'Erastus of Corinth (Romans 16.23): Responding to Recent Proposals on His Rank, Status, and Faith', *NTS* 57: 583–93.
    2012   *Paul as an Administrator of God in 1 Corinthians* (SNTSMS 152; Cambridge: Cambridge University Press).

Green, M.
    1970   *Evangelism in the Early Church* (London: Hodder & Stoughton).

Guijarro, S.
    1997   'The Family in First-Century Galilee', in H. Moxnes (ed.), *Constructing Early Christian Families* (London: Routledge): 42–65.

Hadman, J.
    1978   'Aisled Buildings in Roman Britain', in M. Todd (ed.), *Studies in the Romano-British Villa* (Leicester: Leicester University Press): 187–95.

Harland, P.A.
    2003   *Associations, Synagogues, and Congregations: Claiming a Place in Ancient Mediterranean Society* (Minneapolis, MN: Fortress).
    2009   *Dynamics of Identity in the World of the Early Christians: Associations, Judeans, and Cultural Minorities* (London: T&T Clark/Continuum).

Harmon, D.P.
    1978   'The Family Festivals of Rome', *ANRW* II.16.2: 1592–1603.

Hays, R.B.
    1997   *First Corinthians* (Interpretation; Louisville, KY: Westminster John Knox).

Helgeland, J.
    1979   'Christians and the Roman Army from Marcus Aurelius to Constantine', *ANRW* II.23.1: 724–834.

Helgeland, J., R.J. Daly, and J. Patout Burns
    1985   *Christians and the Military: The Early Experience* (Philadelphia: Fortress).

Hengel, M.
    1971   'Proseuche und Synagoge: Jüdische Gemeinde, Gotteshaus und Gottes- dienst in der Diaspora und in Palästina', in G. Jeremias, H.W. Kuhn, and H. Stegemann (eds.), *Tradition und Glaube: Das frühe Christentum in seiner Umwelt: Festgabe für Karl Georg Kuhn zum 65. Geburtstag* (Göttingen: Vandenhoeck & Ruprecht): 157–84.

Hermansen, G.
    1981   *Ostia: Aspects of Roman City Life* (Edmonton: University of Alberta Press).

Hirshfield, Y.
    1995   *The Palestinian Dwelling in the Roman-Byzantine Period* (Jerusalem: Franciscan).

Hock, R.F.
    1979   'The Workshop as a Social Setting for Paul's Missionary Preaching', *CBQ* 41: 438–50.
    1980   *The Social Context of Paul's Ministry: Tentmaking and Apostleship* (Augsburg: Fortress).

Holloway, P.A.
    2009   *Coping with Prejudice: 1 Peter in Social-Psychological Perspective* (WUNT I/244; Tübingen: Mohr Siebeck).

Holmberg, B.
    1978   *Paul and Power: The Structure of Authority in the Primitive Church as Reflected in the Pauline Epistles* (Coniectanea Biblica, New Testament Series 11; Lund: Gleerup).

Hooker, M.D.
    1991   *The Gospel according to Saint Mark* (BNTC; Peabody, MA: Hendrick- son).

Holtzmann, H.J.
    1901   *Die Apostelgeschichte* (Hand-Commentar zum Neuen Testament;
            Tübingen: Mohr Siebeck)
Horrell, D.G.
    1996   *The Social Ethos of the Corinthian Correspondence: Interests and Ideol-
            ogy from 1 Corinthians to 1 Clement* (SNTW; Edinburgh: T. & T. Clark).
    1998   *The Epistles of Peter and Jude* (London: Epworth).
    2001   'From ἀδελφοί to οἶκος θεοῦ: Social Transformation in Pauline
            Christianity', *JBL* 120: 293–311.
    2004   'Domestic Space and Christian Meetings at Corinth: Imagining New
            Contexts and the Buildings East of the Theatre', *NTS* 50: 349–69.
    2008   'Pauline Churches or Early Christian Churches? Unity, Disagreement, and
            the Eucharist', in A.A. Alexeev, C. Karakolis, and U. Luz (eds.), *Einheit
            der Kirche in Neuen Testament* (WUNT I/218; Tübingen: Mohr Siebeck):
            185–203.
Howell, I. (ed.)
    2005   *Prehistoric Landscape to Roman Villa: Excavations at Beddington,
            Surrey, 1981–7* (Museum of London Archaeology Service Monograph 26;
            London: Museum of London Archaeology Service).
Hurtado, L.W.
    2006   *The Earliest Christian Artifacts: Manuscripts and Christian Origins*
            (Grand Rapids: Eerdmans).
Jackson, D.A., and T. Ambrose
    1978   'Excavations at Wakerley, Northants, 1972–5', *Britannia* 9: 115–242.
Jashemski, W.M.F.
    1979   *The Gardens of Pompeii: Herculaneum and the Villas Destroyed by
            Vesuvius* (New Rochelle, NY: Caratzas Bros.).
    1993   *The Gardens of Pompeii: Herculaneum and the Villas Destroyed by
            Vesuvius. Vol. 2, Appendices* (New Rochelle, NY: Aristide D. Caratzas).
    2007   'Gardens', in J.J. Dobbins and P.W. Foss (eds.), *The World of Pompeii*
            (London: Routledge): 487–98.
Jensen, R.M.
    2008   'Dining with the Dead: From the Mensa to the Altar', in L. Brink and D.
            Green (eds.), *Commemorating the Dead: Texts and Artefacts in Context*
            (Berlin: de Gruyter): 107–44.
    2010   *Living Water: Images, Symbols, and Settings of Early Christian Baptism*
            (Supplements to Vigiliae Christianae; Leiden: Brill).
Jewett, R.
    1993   'Tenement Churches and Communal Meals in the Early Church', *Biblical
            Research* 38: 23–43.
    2007   *Romans* (Hermeneia; Minneapolis, MN: Fortress).
Judge, E.A.
    1960   *The Social Pattern of Christian Groups in the First Century* (London:
            Tyndale).
Kee, H.C.
    1990   'The Transformation of the Synagogue After 70 C.E.: Its Import for Early
            Christianity', *NTS* 36: 1–24.

Kim, C.-H.
    1975   'The Papyrus Invitation', *JBL* 94: 391–402.
Kirsch, J.P.
    1918   *Die römischen Titelkirchen im Altertum* (Paderborn: F. Schöningh).
Kistemaker, S.J.
    1990   'The Speeches in Acts', *Criswell Theological Review* 5: 31–41.
Klauck, H.J.
    1981   *Hausgemeinde und Hauskirche im frühen Christentum* (SBS 103; Stuttgart: Katholische Bibelwerk).
    2008   *The Apocryphal Acts of the Apostles: An Introduction* (trans. B. McNeil; Waco, TX: Baylor University Press).
Kleberg, T.
    1957   *Hôtels, Restaurants et Cabarets dans L'antiquité Romaine: Études Historiques et Philologiques* (Uppsala: Almqvist & Wiksell).
Kloppenborg, J.S.
    1993a   'Edwin Hatch, Churches and Collegia', in B.H. McLean (ed.), *Origins and Methods: Towards a New Understanding of Judaism and Christianity: Essays in Honour of John C. Hurd* (JSNTSup 86; Sheffield: JSOT): 212–38.
    1993b   'Philadelphia, Theodidaktos and the Dioscuri: Rhetorical Engagement in 1 Thessalonians 4.9-12', *NTS* 39: 265–89.
    1996a   'Collegia and *Thiasoi*: Issues in Function, Taxonomy and Membership', in J.S. Kloppenborg and S.G. Wilson (eds.), *Voluntary Associations in the Graeco-Roman World* (London: Routledge): 59–73.
    1996b   'Egalitarianism in the Myth and Rhetoric of Pauline Churches', in E.A. Castelli and H. Taussig (eds.), *Reimagining Christian Origins: A Colloquium Honoring Burton L. Mack* (Valley Forge, PA: Trinity Press International): 247–63.
Kloppenborg, J.S., and R.S. Ascough
    2011   *Greco-Roman Associations: Texts, Translations, and Commentary* (Berlin: de Gruyter).
Koloski-Ostrow, A.O.
    1990   *The Sarno Bath Complex: Architecture in Pompeii's Last Years* (Monograph Series of the Italian Superintendency; Rome: L'Erma di Bretschneider).
    2007   'The City Baths', in J.J. Dobbins and P.W. Foss (eds.), *The World of Pompeii* (London: Routledge): 224–56.
Kraeling, C.
    1967   *The Christian Building* (The Excavations at Dura Europos. Final Report 8.2; New Haven, CT: Dura-Europos Publications).
Krautheimer, R.
    1939   'The Beginning of Christian Architecture', *Review of Religion* 3: 127–48.
    1937–77   *Corpus Basilicarum Christianarum Romae* (5 vols.; Vatican: Pontifical Gregorian Institute).
    1986   *Early Christian and Byzantine Architecture* (New Haven: Yale University Press, 4th edn).

Lampe, P.
    1994   'The Eucharist: Identifying with Christ on the Cross', *Interpretation* 48: 36–49.
    2003   *From Paul to Valentinus: Christians at Rome in the First Two Centuries* (trans. M. Steinhauser; Minneapolis, MN: Fortress).
Lane, W.
    1998   'Social Perspectives on Roman Christianity during the Formative Years from Nero to Nerva: Romans, Hebrews, 1 Clement', in K.P. Donfried and P. Richardson (eds.), *Judaism and Christianity in First-Century Rome* (Grand Rapids: Eerdmans): 196–244.
Lanzoni, F.
    1925   'I titoli presbiteriali di Roma antica nella storia legenda', *Rivista di archeologia Cristiana* 2: 195–257.
Laurence, R., and A. Wallace-Hadrill
    1997   *Domestic Space in the Roman World: Pompeii and Beyond* (JRA 22; Portsmouth, RI: Journal of Roman Archaeology).
Le Cornu, H., and J. Shulam
    2003   *A Commentary on the Jewish Roots of Acts* (Jerusalem: Academon).
Levine, L.I.
    1996   'The Nature and Origin of the Palestinian Synagogue', *JBL* 115: 425–48.
Lieu, J.M.
    2008   *I, II, & III John: A Commentary* (Louisville, KY: Westminster John Knox).
    2009   'Jews, Christians and "Pagans" in Conflict', in A.-C. Jacobsen, J. Ulrich, and D. Brakke (eds.), *Critique and Apologetics: Jews, Christians and Pagans in Antiquity* (Frankfurt: Lang): 43–58.
Longenecker, B.W.
    2009   'Socio-Economic Profiling of the First Urban Christians', in T. Still and D. Horrell (eds.), *After the First Urban Christians: The Social-Scientific Study of Pauline Christianity Twenty-Five Years Later* (London: Continuum): 36–59.
    2010   *Remember the Poor: Paul, Poverty, and the Greco-Roman World* (Grand Rapids: Eerdmans).
Luijendijk, A.
    2008   'Papyri from the Great Persecution: Roman and Christian Perspectives', *JECS* 16: 341–69.
Lynch, J.P.
    1972   *Aristotle's School: A Study of a Greek Educational Institution* (Berkeley: University of California Press).
MacDonald, M.Y.
    1988   *The Pauline Churches: A Socio-Historical Study of Institutionalization in the Pauline and Deutero-Pauline Writings* (SNTSMS 60; Cambridge: Cambridge University Press).
    1996   *Early Christian Women and Pagan Opinion: The Power of the Hysterical Woman* (Cambridge: Cambridge University Press).
    2011   'Children in House Churches in Light of New Research on Families in the Roman World', in C.E. Evans (ed.), *The World of Jesus and the Early Church: Identity and Interpretation in Early Communities of Faith* (Peabody, MA: Hendrickson): 69–86.

MacKnight, J.
  1810   *A New Literal Translation from the Original Greek of All the Apostolical Epistles with a Commentary, and Notes, Philological, Critical, Explanatory, and Practical* (Boston: W. Wells & T.B. Wait), V.
MacMahon, A.
  2003   *The Taberna Structures of Roman Britain* (British Archaeological Reports, British Series 356; Oxford: John & Erica Hedges).
MacMullen, R.
  2009   The *Second Church: Popular Christianity A.D. 200–400* (Atlanta: SBL).
Magness, J.
  2005   'The Date of the Sardis Synagogue in Light of the Numismatic Evidence', *AJA* 109: 443–7.
Maier, H.O.
  1991   *The Social Setting of the Ministry as Reflected in the Writings of Hermas, Clement, and Ignatius* (Dissertations SR; Waterloo, ON: Wilfrid Laurier University Press).
Maiuri, A.
  1939   'La Croce di Ercolano', *Rendiconti della Pontificia Accademia Romana di Archeologia* 15: 193–218.
Malherbe, A.J.
  1977   *Social Aspects of Early Christianity* (Baton Rouge: Louisiana State University Press).
  1993   'Hospitality', in B.M. Metzger and M.D. Coogan (eds.), *The Oxford Companion to the Bible* (Oxford: Oxford University Press): 292–3.
Marshall, I.H.
  1980   *The Acts of the Apostles: An Introduction and Commentary* (TNTC; Leicester: IVP).
Matson, D.L.
  1996   *Household Conversion Narratives in Acts: Pattern and Interpretation* (Sheffield: Sheffield Academic).
Matassa, L.
  2007   'Unravelling the Myth of the Synagogue on Delos', *BAIAS* 25: 81–116.
McKnight, S.
  2011   *The Letter of James* (NICNT; Grand Rapids: Eerdmans).
Meates, G.W.
  1979–87 *The Roman Villa at Lullingstone, Kent* (2 vols.; Chichester: Kent Archaeological Society).
Meeks, W.A.
  1983   *The First Urban Christians: The Social World of the Apostle Paul* (New Haven, CT: Yale University Press).
Meggitt, J.J
  1998   *Paul, Poverty and Survival* (SNTW; Edinburgh: T. & T. Clark).
  2001   'Response to Martin and Theissen', *JSNT* 84: 85–94.
Meiggs, R.
  1973   *Roman Ostia* (Oxford: Oxford University Press, 2nd edn).

Mell, U.
   2010   *Christliche Hauskirche und Neues Testament: Die Ikonologie des
             Baptisteriums von Dura Europos und das Diatessaron Tatians* (Novum
             Testamentum et Orbis Antiquus/Studien zur Umwelt des Neuen Testa-
             ments 77; Göttingen: Vandenhoeck & Ruprecht).
Metzger, B.M.
   1994   *A Textual Commentary on the Greek New Testament: A Companion
             Volume to the United Bible Societies' Greek New Testament* (Stuttgart:
             Deutsche Bibelgesellschaft, 4th edn).
Moeller, W.O.
   1976   *The Wool Trade of Ancient Pompeii* (Leiden: Brill).
Muddiman, J.
   2001   *The Epistle to the Ephesians* (BNTC; London: Continuum).
Murphy-O'Connor, J.
   1992   'Prisca and Aquila: Traveling Tentmakers and Church Builders', *BR* 8:06:
             40–51, 62.
   1995   'The Cenacle: Topographical Setting for Acts 2:44-45', in R. Bauckham
             (ed.), *The Book of Acts in its Palestinian Setting* (The Book of Acts in its
             First Century Setting 4; Grand Rapids: Eerdmans; Carlisle: Paternoster):
             303–21.
   2002   *St. Paul's Corinth: Texts and Archaeology* (Collegeville, PA: Liturgical,
             3rd edn).
   2009   *Keys to First Corinthians: Revisiting the Major Issues* (Oxford: Oxford
             University Press).
Neyrey, J.H.
   2003   '"Teaching You in Public and from House to House" (Acts 20:20):
             Unpacking a Cultural Stereotype', *JSNT* 26: 69–102.
Nielsen, I.
   1990   *Thermae et Balnea: The Architecture and Cultural History of Roman
             Public Baths* (Aarhus: Aarhus University Press).
Oakes, P.
   2009   *Reading Romans in Pompeii* (Minneapolis, MN: Fortress).
Økland, J.
   2004   *Women in their Place: Paul and the Corinthian Discourse of Gender and
             Sanctuary Space* (JSNTSup 269; London: T&T Clark International).
Orr, D.G.
   1978   'Roman Domestic Religion: The Evidence of the Household Shrines',
             ANRW II.16.2: 1557–91.
Osiek, C.
   1999   *Shepherd of Hermas* (Hermeneia; Minneapolis, MN: Fortress).
Osiek, C., and D.L. Balch
   1997   *Families in the New Testament World: Households and House Churches*
             (Louisville, KY: Westminster John Knox).
Osiek, C., and M.Y. MacDonald, with J.H. Tulloch
   2006   *A Woman's Place: House Churches in Earliest Christianity* (Minneapolis,
             MN: Fortress).

Oster, R.E.
    1993   'Supposed Anachronism in Luke–Acts' Use of ΣΥΝΑΓΩΓH: A Rejoinder to H C Kee', *NTS* 39: 178–208.
Packer, J.E.
    1978   'Inns at Pompeii: A Short Survey', *Cronache Pompeiane* 4: 5–53.
Parker, S.T.
    1999   'Brief Notice on a Possible Early 4th C. Church at 'Aqaba, Jordan', *JRA* 12: 372–6.
Pervo, R.I.
    2009   *Acts: A Commentary* (Hermeneia; Minneapolis, MN: Fortress).
Petersen, J.M.
    1973   'Some Titular Churches at Rome with Traditional New Testament Connexions', *ExpTim* 84: 277–9.
Pirson, F.
    1997   'Rented Accommodation at Pompeii: The Insula Arriana Polliana', in R. Lawrence and A. Wallace-Hadrill (eds.), *Domestic Space in the Roman World: Pompeii and Beyond* (JRA Supplement Series 22; Portsmouth, RI: Journal of Roman Archaeology): 165–81.
    2007   'Shops and Industries', in J.J. Dobbins and P.W. Foss (eds.), *The World of Pompeii* (London: Routledge): 457–73.
Richardson, L.
    1988   *Pompeii: An Architectural History* (Baltimore: The Johns Hopkins University Press).
Richardson, P.
    2004a   *Building Jewish in the Roman East* (Waco, TX: Baylor University Press).
    2004b   'Towards a Typology of Levantine/Palestinian Houses', *JSNT* 27: 47–68.
Rickman, G.
    1971   *Roman Granaries and Store Buildings* (London: Cambridge University Press).
Riesner, R.
    1995   'Synagogues in Jerusalem', in R. Bauckman (ed.), *The Book of Acts in the Palestinian Setting* (The Book of Acts in its First Century Setting 4; Grand Rapids: Eerdmans): 179–210.
Rihll, T.
    2003   'Teaching and Learning in Classical Athens', *Greece & Rome*, Second Series 50: 168–90.
Robert, L.
    1969   'Deux décrets d'une association à Athènes', *Achaiologike Ephemeris*: 7–15
Roberts, C., T.C. Skeat, and A.D. Nock
    1936   'The Gild of Zeus Hypsistos', *HTR* 29: 39–91.
Robinson, H.S.
    1962   'Excavations at Corinth', *Hisperia* 46: 111–12.
Rodwell, W.J., and K.A. Rodwell
    1985   *Rivenhall: Investigations of a Villa, Church and Village, 1950–77* (London: Council of British Archaeology).
Rowell, H.T.
    1957   'Satyricon 95-96', *Classical Philology* 52: 217–27.

Runesson, A.
    1999   'The Oldest Original Synagogue Building in the Diaspora: A Response to
              L. Michael White', *HTR* 92: 409–33.
    2001a   *The Origins of the Synagogue: A Socio-Historical Study* (Coniectanea
              biblica, New Testament Series 37; Stockholm: Almqvist & Wiksell).
    2001b   'The Synagogue at Ancient Ostis: The Building and its History from the
              First to the Fifth Century', in B. Olsson, D. Mitternacht, and O. Brandt
              (eds.), *The Synagogue of Ancient Ostia and the Jews of Rome: Inter-
              disciplinary Studies* (Stockholm: Paul Åströms Förlag).
    2002   'A Monumental Synagogue from the First Century: The Case of Ostia',
              JSJ 33: 171–220.
    2007   'Architecture, Conflict, and Identity Formation: Jews and Christians in
              Capernaum From the 1st to the 6th Century', in J. Zangenberg, H.W.
              Attridge, and D. Martin (eds.), *Religion, Ethnicity, and Identity in Ancient
              Galilee* (WUNT I/210; Tübingen: Mohr Siebeck): 231–57.
Runesson, A., D.B. Binder, and B. Olsson
    2008   *The Ancient Synagogue from its Origins to 200 C.E.: A Source Book*
              (Arbeiten zur Geschichte des antiken Judentums und des Urchristentums
              72; Leiden: Brill).
Safrai, S.
    1976   'Home and Family', in S.Safrai and M.Stern (eds.), *The Jewish People in
              the First Century: Historical Geography, Political History, Social,
              Cultural and Religious Life and Institutions* (2 vols.; Assen: Van Gorcum;
              Philadelphia: Fortress): II: 728–92.
Saller, R., and B. Shaw
    1984   'Tombstones and Roman Family Relations in the Principate: Civilians,
              Soldiers and Slaves', *JRS* 74: 124–56.
Sande, S.
    1999   'Huskirker og tituluskirker – salmer i heimen eller i badet?', *Kirke og
              Kultur* 104: 7–18.
Schneider, G.
    1980   *Die Apostelgeschichte* (Freiburg: Herder).
Schoedel, W.R.
    1985   *Ignatius of Antioch: A Commentary on the Letters of Ignatius of Antioch*
              (Hermeneia; Philadelphia: Fortress).
Schüssler Fiorenza, E.S.
    1983   *In Memory of Her: A Feminist Theological Reconstruction of Christian
              Origins* (New York: Crossroads).
Scobie, A.
    1986   'Slums, Sanitation and Mortality in the Roman World', *Klio* 68.2: 399–
              433.
Sessa, K.
    2009   'Domus Ecclesiae: Rethinking a Category of Ante-Pacem Christian
              Space', *JTS* 60: 90–108.
Shiner, W.
    2003   *Proclaiming the Gospel: First-Century Performance of Mark* (Harrisburg,
              PA: Trinity Press International).

Slane, K.W.
    1986   'Two Deposits from the Early Roman Cellar Building, Corinth', *Hesperia* 55.3: 271–318.

Smith, D.E.
    2003   *From Symposium to Eucharist: The Banquet in the Early Christian World* (Minneapolis, MN: Fortress).
    2012   'The House Church as Social Environment', in C. Osiek and A.C. Niang (eds.), *Text, Image, and Christians in the Graeco-Roman World: A Festschrift in Honor of David Lee Balch* (Princeton Theological Monograph Series; Eugene, OR: Wipf & Stock): 3–21.

Snyder, G.F.
    2003   *Ante-Pacem: Archaeological Evidence of Church Life Before Constantine* (Macon, GA: Mercer University Press).

Snyder, H.G.
    2007   '"Above the Bath of Myrtinus": Justin Martyr's "School" in the City of Rome', *HTR* 100: 335–62.

Sordi, M.
    1986   *The Christians and the Roman Empire* (London: Croom Helm).

Stefani, G.
    2005   'Pompei. Un Panificio', in G. Stefani (ed.), *Cibi e sapori a Pompei e dintorni: Antiquarium di Boscoreale, 3 febbraio–26 giugno 2005* (Pompei: Flavius): 139–40.

Stegemann, E., and W. Stegemann
    1999   *The Jesus Movement: A Social History of its First Century* (Edinburgh: T. & T. Clark).

Stambaugh, J.E.
    1988   *The Ancient Roman City* (Baltimore, MD: The Johns Hopkins University Press).

Stowers, S.K.
    1984   'Social Status, Public Speaking and Private Teaching: The Circumstances of Paul's Preaching Activity', *NovT* 26: 59–82.

Strange, J.F., and H. Shanks
    1982   'Has the House Where Jesus Stayed in Capernaum Been Found?', *BARev* 8: 26–37. Online: http://members.bib-arch.org/publication.asp?PubID= BSBA &Volume=8&Issue=6&ArticleID=4 (accessed 11 December 2012).

Swift, E.H.
    1951   *Roman Sources of Christian Art* (New York: Columbia University Press).

Taylor, J.E.
    1993   *Christians and the Holy Places: The Myth of Jewish-Christian Origins* (Oxford: Oxford University Press).
    2003   'Where Was Gethsemane?', in M.D. Meinhardt (ed.), *Jesus: The Last Day* (Washington: Biblical Archaeological Society) 23–38.

Tchalenko, G.
    1953   *Villages antiques de la Syrie du Nord: le massif du Bélus à l'époque romaine* (Bibliothèque archéologique et historique, Paris: Geuthner), I.

Telbe, M.
    2009   *Christ-Believers in Ephesus: A Textual Analysis of Early Christian Identity Formation in a Local Perspective* (WUNT I/242; Tübingen: Mohr Siebeck).

Tepper, Y., and L. Di Segni
    2006   *A Christian Prayer Hall of the Third Century CE at Kefar 'Othnay (Legio): Excavations at the Megiddo Prison 2005* (Jerusalem: Israel Antiquities Authority).

Theissen, G.
    1982   *The Social Setting of Pauline Christianity: Essays on Corinth* (Edinburgh: T. & T. Clark).

Thiselton, A.C.
    2000   *The First Epistle to the Corinthians* (NIGTC; Grand Rapids: Eerdmans; Carlisle: Paternoster).

Thomas, J.P.
    1987   *Private Religious Foundations in the Byzantine Empire* (Washington, DC: Dumbarton Oaks).

Tidball, D.T.
    1983   *An Introduction to the Sociology of the New Testament* (Exeter: Paternoster).

Torjesen, K.J.
    1995   *When Women Were Priests: Women's Leadership in the Early Church and the Scandal of their Subordination in the Rise of Christianity* (New York: HarperCollins).

Toynbee, J.M.C.
    1971   *Death and Burial in the Roman World* (London: Thames & Hudson).

Trebilco, P.
    2004   *The Early Christians in Ephesus from Paul to Ignatius* (WUNT I/166; Tübingen: Mohr Siebeck).

Trümper, M.
    2004   'The Oldest Original Synagogue Building in the Diaspora: The Delos Synagogue Reconsidered', *Hesperia* 73: 513–98.

Tulloch, J.H.
    2006   'Women Leaders in Family Funerary Banquets', in C. Osiek and M.Y. MacDonald (eds.), *A Women's Place: House Churches in Earliest Christianity* (Minneapolis, MN: Fortress): 164–93.

Tzaferis, V.
    2007   'Inscribed to "God Jesus Christ": Early Christian Prayer Hall Found in Megiddo Prison', *BARev* 33.2: 38–49.

Vermaseren, M.J., and C.C. Van Essen
    1965   *The Excavations in the Mithraeum of the Church of Santa Prisca in Rome* (Leiden: Brill).

Verbrugge, V.D.
    1998   *Early Church History* (Grand Rapids: Zondervan).

Verner, D.C.
    1983   *The Household of God: The Social World of the Pastoral Epistles* (Chico, CA: Scholars Press).

Walbank, M.E.H.
    1997   'The Foundation and Planning of Early Roman Corinth', *JRA* 10: 95–130.

Wallace-Hadrill, A.
    2003   'Domus and Insulae in Rome: Families and Housefuls', in D.L. Balch and C. Osiek (eds.), *Early Christian Families in Context: An Interdisciplinary Dialogue* (Grand Rapids: Eerdmans): 3–18.

Ward, R.B.
    1992   'Women in Roman Baths', *HTR* 85.2: 125–47.

Ward-Perkins, J.B.
    1954   'Constantine and the Origins of the Christian Basilica', *Papers of the British School at Rome* 22: 69–90.

Weissenrieder, A.
    2012   'Contested Spaces in 1 Corinthian 11:17–34 and 14:30: Sitting or Reclining in Ancient Houses, in Associations and in the Space of the *Ekklēsia*', in D.L. Balch and A. Weissenrieder (eds.), *Contested Spaces: Houses and Temples in Roman Antiquity and the New Testament* (WUNT I/285; Tübingen: Mohr Siebeck): 59–107.

Wild, R.A.
    1981   *Water in the Cultic Worship of Isis and Sarapis* (Leiden: Brill).

White, L.M.
    1990   *The Social Origins of Christian Architecture*. Vol. 1, *Building God's House in the Roman World: Architectural Adaptation among Pagans, Jews, and Christians* (Harvard Theological Studies 42; Valley Forge, PA: Trinity Press International).
    1997   *The Social Origins of Christian Architecture*. Vol. 2, *Texts and Monuments of the Christian Domus Ecclesiae in its Environment* (Harvard Theological Studies 42; Valley Forge, PA: Trinity Press International).
    1999   'Reading the Ostia Synagogue: A Reply to A. Runesson', *HTR* 92: 435–64.
    2000   'Architecture: The First Five Centuries', in P.F. Esler (ed.), *The Early Christian World* (2 vols.; London: Routledge), II: 693–746.
    2012   'The Changing Face of Mithraism at Ostia: Archaeology, Art and the Urban Landscape', in D.L. Balch and A. Weissenrieder (eds.), *Contested Spaces: Houses and Temples in Roman Antiquity and the New Testament* (WUNT I/285; Tübingen: Mohr Siebeck): 435–92.

Wilken, R.L.
    1970   'Toward a Social Interpretation of Early Christian Apologetics', *Church History: Studies in Christianity and Culture* 39: 437–58.
    1984   *The Christians as the Romans Saw Them* (New Haven: Yale University Press).

Williams, C.K.
    1977   'Corinth 1976: Forum Southwest', *Hesperia* 46: 40–81.

Wiseman, J.R.
    1979   'Corinth and Rome I: 228 B.C.–267 A.D.', *ANRW* II.7.1: 438–548.

Wiseman, T.P.
    1985   'Who Was Crassicius Pansa?', *Transactions of the American Philological Association* 115: 187–96.

Witherington, B.
    1995   *Conflict and Community in Corinth: A Socio-Rhetorical Commentary on 1 and 2 Corinthians* (Grand Rapids: Eerdmans).
    1998   *The Acts of the Apostles: A Socio-Rhetorical Commentary* (Grand Rapids: Eerdmans).

Wright, K.S.
    1980   'A Tiberian Pottery Deposit from Corinth', *Hesperia* 49: 135–77.

Wycherley, R.E.
    1953   'The Painted Stoa: "Sapiens bracatis inlita Medis porticus": Persius 3.53-43', *Phoenix* 7: 20–35.
    1961   'Peripatos: The Athenian Philosophical Scene 1', *Greece & Rome*, Second Series 8: 152–63.
    1962   'Peripatos: The Athenian Philosophical Scene II: The Gymnasia and the Philosophical Schools', *Greece & Rome*, Second Series 9: 2–21.
Yegül, F.
    1992   *Baths and Bathing in Classical Antiquity* (New York: Architectural History Foundation; Cambridge, MA: MIT Press).
    2010   *Bathing in the Roman World* (Cambridge: Cambridge University Press).

INDICES

INDEX OF REFERENCES

INDEX OF AUTHORS

Lightning Source UK Ltd.
Milton Keynes UK
UKHW021021030620
364356UK00003B/134